OLD TESTAMENT MESSAGE

A Biblical-Theological Commentary

Carroll Stuhlmueller, C.P. and Martin McNamara, M.S.C.

EDITORS

Old Testament Message, Volume 8

ISAIAH 1-39

Joseph Jensen, O.S.B.

Michael Glazier, Inc.
Wilmington, Delaware

ABOUT THE AUTHOR

Joseph Jensen, O.S.B., studied theology at Collegio Sant'Anselmo, Rome. He did his graduate Scripture work at the Pontifical Biblical Institute and at Catholic University where he is currently teaching. He is Executive Secretary of the Catholic Biblical Association. His publications include *God's Word to Israel*.

Second Printing 1989

First published in 1984 by MICHAEL GLAZIER, INC. 1935 West Fourth Street, Wilmington, Delaware 19805

Distributed outside U.S., Canada & Philippines by: GILL & MACMILLAN, LTD., Goldenbridge, Inchicore, Dublin 8, Ireland

Library of Congress Cataloging in Publication Data

Jensen, Joseph, 1924-
    Isaiah 1-39.
    Bibliography: p. 307.
    I. Bible. O.T. Isaiah I-XXXIX—Commentaries.
I. Bible. O.T. Isaiah I-XXXIX. English. 1984.
II. Title.
BS1515.3.J46 1984 224'.1077 83-83252
ISBN 0-89453-408-4
ISBN 0-89453-243-X (pbk.)

7171-1172-5 (Gill & MacMillan, Ltd.)

Typography by Richard Reinsmith

Printed in the United States of America

To my sister Harriet

List of Abbreviations

ANET: James B. Pritchard, *Ancient Near Eastern Texts Relating to the Old Testament* (2d ed.; Princeton, NJ: Princeton University Press, 1955).

HI: John Bright, *A History of Israel* (3d ed.; Philadelphia: Westminster, 1981).

NAB: New American Bible

OAB: Oxford Annotated Bible

OTA: Old Testament Abstracts, a periodical published by the Catholic Biblical Association, Catholic University, Washington, DC. References are to volume and abstract number and direct the reader to bibliographical data on articles on the topic discussed, along with a summary of their contents.

RSV: Revised Standard Version (the Bible translation which is set forth in this commentary)

TABLE OF CONTENTS

Editors' Preface

Old Testament Message brings into our life and religion today the ancient word of God to Israel. This word, according to the book of the prophet Isaiah, had soaked the earth like "rain and snow coming gently down from heaven" and had returned to God fruitfully in all forms of human life (Isa 55:10). The authors of this series remain true to this ancient Israelite heritage and draw us into the home, the temple and the market place of God's chosen people. Although they rely upon the tools of modern scholarship to uncover the distant places and culture of the biblical world, yet they also refocus these insights in a language clear and understandable for any interested reader today. They enable us, even if this be our first acquaintance with the Old Testament, to become sister and brother, or at least good neighbor, to our religious ancestors. In this way we begin to hear God's word ever more forcefully in our own times and across our world, within our prayer and worship, in our secular needs and perplexing problems.

Because life is complex and our world includes, at times in a single large city, vastly different styles of living, we have much to learn from the Israelite Scriptures. The Old Testament spans forty-six biblical books and almost nineteen hundred years of life. It extends through desert, agricultural and urban ways of human existence. The literary style embraces a world of literature and human emotions. Its history began with Moses and the birth-pangs of a new people, it came of an age politically and economically under David and Solomon, it reeled under the fiery threats of prophets like Amos and Jeremiah. The people despaired and yet were re-created with new hope during the Babylonian exile. Later reconstruction in the homeland and then the trauma of apocalyptic movements prepared for the revelation of "the mystery hidden for ages in God who created all things" (Eph 3:9).

While the Old Testament telescopes twelve to nineteen hundred years of human existence within the small country of Israel, any single moment of time today witnesses to the reenactment of this entire history across the wide expanse of planet earth. Each verse of the Old Testament is being relived somewhere in our world today. We need, therefore, the *entire* Old Testament and all twenty-three volumes of this new set, in order to be totally a "Bible person" within today's widely diverse society.

The subtitle of this series—"A Biblical-Theological Commentary"—clarifies what these twenty-three volumes intend to do.

Their *purpose* is theological: to feel the pulse of God's word for its *religious* impact and direction.

Their *method* is biblical: to establish the scriptural word firmly within the life and culture of ancient Israel.

Their *style* is commentary: not to explain verse by verse but to follow a presentation of the message that is easily understandable to any serious reader, even if this person is untrained in ancient history and biblical languages.

Old Testament Message—like its predecessor, *New Testament Message*—is aimed at the entire English-speaking world and so is a collaborative effort of an international team. The twenty-one contributors are women and men drawn from North America, Ireland, Britain and Australia. They are scholars who have published in scientific journals, but they have been chosen equally as well for their proven ability to communicate on a popular level. This twenty-three book set comes from Roman Catholic writers, yet, like the Bible itself, it reaches beyond interpretations restricted to an individual church and so enables men and women rooted in biblical faith to unite and so to appreciate their own traditions more fully and more adequately.

Most of all, through the word of God, we seek the blessedness and joy of those

who walk in the law of the Lord!...

who seek God with their whole heart (Ps. 119:1-2).

Carroll Stuhlmueller, C.P.   Martin McNamara, M.S.C.

INTRODUCTION

The book of Isaiah comprises sixty-six chapters and is the longest of the prophetic books and one of the longest of the Old Testament. In the days when books were published only in scroll form, it required a scroll that reached the outermost limits of manageability; the Isaiah A scroll from Cave 1 at Qumran is 24.5 feet long. Yet closer inspection reveals that not all this material is attributable to the great prophet of the eighth century, Isaiah of Jerusalem. By the latter part of the eighteenth century, at least, scholars had begun to distinguish chapters 1-39, sometimes called Proto-Isaiah or First Isaiah, from chapters 40-66, called Deutero-Isaiah or Second Isaiah; later study led to the further division of chaps. 40-66 into chaps. 40-55 and chaps. 56-66, now called Deutero-Isaiah (or Second Isaiah) and Trito-Isaiah (or Third Isaiah), respectively. The basis for these distinctions is the conviction that while chaps. 1-39 represent, in the main, the collected oracles of Isaiah of the eighth century, the other chapters represent the work of much later times, namely, of the exilic period (chaps. 40-55) and the postexilic period (chaps. 56-66). The conviction rests on the results of extensive historical and literary analysis of the book. Sometimes these results derive from studies of vocabulary and style of the Hebrew text, and sometimes they relate to theological themes that would require too lengthy a treatment to cover here. But some of them, especially those which relate to historical matters, are fairly obvious. So, for example, chaps. 1-39 mention Isaiah frequently by name, the later chapters never. In chaps. 1-39 the mighty Assyrian empire hovers over the action, with its kings Sargon (II) and Sennacherib sometimes mentioned by name, while chaps. 40-55 have as their background the Babylonian captivity, though it is clear that Babylon's days are numbered, and its conqueror-to-be, Cyrus (the Persian), is named (45:1). These few examples will have to suffice. Deutero- and Trito-Isaiah are dealt with in a separate volume in the *Old Testament Message* series (*OTM*, Vol. 12).

A Collection of Collections

Even chaps. 1-39 are not all attributable to Isaiah and to his time, and the development and arrangement of the collection is a very complex thing; many aspects of it remain the subject of doubt and/or dispute. We can, with truth, speak of a "collection of collections," and can distinguish at least the following ones:

A.   Chaps 1-12: oracles concerning Judah and Jerusalem
B.   Chaps. 13-23: oracles against the nations
C.   Chaps. 24-27: the Apocalypse of Isaiah
D.   Chaps. 28-33: later oracles of Isaiah
E.   Chaps. 34-35: the vindication of Zion
F.   Chaps. 36-39: historical appendix

Only in sections A and D are we dealing, in the main, with the words of Isaiah; sections C and E are wholly from later times, whereas section F is narrative about Isaiah taken from 2 Kgs 18:13-20:19. Section B contains a number of authentic oracles of Isaiah (and one narrative about him — chap. 20) but is in large part made up of later compositions.

Each of these sections had a complex history of its own and some of them are composed of smaller, earlier collections. Thus in Section A there is an inscription at 1:1 and another at 2:1. The one at 2:1 would be pointless unless it originally stood at the beginning of a section; thus we can conclude that chap. 1 was placed before it at some later point and was provided with an inscription which would do for the whole book (or whatever comprised it at that time). Furthermore, we would expect Isaiah's call narrative to stand at the beginning of the collection in which it is found rather than in the middle (chap. 6). In fact, many scholars agree that chap. 1 is a collection of representative oracles of Isaiah put together as an introduction to the book as a whole and was tacked on in front of a collection that comprised 2:1-4:1 (with 4:2-6 being a later addition to it), with another beginning at 5:1. There is also much agreement that 6:1-8:18 forms a special collection, the so-called "Memoirs of Isaiah" (thus the call narrative did indeed stand at the beginning of the collection to which it pertains), completed by the addition of 8:19-9:7. Yet the fact that the series of "woes" found in 5:8-24 is continued in 10:1-4a and that 9:7-20 and 5:25-30 belong together (as revealed by the same refrain running through both parts) indicates that these "Memoirs" were inserted into an already existing collection (which began at 5:1 and extended at least to 10:4a). Thus even by this somewhat simplified account, section A would have a rather complex history.

The "Memoirs" just referred to (comprising most of the material in 6:1-8:18) may very well have been compiled by Isaiah himself (see below, p. 82). This material would date to the period of the Syro-Ephraimitic War (735-732). Some think that what Isaiah spoke of writing down as "a witness for ever" in 30:8 refers to much of the material in chaps. 28-31; in this case we would have another extensive compilation from Isaiah himself, this one dating largely to the period of Hezekiah's revolt against Assyria (705-701). Much of the material in 2:1-4:1 and that which surrounds the "Memoirs" in 5:1-10:4 may come from the beginning of Isaiah's ministry, before the events of 735-732. This suggests that the principal Isaianic materials in chaps. 2-11 consisted first of all of oracles from his early years (the authentic material in 2:6-5:29 and 9:8-10:4), into which was inserted 6:1-8:18(9:7) from the time of the Syro-Ephraimitic War and sometime thereafter. The collection comprising chaps. 28-31 would then relate to a later period of his ministry (705-701). At various times other materials were inserted to bring those two collections to the full content they presently have. Such materials would include authentic oracles of Isaiah originally transmitted apart from these collections, pieces composed by others but thought to be relevant by the editors (e.g., 4:2-6; 11:12-12:6), and additions tacked on by editors or copyists by way of expansion, commentary, etc. (e.g., 2:5, 22; 8:19-20; 11:10-11). That is why the sum of the parts here identified by chapter and verse does not equal the full extent of the collections described.

Section B, the oracles against the nations (chaps. 13-23), appears to have grown up in a rather different way. Most of the non-Isaianic material can be dated to the late monarchy or the early exile; this is clearly the case with the oracles against Babylon (chaps. 13-14, 21), which must have been written before the fall of the Babylonian empire, and it is probable that the demise of Babylon was the primary interest of the collection. Oracles against other nations were added to it, however, and the editor or collector provided each piece with the formula "an oracle concerning. . ." as introduction (see below, p. 139). At this point the collection existed apart from any prophetic book and contained no oracles from Isaiah. The collection was then put under the aegis of Isaiah by inserting it into the Isaiah collection with the introduction "The oracle concerning Babylon which Isaiah the son of Amoz saw" (13:1). At the same time there were transferred into this new section of the book genuine oracles of Isaiah that dealt with foreign nations (especially Assyria and Egypt) but previously dispersed among the materials of chaps. 1-12 and 28-31; these were also provided (though not consistently) with the "an oracle concerning. . ." introduction. Here we can list in particular 14:24-27 (against Assyria), 14:28-32 (a warning to Philistia), 17:1-11 (against Damascus), 17:12-14 (against the nations), 18:1-6 (against Egypt/Ethiopia), 19:1-4, 11-14 (against Egypt), and chap. 20 (a narrative which involves Egypt/Ethiopia).

Many would see Isaiah 1-35 (before the addition of the

historical appendix from 2 Kings) as composed of three main sections, namely, chaps. 1-12, chaps. 13-23, and chaps. 24-35, which would then exhibit a three-part structure of oracles against Judah and Jerusalem, oracles against the nations, and oracles (mainly) of promise. This would correspond to the broad structure found in the book of Ezekiel and in that of Jeremiah in the Septuagint (not, however, in the Hebrew text nor in translations dependent on it). This is possible, though in fact the third section would contain a great deal of material (including almost all of that which is genuinely Isaianic, i.e., much of chaps. 28-31) which threatens rather than promises. It is to be conceded, however, that the two lengthy non-Isaianic sections that are included in that section (chaps. 24-27, the so-called Apocalypse of Isaiah, and chaps. 34-35, here dubbed "the vindication of Zion") are directed to promises of a glorious future.

Authenticity

From the preceding explanation of the origins of the Isaiah collection, it is clear that much of the material, even in chaps. 1-39, does not stem from Isaiah of Jerusalem of the eighth century. This does not in any way diminish its value as part of the canon of Scripture or as God's inspired word. It does mean that we would often mislead ourselves if we attempted to interpret these parts as Isaiah's words; it also means that in any attempt to give an account of Isaiah's own teaching we would want to restrict ourselves to those oracles which really came from him.

The attempt to distinguish the authentic words of Isaiah from others which have been added to the collection is not an easy one. The criteria on which judgments of this sort are based include such things as historical allusion, vocabulary, and characteristic teachings. The problem arises to some extent in all the prophetic books, as well as in the case of some of the other biblical writings (e.g., the epistles of St. Paul), but it seems to be particularly acute in the case of Isaiah. Depending on whether one judges certain passages to be authentic or not, various commentators have come up with quite different ideas of what Isaiah taught concerning the Zion tradition, the Davidic dynasty, the fate of Assyria, Israel's future hope, etc. There is obviously much room for circular reasoning in applying the criterion of "characteristic teachings," and so it is important to utilize primarily the more objective criteria. Fortunately, there are fairly extensive materials in Isaiah 1-39 that fit perfectly into eighth century Judah and that relate directly to the events in which Judah's leadership and Isaiah himself were involved, so that virtually all agree in attributing them to Isaiah. From this body of material it is possible to learn much of Isaiah's vocabulary, literary technique, and thought as a basis for judging other materials in the Isaiah collection. Yet there are, for example, a number of commentators who are convinced, whether on the basis of solid evidence or not, that the prophetic concept of a new order of salvation arose only in exilic times and that therefore any passages in the Isaiah collection which manifest this concept could not come from Isaiah but had to be added later. This is not the approach taken in the present commentary, but discussion of individual texts will normally make reference to contrary views.

Also relevant to the matter of authenticity are various theories concerning the editing of the collection. There are some, for example, who believe the collection went through an editing in the days of King Josiah, when Assyria's end was near, that was responsible for a number of passages which speak or are alleged to speak of judgment on Assyria (14:24-27; 17:12-14; 28:23-29, etc.), as well as others; these passages will be dealt with individually in the commentary, but by and large there seems no reason for refusing to attribute them to Isaiah. With better reason one can argue for separate reworkings of the book during the exilic or postexilic period to emphasize judgment or salvation. The first of these reworkings would have added brief but pointed threats, usually of one or two verses only, to passages that already spoke of judgment (e.g., 2:10-11; the opening lines of 6:13). The second of these reworkings tended in the opposite direction, usually softening the import of certain oracles of judgment by suggesting mercy or promising later restoration (e.g., 1:27-28; 2:22; 3:10-11); again, these are regularly very brief additions. Reference to such editing will be made at appropriate places in the commentary.

Since this is intended as a commentary on the whole of Isaiah 1-39 there can be no question of shortchanging those passages which are judged to be from authors other than Isaiah. As inspired Scripture they deserve to be read and studied and valued for their contributions to biblical revelation and the history of religious thought.

Textual Criticism

Any translation of the Bible is designed to read smoothly and therefore will seldom betray the complications that sometimes lurk beneath the surface, i.e., in the Hebrew text. It happens not infrequently that the Hebrew text is obscure or, occasionally, virtually untranslatable. Most often this happens because of an error in the transmission of the Hebrew text. In such cases scholars resort to various expedients to attempt to recover the original reading. The most common expedient is the use of very early translations, most especially the Septuagint, the rendering of the Hebrew text into Greek made before the end of the Old Testament period; on the basis of its Greek rendering it is often possible to reconstruct the faulty Hebrew text. Other early translations, such as the Syriac and Latin, may also be of use. Although the Hebrew text was standardized early in the Christian era to produce the traditional or Masoretic text, the famous Isaiah A scroll from Qumran Cave 1, although basically conforming to the Masoretic text, contains a number of divergent readings that help clarify difficulties. If such helps from textual criticism do not provide a solution, scholars may resort to conjecture, i.e., an educated guess as to what originally stood in the text. This procedure is not as arbitrary as it may sound. Often the context demands a word very similar to the one which stands in the text (as if in English we read "the fly was attracted to the money jar"), especially if the shift involves Hebrew letters that scribes often confuse. Other frequent scribal errors involve the accidental repetition of a word or phrase or the omission of material because the eye has skipped from one word to another similar or identical to it. Occasional reference will be made in the commentary to uncertainty or obscurity in the Hebrew text to explain why the interpretation adopted may not seem to be supported by the wording of the *RSV* (or other English text).

The Prophet and His Times

Nothing is known about the man Isaiah aside from hints contained in the book (which are tantalizingly few) and what can be gathered from his general historical and cultural background. He received his call in the Jerusalem Temple and seems to have exercised the whole of his prophetic ministry in or near that city. He was married to a woman who is designated as a prophetess (8:3); two sons are mentioned to whom he gave the symbolic names Shear-jashub (7:3) and Maher-shalal-hash-baz (8:3), though there may have been others who were not mentioned. On the basis of his easy access to the king, his immense literary ability, and his knowledge of history and current events, it is often argued that he was a member of the aristocracy; while his social standing is a matter of conjecture, there can be little doubt that he was among the educated classes; this is seen also in the not infrequent contacts with the wisdom tradition that are manifested in his oracles.

Isaiah's theological concerns are primarily those of Judah and Jerusalem. There is no reference to Moses, Sinai, or covenant in the authentic words of Isaiah and perhaps only an allusion or two to the exodus; nor is it possible to establish any clear link with the law codes we know from the Old Testament. Similar statements could not be made, e.g., of his near contemporary in Israel to the north, Hosea, nor of Jeremiah, who preached in Jerusalem more than a century later but whose roots lay in the northern traditions of his home in Anathoth of Benjamin. Isaiah manifests interest in the Davidic dynasty, the Temple of Jerusalem and the "Zion tradition" generally, and Israel's holy war tradition. His teaching concerning moral obligations would have been drawn in part from general norms of behavior embodied in Israel's wisdom tradition, with its strong concern for safeguarding the rights of the weak and helpless members of society; such norms would have been included in the education received by the youth of Jerusalem's upper class, those who were destined to rule and upon whom the obligation of administering justice would fall. But in part Isaiah's teaching would have sprung from his prophetic call and the experience of God that went with it. The one who has experienced the holiness of God is immediately aware of the sinfulness of which he and the whole people are guilty (6:3-6). In the light of this holiness not only oppression of the poor but also any form of human pride and resistance to God's will become intolerable sins which invite destruction.

God's holiness, in Old Testament thought, implies power even more than it implies moral goodness, and the one who experiences it knows the futility of looking elsewhere for effective policy and action: they will come from God alone, and to forsake him to look for other help is like abandoning the powerhouse in order to buy a flashlight. So strong was Isaiah's insistence on trust in Yahweh and his condemnation of seeking help elsewhere that he has not infrequently been called utopian. Yet Assyria would have crushed the rebellion behind the Syro-Ephraimitic War whether Ahaz had called for help or not, and Hezekiah's revolt against Assyria, trusting in Egypt's help, brought only disaster.

Isaiah was called to the prophetic ministry "in the year that King Uzziah died" (6:1), probably 742 (on the chronological problem, see below). According to the inscription of his book (1:1), he prophesied in the days of Uzziah, Jotham, Ahaz, and Hezekiah. However, the inscription is from a later hand and, in any case, he would have had little or no time under Uzziah. There are a number of oracles that can probably be dated to the period before Ahaz (see above on the formation of the Isaiah collection); these are concerned mainly with what we would call "social justice" (treatment of the weak and poor), human pride, and Yahweh's reaction to such failings. There are a number of oracles from the days of Ahaz that relate especially to the Syro-Ephraimitic War, a time followed apparently by a lengthy period of silence (cf. 8:16-18); with the exception 28:1-4 (which probably falls between 732 and 722), no oracles can be dated with confidence to the next eighteen years. In chap. 20 we have unmistakable proof that Isaiah vigorously opposed any entry of Judah into Ashdod's rebellion against the Assyrians (714-711); and other oracles that probably date from this period bear witness to the same message (18:1-6; 19:1-15). A fourth period of activity, much better attested than the third, came during Hezekiah's rebellion against Sennacherib in 705-701 (see especially chaps. 28-31) and the immediate aftermath (1:4-9; 22:1-14).

Although it is not obvious from the oracles of his first period, the whole time of Isaiah's prophetic ministry was overshadowed by the brooding presence of the Assyrian empire, its might, and its ambitions; in one way or another almost all the material of his second, third, and fourth periods testifies to the pervasive concern created by the threat of the domination of this Mesopotamian power (see Map 3). Assyria's ninth-century attempt to expand to the west had been held in check by a coalition of smaller states (the so-called anti-Assyrian coalition), including Syria (Aram) and Israel, and a period of weak Assyrian rulers coincided with the rise of Urartu, in the Armenian mountains. But the weak Assyrian dynasty was swept away by revolt and there emerged as the new leader the vigorous and able Tiglath-pileser III (745-727). Only two years after his accession he appeared with his army at Arpad to claim the homage of those kings who acknowledged Assyrian overlordship and to direct campaigns against kings of Anatolia, Syria, and Palestine who did not submit. Among the latter is listed a certain "Azriyau of Yaudi" (*ANET* 282-83), who was probably Uzziah (Azariah) of Judah. Judah was sufficiently remote to be left in peace for the moment. Menahem (745-737), king of Israel, was among those who submitted.

Unfortunately, Israel was not able to hold consistently to any policy with regard to Assyria, and the frequent change of king and dynasty between 746 and the destruction of the nation in 722/1 reflected and was in large part the result of the weathervane-like alternations between submission and resistance.

Judah was drawn back into the picture on the occasion of the so-called Syro-Ephraimitic War (735-732; "Ephraimitic" from Ephraim, which, being one of the largest of the tribes of northern Israel, sometimes gives its name to the whole). On this occasion Israel, under Pekah (736-732), joined with Syria (Aram), under Rezin (740-732), in revolting against Assyria, to which they stood in the relation of vassals. If Uzziah (Azariah) (783-742) had formerly joined in resistance to Assyria, his grandson Ahaz, the then king of Judah (735-715), was more circumspect. But Syria and Israel, fearing that a neutral or possibly hostile Judah to the south would compromise their defense strategy in the face of the expected Assyrian bid to reassert control, invaded Judah's territory; part of the plan, apparently, was to replace Ahaz with a man who would be more amenable to their designs. In these circumstances Ahaz thought he had no choice except to voluntarily submit to Assyria and ask for their help (2 Kgs 16:5-8), a course of action bitterly opposed by Isaiah (see below on chaps. 7-8).

The Assyrians, who could not in any case have ignored the defection of their vassals, first swept down the Palestine coast, subduing the Philistines and cutting off any help the Egyptians might have attempted to send. They occupied Israelite territory in both Transjordan and Galilee, destroyed some of the cities, and, consistent with the usual policy for rebellious vassals, deported a large part of the population. Of what had been the northern kingdom of Israel they left only Samaria and some of its surrounding territories; the rest they divided into three provinces (Gilead, Megiddo, including Galilee, and Dor) which they incorporated into the Assyrian empire. Pekah was assassinated by Hoshea, who himself became king and promptly submitted to Assyria. Rezin was executed by Tiglath-pileser, much of Syria's population was deported, its territory was divided into four Assyrian provinces, and Damascus, its capital, was sacked.

One might have thought this would end Israel's resistance permanently, but such was not the case. After the death of Tiglath-pileser III and the succession of his son Shalmaneser V (726-722), Hoshea (732-724), acting with the understanding of help from Egypt, refused submission to Assyria and so brought on the end of the northern kingdom. In the event, no help came from Egypt, which was weak and divided at this time under the Twenty-fourth Dynasty, and Hoshea quickly surrendered to Shalmaneser in 724 and was taken prisoner. But Samaria continued to hold out and fell only in the year 722/721; again a large number were deported and the remaining territory became a province in the Assyrian empire. Israel, which was, after all, with Judah, God's chosen people, loomed importantly in Isaiah's thought. The schism between Judah and Israel, which had occurred almost two centuries before he came on the scene, he considered a great calamity (7:17), and he chastises Israel for their vice and folly, threatening the destruction that finally did overtake them (28:1-4).

Judah, in the meantime, as a result of Ahaz's action, had become an Assyrian vassal. One of the disadvantages of this (besides the heavy annual tribute which had to be paid) was the recognition of the Assyrian gods, at least in the oath of loyalty Ahaz had to swear. The new altar which Ahaz caused to be built, after having seen a model of it at Damascus, where he went to make his submission to Tiglath-pileser III, reflects this new situation (2 Kgs 16:10-16). The introduction of Assyrian elements into the cult no doubt also encouraged the revival of native forms of paganism; of Ahaz it is said that he sacrificed his son (2 Kgs 16:3), a pagan practice frequently condemned in the Old Testament (Lev 20:2-5; 2 Kgs 23:10; Jer 7:31; 32:35; Ezek 16:20-21). Such weakening of Judah's loyalty to Yahweh would also have had a deleterious effect on other aspects of their religious life, especially through the corruption of their sense of justice and compassion toward the weaker members of society, a point on which Isaiah has much to say.

Assyria continued virtually invincible, even though there were signs that could be interpreted as the beginnings of decay. After the death of Shalmaneser V and the accession of Sargon II (721-705), Babylonia, which Tiglath-pileser III had quelled, making himself king there, now rebelled under the leadership of Merodach-baladan (Marduk-apla-iddina). Merodach-baladan was dealt with rather quickly on this occasion (though he continued to be a problem — see below on 39:1-8), but new campaigns were necessary against Urartu to the north (they had been defeated by Tiglath-pileser and now Sargon finally crushed them), against the Medes to the east in Iran, against Carchemish and others. And around 716 in Egypt the new and vigorous Twenty-fifth Dynasty (Ethiopian), founded by Piankhi, replaced the ineffectual Twenty-fourth Dynasty (*HI*, 281).

Ahaz's successor, Hezekiah (715-687), was much more interested in independence than in continued submission. His preparations for revolt were careful and far-ranging. An important element was his religious reform: he removed pagan cult objects from the Temple (even Israelite ones that were suspect — see 2 Kgs 18:4) and closed local shrines; apparently this reform was extended even into the northern territories that had previously been Israel, whose inhabitants he invited to come to Jerusalem to worship. In all this he made himself a favorite of the deuteronomic historians (see 2 Kgs 18:1-6). To strengthen Jerusalem's ability to withstand a siege, Hezekiah had his famous tunnel dug (1,749 feet through solid rock) to bring water from the spring Gihon to a reservoir within the city of Jerusalem. In addition, though we know of it only through hints in Isaiah's oracles, negotiations were conducted between Egypt and Judah concerning Egyptian help in repelling the Assyrian troops that could be expected in the event of a rebellion by Judah. Egypt was not a vassal of Assyria, but Sargon had conducted a campaign that brought him to the very border of Egypt in 716-715, and this raised the fears of an eventual invasion of Egypt (which did, in fact, take place in 663 under Asshurbanapal), prompting Egypt to encourage any activity that would weaken Assyria.

Isaiah would undoubtedly have applauded Hezekiah's religious reforms, as well as the desire for independence. Nevertheless, Hezekiah's plans for revolt hardly left room for any policy that Yahweh might have had — and Isaiah was quite convinced that he did. Assyria had a place in Yahweh's intention, initially, at least, as his instrument to punish a sinful Judah; but as king of all the earth, his plan was all-encompassing, and it included the eventual disposal of Assyria and its arrogant boasting. Furthermore, Judah's inclusion of Egyptian help in its machinations was an implicit denial that it was Yahweh's power that would determine the outcome. Although such lofty theological considerations might seem to ignore God's use of secondary causes, or perhaps to treat them one-sidedly, behind them lay also the quite realistic assessment that Assyria was strong enough to remain in control and that any trust in Egypt would be disastrously misplaced.

In any event, we find Isaiah strenuously warning against revolt against the Assyrians in the period of 714-711, a time at which the Philistine city of Ashdod revolted. Other Philistine cities joined in; from Assyrian documents, we learn that Judah, along with Edom and Moab, was invited to join, and from chap. 20 we know that Egypt had promised help. Hezekiah did not participate in the revolt on this occasion, and it seems probable that Isaiah's opposition had some influence on the decision not to. Yet Hezekiah does not seem to have been consistently amenable to Isaiah's urgings, for it was certainly in the face of most strenuous opposition from Isaiah that he revolted from Assyria in 705. The occasion was the death of Sargon II and the accession of a new Assyrian king, Sennacherib (704-681). Judah's revolt was only one part of a concerted and widespread rebellion, but Sennacherib was capable of dealing with it. He first subdued Babylon, again led by Merodach-baladan, and then moved against Tyre; and with the conquest of Tyre many of the rebel kings surrendered. Sennacherib then moved against the Philistine cities that had been members of the conspiracy and, in the course of reducing them, defeated the Egyptian army that came out to offer support. The devastation in Judah was terrible. Assyrian records tell of forty-six walled cities being reduced, as well as many other smaller towns; Judah was stripped of much of its territory and more than 200,000 inhabitants deported — though that figure is almost certainly an exaggeration. Finally Jerusalem alone was left, and Hezekiah surrendered, paying an enormous tribute in order to save the city (2 Kgs 18:13-16). The legendary account of Jerusalem's deliverance on this occasion given in 2 Kgs 18:17-19:37 // Isa 36:2-37:38 is dealt with in the commentary and will not be discussed here. (And, in general, many of the events touched on briefly in this historical summary are discussed in greater detail in the commentary on the relevant passages.)

The dates assigned to reigns and events in the preceding summary follow the conclusions reached by W. F. Albright and defended by John Bright, D. N. Freedman, E. F. Campbell, and others, but the reader should be warned that precisely for the period under discussion there are uncertainties which have a bearing on our understanding of the events reported. The kings of Judah for the period in question, with their regnal years according to Albright-Bright chronology, are the following:

Uzziah (Azariah): 783-742
Jotham   : 750-735 (coregent with Uzziah 750-742)
Ahaz   : 735-715
Hezekiah   : 715-687

Although 1-2 Kings gives us detailed information about the reigns of the kings of Judah and Israel, in terms of when each one began to reign and how long he reigned, there are inconsistencies which warn us that not all the information is accurate. Furthermore, the "when each one began to reign" is not given with respect to a fixed date but in terms of the year of rule of his opposite number in the other kingdom (i.e., X became king of Judah in the Nth year of Y, king of Israel, and he ruled N years in Jerusalem). In order to translate this information into dates, scholars make use of events to which we have already been able to fix a date, and which coincide with other events which we wish to date (synchronism). Assyrian sources make it possible to construct precise Assyrian regnal lists from 911 to the middle of the seventh century; and by the happy event that a solar eclipse is precisely located within that period, absolute dates are assignable for the whole series. When an event from those records coincides with one mentioned in the Bible, we have a synchronism that allows the dating of the biblical event.

Sennacherib's invasion, on the basis of Assyrian records, is dated to 701; in 2 Kgs 18:13 // Isa 36:1 we are told that this was the fourteenth year of Hezekiah, and this leads to the conclusion that he came to the throne in 715. If we allow Ahaz the sixteen years of rule that 2 Kgs 16:2 gives him, he then would have begun to reign in 730; but on the basis of Assyrian records the Syro-Ephraimitic War must have begun in 735, when we know Ahaz was king, and thus he must have ruled at least twenty years, from 735. A further complication comes from 2 Kgs 18:1, which dates Hezekiah's accession to the throne in the third year of Hoshea, king of Israel; since it is clear that Hoshea began to rule about the time the Assyrians ended Pekah's rebellion (i.e., 732), this would place the beginning of Hezekiah's rule about 728. (This chronology is reinforced by 2 Kgs 18:9-10, which has Samaria besieged in the fourth year of Hezekiah and taken in his sixth year, events dated to 724 and 722 by Assyrian records.) There is also the fact that Isa 14:28-32 probably refers to the death of Tiglath-pileser III, and the oracle is dated "in the year that King Ahaz died"; since Tiglath-pileser III died in 727, this would date Ahaz's death in that same year (and his accession to the throne around 742, since, according to 2 Kgs 16:2, he ruled for sixteen years). Thus it is clear that the biblical data are not consistent and that choices need to be made. As indicated above, the Bright-Albright dating accepts the accuracy of 2 Kgs 18:13 (that Sennacherib's invasion of 701 occurred in the fourteenth year of Hezekiah). Others have supposed that there is a scribal error in that verse, that we should read "twenty-fourth year," and that Hezekiah therefore began to rule in 725. Still others suppose that the dating in that verse has been invented on the basis of the account of Hezekiah's illness and the fifteen years of additional life that he is promised (see below on chap. 38) and is to be disregarded; this would leave the testimony of 2 Kgs 18:1, 9-10, on the basis of which the beginning of his reign would be dated to 727 or 728. The Bright-Albright chronology involves a coregency of Jotham with Uzziah, for which there is good biblical basis, since we are told that Uzziah became a leper and that Jotham "was over the household, governing the people of the land" (2 Kgs 15:5). One of the systems that proposes an accession date of 725 for Hezekiah and a sixteen-year reign for Ahaz needs to postulate that all of Jotham's reign and part of Ahaz's were coregency with Uzziah, though this is not based on biblical data.

One of the questions that hinges on the solution given to these problems has to do with the date of Isaiah's call, which came "in the year that King Uzziah died" (6:1), which would be 742 according to the Bright-Albright chronology, but as early as 747 or as late as 735 according to others. Another question that relates to chronology is whether Hezekiah could be the child whose birth Isaiah foretells in the Immanuel oracle of 7:14, delivered about 735. *If* 2 Kgs 18:1 is correct in putting Hezekiah's age at twenty-five at the beginning of his reign, then an accession year of 715 would have him born in 740, an accession year of 725 would put his birth in 750, and an accession year of 728 would put his birth in 753. Any of those birthdates would make it difficult for Hezekiah to be Immanuel. (One system that dates Hezekiah's accession to the throne in 728, however, postulates that Ahaz ruled for only six — not sixteen — years and that Hezekiah came to the throne at the age of five — not twenty-five — and this would have him born in 733. Errors of this sort in the transmission of numbers do occur, but obviously it is difficult to know if they did in the case at hand and which ones.)

A third question that hinges on chronology relates to

whether the "two campaigns" theory is the best solution to the problems that surround Sennacherib's invasion as described in 2 Kgs 18:13-19:37 // Isa 36:1-37:38. Those who postulate a second campaign date it around 688, and this is compatible with an accession date for Hezekiah in 715 (and the reign of twenty-nine years that 2 Kgs 18:2 gives him), but it is not compatible with an accession in 725 or 728, for his twenty-nine year reign (and presumably his life) would have ended long before that. (On the "two campaigns" theory, see below on chaps. 36-37.)

Teachings

To explain what Isaiah taught will be a principal goal of the commentary itself, and all that can be attempted here is a brief systematic summary of some of the more salient features of his message. Even such a limited attempt is complicated by a number of factors, not least of which is the question of the authenticity of particular passages. We can begin, at least, with matters that occasion little or no dispute.

Like Amos, his predecessor in the north, and Micah, his younger contemporary in Judah, Isaiah gives attention to the plight of the poorer members of society. To some extent they were the victims of social revolution, of the change from an egalitarian society of small landowners, primarily agricultural, to a much more stratified society with royalty, nobility, and a wealthy merchant class and an emerging latifundism (i.e., heaping up of large landed estates). This is not something which happened overnight, but the process is seen to be well along the way in the three prophets referred to. Often these changes were brought about by legal means, though references to judicial bribery and other abuses indicate that this was not always the case. But whether legal or not, the cost of such "progress," in terms of human misery, was something the prophets thought worthy of condemnation. Thus Isaiah sees as an evil the insouciance with which the affairs of the weaker members of society were treated

(1:17, 23; 5:23; 10:1-2) and condemns the accumulation of property (5:8-10), no doubt because that involved the dispossession, by one means or another, of the previous owners; according to some this would also have meant loss of representation in the legal assemblies.

Because Judah did not have an evolved judicial organization, administration of justice would have been in the hands of ordinary government officials, the nobility, and the prominent citizens of city and village. It is difficult to know what, if any, detailed collection of laws might have been in force in Isaiah's day; the Covenant Code (Exod 20:22-23:33) seems to have been primarily a northern collection, the Deuteronomic Code (Deuteronomy 12-26) came to light in Judah only after Isaiah's time (*OTM*, Vol. 4, pp. 1-3), and the Holiness Code (Leviticus 17-26), although containing some moral and humanitarian provisions (mainly in chap. 19), some of them old, is a later compilation that, in the main, is concerned with cultic and other matters that find little echo in Isaiah. But those who administered justice would have been imbued with the ethics of the wisdom tradition, in which they would have received their training, and some of Isaiah's criticisms indicate they neglected the lofty ideals of their training; violence replaces justice (5:7) and those in authority pervert power to their own gain (10:1-2).

Isaiah sees Yahweh as king, not simply of Judah, but of all the earth. He is the Lord, Yahweh of hosts, the Holy One of Israel. Other nations, even the mightiest, are subject to him and do his bidding when he calls; they are but instruments to be wielded by him. Furthermore, he does not simply react to man but is himself the Lord of history and, as is fitting, has a policy or plan that he implements. Since this is so, attempts to force events through military might or foreign alliances are doomed to failure — or, more accurately, achieve only that success which accords with Yahweh's will. It is for this reason that Isaiah strenuously opposed both Ahaz's appeal to the Assyrians for help at the time Judah was invaded by Syria and Israel in 735 and Hezekiah's plans to revolt against Assyria in 705. In either case it was a question of attempting to control events through human forces without regard to what Yahweh could and would do.

There was also the matter of Yahweh's concern for the Davidic dynasty, assured by his firm promise, and for Jerusalem, the city of his choice (though here we touch on points not agreed upon by all). On the former, see the commentary especially on 7:1-16; 9:1-7; and 11:1-9. On the latter, it may be pointed out that Jerusalem occupies a place of central interest for Isaiah. This can be seen, in the first instance, in the number of references he makes to it. Judah is hardly mentioned except in conjunction with Jerusalem. The city is referred to under a number of other titles: Zion, Mount Zion, Daughter Zion, the Mount of Yahweh, and the Mount of the house of Yahweh; the Lord is "Yahweh of hosts who dwells on Mount Zion" (8:18). Judah and its leaders would be safe if they turned to him with the requisite faith, i.e., with the efficacious faith that renounced political machinations and trust in foreign powers in favor of the trust that would allow him to manifest his power in his own way. When leaders and people as a whole turn aside from the way of faith which Yahweh has marked out for them through his prophet, those who remain faithful by "waiting for the Lord" (8:16-18) constitute a sort of remnant of faith: even after Judah's earlier rejection, the invitation to build on this precious cornerstone of faith (28:16) and to find salvation and strength "in quietness and trust" (30:15) is renewed. Thus Isaiah accepts and builds on the Zion tradition, a tradition which undoubtedly antedated him, but he sees Yahweh's help and protection conditional on Judah's trust in his power to save.

Judah's failures in the two areas referred to, social justice and international relations, led Isaiah to pronounce many threats against the nation. In some cases these may be couched quite clearly in conditional terms, as when the alternatives of peace and the sword are offered (1:19-20), but even those sayings which seem to threaten unconditional judgment are often calls to repentance and conversion. In the same way, punishment already inflicted should lead to the contrition which brings healing — though often enough does not (1:5-6; 22:1-14). It is in this context of punishment of Judah's sin that Assyria's role is most clearly defined. Isaiah neither dismissed Assyria's might nor was he in awe of it. If Assyria had been raised to heights of power it was because Yahweh had done it for his own purpose; and part of that purpose, Isaiah knew, was the chastisement of Judah (10:5-6). The fact that Assyria did not recognize the limited nature of the role assigned to it by Yahweh indicated foolishness and pride and pointed to its eventual demise (10:7-15; 14:24-27).

But punishment need not always be tied to military defeat at the hand of Assyria or some other nation; Isaiah could speak of Yahweh's punitive action in more direct terms, as in his "day of the Lord" oracle (2:6-21); here the sin which calls forth punishment is especially that of pride, for it is a day against everything that is lifted up so that it may be brought low. On many other occasions, too, Isaiah returns to this matter of pride and its punishment (in addition to 2:11-12, 17, see 3:16; 5:15-16; 9:8-9; 10:7-15; 28:1-4). The special evil of pride, no doubt, is that it stands in such opposition to the attitude one ought to have before the holy God. Yahweh's holiness is the quality that comes most to the fore in Isaiah's teaching, receiving a certain emphasis already in his call narrative (6:3). "The Holy One of Israel" occurs frequently and is one of Isaiah's favorite titles for the Lord.

But the "of Israel" in that title is revealing, for it indicates Isaiah's awareness of election enjoyed by God's people: Yahweh, Lord of all the earth, stands in a particular relationship to one people. (The name "Israel" in this expression — and in some others used by Isaiah — does not designate the northern kingdom, which he is more apt to designate as "Ephraim," but God's chosen people as such. In practice, since in some passages he sees the northern kingdom as already written off — e.g., 7:4-9; 8:1-4; 28:1-4 — "Israel" can designate the part of the chosen people he sees as the object of God's special care, namely, Judah; this is more clearly the case after the fall of Samaria.) In a few places the people of

Judah are Yahweh's "children" (1:2; 30:1, 9), but more frequently are designated "my people," so that when they are referred to as "this people," it is a sign of Yahweh's displeasure (6:9-10; 8:6, 11;28:11). Because of this special relationship of Judah to Yahweh, Isaiah can hold out to them hope of a future restoration and even of a golden age (though this is a point on which not all agree). Actual or threatened punishments are not intended as destruction but can have a medicinal effect. Even the fearful "day of the Lord" is said to be intended for the humbling of human pride (2:11, 17), and the Assyrians are given a commission limited to chastising Judah, and thus they are Yahweh's "rod" and "staff" but not his sword (10:5-7). Assyria may one day perish for its arrogance, but for Judah the trial to come is a way of bringing it to an idyllic state, which is sometimes likened to ideal days gone by (1:21-26; and see comments on "Immanuel" in 7:10-17).

Isaiah's universalistic view of Yahweh as Lord of all the earth leads him to one of the most beautiful visions of the future to be found in any literature, namely, the pilgrimage of the nations to Mt. Zion to receive Yahweh's *torah* and to transform their weapons of war into implements of peace (2:2-4). By comparing this passage with 30:8-14 we can discover the basis for the difference between the evils of the present age and the blessings of the future age. In the former passage (and present age) people reject Yahweh's *torah* (instruction) and so come to the destruction their folly brings upon themselves; but in the age to come the acceptance of Yahweh's *torah* results in the wise and obedient behavior that leads to peace. That Isaiah would expect obedience in the future in place of the disobedience he experienced during his lifetime suggests a new force from God that is capable of transforming the human heart — something we would call "grace" but which Isaiah would be more likely to call "spirit." (*OTA*, 4, #803.)

Unlike Ezekiel (see Ezek 36:26; and cf. Jeremiah's "new heart" and *torah* placed in the heart, Jer 31:33), Isaiah does not speak of the bestowal of the "spirit" in this generalized sense, but he does speak of a future son of David who would have the spirit as his special gift. In the circumstances of the Syro-Ephraimitic War, basing himself upon God's promise to the house of David and the developments generated therefrom, Isaiah assured Ahaz of safety in the attack and foretold a new successor in David's line in whom expectation would come to fruition. Isaiah appears to have expected someone for the contemporary situation, and the description of an ideal ruler in 9:6-7 seems to date from the same historical context. Whether any of this can be applied to the one who was in fact Ahaz's immediate successor, Hezekiah, is problematical, especially in view of the chronological uncertainties (see above). If Hezekiah was the one on whom Isaiah's expectations centered in the first instance, he must have come to have other views; Hezekiah's revolt in 705 certainly flew in the face of what Isaiah was preaching at that time and, although the texts do not directly witness to it, there may have been bitter conflict between them. Yet Isaiah's faith in the coming of an ideal Davidic king did not disappear, as the portrait found in 11:1-9 bears witness. Here would be a recipient of the spirit of Yahweh who, because of this spirit, would be capable of bearing the four names predicated in 9:6, of ruling over a renewed Judah (and world) in which the peace looked for in 2:4 would be a reality. It is only the king who, in 11:2, is said to receive the spirit, but clearly the power and effects of that spirit are communicated through him to his subjects and to all creation so that peace reigns on God's "holy mountain" in the new age come at last. It was not experience with the historical kings of Judah that led the prophet to this vision but rather faith in Yahweh's plan and his power to bring it to pass. From this we know that the prophet did not lack the faith that he so constantly demanded from others.

AN INTRODUCTORY COLLECTION: CHAPTER 1

As has already been pointed out (Introduction, p. 15), Isaiah 1 stands somewhat apart from the larger collection to which it is generally associated (chaps. 1-12); this is seen most strikingly in the new inscription at 2:1. The oracles that make up chap. 1, unlike some of the other Isaiah material, are not given any particular context — historical, chronological, or literary. They seem, in fact, to come from different periods of Isaiah's ministry, though only one of them, vv 4-9, which almost certainly belongs to 701, can be dated with any confidence. The view which is most widely accepted is that these oracles were specifically selected out of the larger Isaianic collection to stand as a sample of and an introduction to Isaiah's preaching. Thus (leaving aside the inscription of 1:1, on which see below) we find here an exposition of Israel's sin (vv 2-3), God's judgment upon it (vv 4-9), false and true ways of making amends (vv 10-17), the choice which confronts God's people (vv 18-20), and restoration through judgment (vv 21-26). (Verses 27-28 and vv 29-31 are not by Isaiah; vv 27-28 may have been added by the editor who compiled the chapter from Isaiah's words, but vv 29-31 were appended at a later date.) The oracles of this chapter, because of careful selection and skillful editing, fit together very well, but attempts to demonstrate they are an original (as distinct from redactional) unity are not convincing. (*OTA*, 1, #522; 4, #500; 5, #839.)

THE INSCRIPTION: 1:1

> **1** The vision of Isaiah the son of Amoz, which he saw concerning Judah and Jerusalem in the days of Uzziah, Jotham, Ahaz, and Hezekiah, kings of Judah.

Most prophetic books (as well as most psalms) have a prefixed "inscription," i.e., a note by an editor of the composition to indicate who the author of the composition was and to provide other enlightening bits of information. Were it not for the inscription we might not even know whose words we are dealing with, for the ancient scrolls did not have the sort of titles and tables of contents (not to mention the running heads) that we find in modern books.

The designation of Isaiah's message as *vision* (*hazon*) is somewhat unexpected, for the usual term is "word" or "words" for a prophetic book; but "vision" (or the verb *hazah*, "to see a vision") is found in the inscriptions at Isa 2:1; Obad 1; Nah 1:1; and Hab 1:1. On the chronology of Bright-Albright followed in this commentary (see Introduction, p. 27), the reigns of the kings under whom Isaiah is said to have prophesied covered the period from 783 to 687/6 (Uzziah 783-742; Jotham, coregent 750-742, king 742-735; Ahaz 735-715; Hezekiah 715-687/6). However, from Isaiah's vocation narrative (see 6:1), we learn that he was called to prophesy in "the year King Uzziah died" (742), which is therefore the upper limit of his prophetic ministry. The last clearly datable oracles relate to the events connected with Hezekiah's revolt and Sennacherib's invasion (705-701). Most of Isaiah's prophetic activity seems to pertain to the reigns of Ahaz and Hezekiah. There is some material in chaps. 1-12 that probably antedates the Syro-Ephraimitic War, and this would have come in the days of Jotham, depending on the chronological system followed.

The prophet's name means something like "Yahweh is salvation," the -iah ending being a shortened form of Yahweh and the first part being a form derived from *yasha'*, the common verb for "to save." Isaiah's father, Amoz, is not otherwise known. (See further on Isaiah and his background in Introduction, pp. 20-30.)

YAHWEH'S SENSELESS CHILDREN: 1:2-3

2 Hear, O heavens, and give ear, O earth;
    for the LORD has spoken:
"Sons have I reared and brought up,
    but they have rebelled against me.
3 The ox knows its owner,
    and the ass its master's crib;
But Israel does not know,
    my people does not understand."

In this brief piece, which may be classified as a complaint, Isaiah exposes the root problem with Yahweh's people: they do not understand. With attention-arresting alliteration (*shime'u shamayim*), Yahweh calls upon the *heavens* and the *earth* to note that he has lavished upon his *people* the care of a parent for children only to find them rebellious and disobedient. Thus in this opening, programmatic oracle Yahweh is depicted in a parent-child relationship with his people (see also 30:1, 9). In near Eastern culture, even more than in our own, obedience to parents is expected not only in childhood but also in adulthood (cf. the "honor your father and your mother" of the Decalogue — Exod 20:12 —which is directed much more to adults than to children); but to say that Israel has *rebelled* indicates something far beyond simple disrespect or disobedience.

At other important junctures, too, in Isaiah's book, Judah's problem is depicted, as here (v 3), as a failure to *know* or *understand* (see 5:13; 6:9-10); here Judah's incomprehension is unfavorably contrasted with that of the ox and the ass, animals proverbial for stupidity or stubbornness (see Prov 7:22; 26:3; Ps 32:9). In his use of proverb, in his vocabulary,

and in identifying the problem as Judah's failure to know/
understand, especially in terms of the parent-child relationship, Isaiah here betrays something of the peculiar relationship in which he stood to the wisdom tradition (see below on
1:10-17; 2:3; 3:11; 5:18-23; 10:5-7; 14:27; 11:2; 28:23-29;
29:13-14, 15-16; 30:9). On this point it is specially to be
noted that it is not said Israel *does not understand* this or
that (not even Yahweh or the prophet's word); this lack of
specification leaves their want of knowledge and understanding quite universal. God's people have not even
grasped the sort of thing that brute beasts know instinctu-
ally. The general tone of the piece is sadness rather than
threat, though rebellious and stupid children do not long
avoid catastrophe. The attempt made by some, to see in the
invocation of the *heavens* and *earth* in v 2 the beginning of a
covenant lawsuit, is to be rejected; Isaiah nowhere makes
reference to the covenant nor to those traditions closely
connected with it. The *heavens* and *earth* are designated
because when Yahweh speaks all creation pays heed; in this
we can see a deliberately marked contrast to the neglect of
those he has made his children.

CHASTISED BUT UNREPENTANT: 1:4-9

> 4 Ah, sinful nation,
> > a people laden with iniquity,
> offspring of evildoers,
> > sons who deal corruptly!
> They have forsaken the LORD,
> > they have despised the Holy One of Israel,
> > they are utterly estranged.
>
> 5 Why will you still be smitten,
> > that you continue to rebel?
> The whole head is sick,
> > and the whole heart faint.
> 6 From the sole of the foot even to the head,
> > there is no soundness in it,

but bruises and sores
and bleeding wounds;
they are not pressed out, or bound up,
or softened with oil.

7 Your country lies desolate,
your cities are burned with fire;
in your very presence
aliens devour your land;
it is desolate, as overthrown by aliens.
8 And the daughter of Zion is left
like a booth in a vineyard,
like a lodge in a cucumber field,
like a besieged city.

9 If the LORD of hosts
had not left us a few survivors,
we should have been like Sodom,
and become like Gomorrah.

This piece almost certainly dates to the events of 701; the devastation described is that wrought by the Assyrian king Sennacherib in punishment for Hezekiah's rebellion against him (2 Kgs 18:13-14), an act Isaiah had strenuously opposed (see below on chaps. 28-31). This piece, too, begins with attention-getting alliteration and assonance (*hoy goy hote'*), and again God's people are referred to as *children*, this time corrupt ones. Isaiah runs through three other terms progressively more intimate (*nation, people, off-spring*) before reaching the poignant climax of *children*. Judah's sin is here no more clearly specified than in the preceding piece, but if this oracle does indeed relate to the events of 701, their sin would be a failure to respond in faith to Yahweh, turning to Egypt for help, and rejecting the word of God through his prophet (see further on chaps. 28-31); it is in this way, especially, that *they have despised the Holy One of Israel* (v 4). (On this title and Yahweh as the Holy One, see below on 6:3).

After the opening (v 4) there follows a central section, vv 5-7, which presents a personification of Judah as a human individual who has been beaten bloody; since v 4 had spoken of *sons*/children, it is probable that the image is that of a son who has been severely chastised for rebellion and disobedience. Again we are brought into touch with the wisdom tradition, here because of its advocacy of the rod as a means of correcting and disciplining (see Prov 10:13; 13:24; 22:15; 23:13, 14; 26:3; 29:15; and see especially 20:30 for close verbal contacts with this passage). In the case at hand the punishment has had to be administered because of repeated rebellions, so that it is said ironically (still consistent with the personification being used) that there is no longer any sound spot to receive new blows — a vivid description of the ravaged condition of the land when Sennacherib had completed his work.

Turning from the image of a body covered with wounds, Isaiah now depicts the stark reality of a land devastated, both city and countryside (v 7). To say that foreigners *devour the land* may be vivid imagery to describe the takeover by the enemy, but it reminds us that invading troops live off the produce of the land and denude it by their plundering, thus leaving precious little to the natives for meeting even their basic needs. The final phrase (*it is desolate...*) is probably a later addition.

A new personification confronts us in v 8: Jerusalem as *Daughter of Zion* (or, probably more correctly, "Daughter Zion"; see *NAB*). The broader Near Eastern background suggests that this "daughter" terminology (sometimes "virgin daughter") derives from the conception of the city as a woman married to the patron deity. The two structures Zion is likened to evoke a picture of isolation and insecurity (for both are flimsy structures). The final characterization as a *besieged city* brings us again to cold reality. Yet in spite of the gloomy picture, Daughter Zion *is left*, so hope is not totally cut off. The fact that Jerusalem was spared in the general destruction visited upon Judah in retaliation for the rebellion against Assyria (Assyrian records speak of bringing down forty-six walled cities with their adjacent villages) is indeed worth remarking upon. (Historically speaking there are problems surrounding the deliverance of Jerusalem and some sources present the escape as a miracle of sorts. On the problems involved, see below on chaps. 36-37.)

The bipolar aspect of v 8 (devastation, yet survival) is continued in v 9. Judah's devastation is so great that its situation is likened to that of *Sodom* and *Gomorrah*, cities proverbial for their wickedness and paradigms of God's destructive retribution (Gen 18:16-19:28). Judah's guilt is comparable to that of these cities (see the indictment above, "sinful nation," in v 4 and the additional reference to Sodom and Gomorrah below in v 10). Nevertheless, the Lord has *left* (cf. the *is left* of v 8) a scanty remnant, so at least destruction is not complete. There is room for hope, and in this sense Judah has fared far differently than Sodom and Gomorrah. Sons, even corrupt sons (v 4), may be beaten bloody, but they are not destroyed, nor is Daughter Zion's hope extinguished. The Hebrew word translated *survivors* (*sarid*) does not occur elsewhere in Isaiah and is therefore not related, at least linguistically, to any remnant theme of his. When it occurs elsewhere in the Old Testament, it is most commonly in expressions which speak of "no survivor"; but cf. Judg 5:13; Jer 31:2; and Joel 2:32 (Heb. 3:5).

WITHOUT MERCY AND RIGHTEOUSNESS THERE IS NO WORSHIP: 1:10-17

10 Hear the word of the LORD,
    you rulers of Sodom!
  Give ear to the teaching of our God,
    you people of Gomorrah!
11 "What to me is the multitude of your sacrifices?
    says the LORD;
  I have had enough of burnt offerings of rams
    and the fat of fed beasts;
  I do not delight in the blood of bulls,
    or of lambs, or of he-goats.

12 "When you come to appear before me,
    who requires of you
    this trampling of my courts?
13 Bring no more vain offerings;
    incense is an abomination to me.
  New moon and sabbath and the calling of assemblies—
    I cannot endure iniquity and solemn assembly.

¹⁴ Your new moons and your appointed feasts
    my soul hates;
  they have become a burden to me,
    I am weary of bearing them.
¹⁵ When you spread forth your hands,
    I will hide my eyes from you;
  even though you make many prayers,
    I will not listen; your hands are full of blood.
¹⁶ Wash yourselves; make yourselves clean;
    remove the evil of your doings from before my eyes;
  cease to do evil,
¹⁷   learn to do good;
  seek justice,
    correct oppression;
  defend the fatherless,
    plead for the widow.

The placing of this oracle after 1:9 is often given as a classic example of the "catch-word" principle; i.e., this passage is placed where it is because its opening reference to *Sodom* and *Gomorrah* occasioned its being placed after the mention of the same cities at the end of the previous piece. Although the opening address refers to both *rulers* and *people*, the contents make it clear that it is primarily the ruling class which is intended, those who are responsible for the oppression and lack of just judgment that is here being condemned. The piece is important for its religious and ethical content. Isaiah says, in effect, as do the other prophets (see Amos 5:21-24; Hos 6:6; Jer 7:1-15) that sacrifice and religious observance are unacceptable to God when they are offered by those who have no concern for the rights and needs of other people, especially the poor and downtrodden. Isaiah is not pointing here to any particular law or code of laws but draws his teaching from the broader ethical instruction to be found in Judah, especially that of the wisdom tradition. In fact, many of the concerns and much of the diction of the piece relate to the wisdom tradition, in which Isaiah was well versed (see on 1:2-3 above and on other texts listed there).

The opening verse, like 1:2, is a call to attention, but this one resembles the address of a teacher in the wisdom tradition, and Isaiah characterizes what is to follow as the *torah* (*teaching*, instruction) *of our God*. It is wise instruction, but because it is also *the word of the Lord*, it comes with the full authority of Yahweh, whom alone Isaiah acknowledges to be wise and source of wisdom (see below on 11:2). Those he addresses as *rulers* (*qesinim*) would probably have been among those who received the education and instruction designed for aspiring scribes and court officials, as well as for the sons of well-to-do families.

In v 11 Yahweh is introduced speaking in the first person, whereas in the call to attention he was referred to in the third person. Yahweh opens his discourse with a rhetorical question, and the pattern which occurs here, i.e., the call to attention followed by a rhetorical question, is one found frequently in wisdom compositions (cf. Job 13:6: 21:2; 34:16; 37:14; Ps 49:2-6; Isa 28:23-24). Although it is a rhetorical question, Yahweh answers it, and the response allows him to list in great detail the *multitude of your sacrifices* that he is more than sated with, a list which begins in the second half of v 11 and continues through v 15.

The tedium which Yahweh experiences in such multiplication of observances is well expressed in the lines which describe them, with their lengthy listing of sacrificial animals and rites. A rhetorical aspect of the piece is the progression of what Yahweh rejects, for the listing goes from external rites (sacrifices, food offerings, incense — vv 11-13a) to the less tangible matters of feasts and assemblies (vv 13b-14) to prayer itself (v 15). In addition, there is an intensification in the expressions of rejection: *I am full* (v 11a), *I do not want* (v 11b), *I cannot endure* (v 13), and *my soul hates* (v 14). Isaiah is not here intending to condemn sacrifice and other rites and observances in themselves, for if that were the case he would, by the same token, be rejecting prayer itself. Verse 15b is, in fact, quite a reversal of standard Israelite piety on the subject of Yahweh hearing and answering prayers; typical is the assertion, "On the day I called, thou didst answer me" (Ps 138:3; cf. Ps 5:3; 6:8, 9;

10:17; 18:6; 22:24; 28:6; 31:22; 34:6; 40:1; 55:17, 19; 69:33; 106:44; 116:1; 145:19). However, the supposition in such cases is that the supplicant is just in God's eyes (cf. Ps 34:17: "When the righteous cry for help, the Lord hears"). But those who close their eyes to oppression and to the need of the widow and the orphan can claim no such dispositions. In dramatic words Isaiah accuses them of violence: these *hands* of theirs — even now spread out in prayer — *are full of blood* (v 15)!

The remedy for the evil situation is proposed in vv 16-17, first in abstract and general (and, in part, symbolic) terms. When Isaiah says *wash yourselves; make yourselves clean*, he is not prescribing some ritual ablutions; they had rituals enough and their confidence in them was a major part of the problem. More directly he tells them to turn from evil to good.

The "conversion" demanded is then set forth in quite concrete terms of concern for the helpless members of society. The officials who are primarily addressed are those responsible for judgment. The ethic in which they were trained had a large place for this sort of concern. It is seen in the wisdom tradition which would have provided the curriculum of the school in which such officials were instructed (cf. Prov 14:31; 15:25; 19:17; 22:9; 22:22-23; 23:10-11; 29:14), which itself reflects the earlier Egyptian wisdom tradition (cf. "The Instruction of Meri-ka-Re," *ANET* 415, and "The Instruction of Amen-em-ope," *ANET* 422, 424). The Old Testament laws which reflect this sort of concern (e.g., Exod 22:20-23; 23:6-9; Deut 24:17) may simply represent a taking over into the legal tradition of such prescriptions of the wisdom ethic. What is enjoined is not so much strict legal justice with regard to the poor (though often even this was sadly lacking — see Amos 2:6; 5:7, 12; Isa 5:7, 23) as a compassionate consideration for them in their need. In saying that God abhors the sacrifices and prayers of those who oppress the poor, Isaiah is very close to the wisdom dictum of Prov 14:31: "He who oppresses a poor man insults his maker."

THE CHOICE: 1:18-20

18 "Come now, let us reason together,
  says the LORD:
 though your sins are like scarlet,
   they shall be as white as snow;
 though they are red like crimson,
   they shall become like wool.
19 If you are willing and obedient,
   you shall eat the good of the land;
20 but if you refuse and rebel,
   you shall be devoured by the sword;
 for the mouth of the LORD has spoken."

This short, seemingly simple, piece is fraught with difficulties. Some commentators wish to join these verses to the
preceding passage as its conclusion. There is also disagreement concerning the sense of the references to sins becoming
white in v 18; some commentators take these to be rhetorical
questions, the answer to which is "no!" The position taken
here is that the *RSV* arrangement and translation is substantially correct, i.e. that God is stating that forgiveness is
possible. What is unambiguously clear is that the people of
Judah are being offered a choice, the alternatives of destruction (*the sword*) and prosperous deliverance from danger
(*the good of the land*), depending on whether their response
is obedience or refusal to the word of the Lord. Although
the *says the Lord* at the beginning and the *for the mouth of
the Lord has spoken* at the end are as authoritative as any
prophetic oracle ever spoken, the passage clearly and explicitly emphasizes the *conditional* nature of many prophetic
threats. This aspect comes from the Lord's invitation to
"reason together" and from the grammatical construction
of the four central lines. The regularity and balance of these
lines is seen more easily in the original than in translation.
Each of them begins with the Hebrew word for *if*, though it
is only with the third one that the condition itself (obedience) appears. Each of the first three lines holds out favorable possibilities, but whereas the first two lines *seem* to

speak of something that will certainly happen (the *if* has to do with their sinful state, and of that there is no doubt), the third line connects the *if* with something less certain, namely, the obedience of the hearers: the decision is up to them. This in turn colors the meaning of the first two lines, for if that obedience is lacking, those sins surely will not be forgiven. At the same time this third line stands as an antithesis to the fourth *if*, which, expressing the disastrous consequences that will follow from disobedience, stands in sharp contrast to all that has preceded (*but if*). The alternatives are placed simply as "to eat" or "to be eaten (by the sword)."

Although the obedience here required is often understood as relating to general ethical norms, the alternatives of *eating the good things of the land* and *being devoured by the sword* suggest the threat of invasion and therefore more easily relates to Isaiah's word for the Assyrian crisis (see below on chaps. 7-8) or to some similar situation.

ZION RESTORED: 1:21-26(28)

21 How the faithful city
    has become a harlot,
      she that was full of justice!
    Righteousness lodged in her,
      but now murderers.
22 Your silver has become dross,
    your wine mixed with water.
23 Your princes are rebels
    and companions of thieves.
    Every one loves a bribe
      and runs after gifts.
    They do not defend the fatherless,
      and the widow's cause does not come to them.

24 Therefore the Lord says,
    the LORD of hosts,
    the Mighty One of Israel:
    "Ah, I will vent my wrath on my enemies,

and avenge myself on my foes.
25 I will turn my hand against you
   and will smelt away your dross as with lye
   and remove all your alloy.
26 And I will restore your judges as at the first,
   and your counselors as at the beginning.
   Afterward you shall be called the city of righteousness,
   the faithful city."

27 Zion shall be redeemed by justice,
   and those in her who repent, by righteousness.
28 But rebels and sinners shall be destroyed together,
   and those who forsake the LORD shall be consumed.

Many of Isaiah's oracles insist on Judah's sinfulness and on the punishment Yahweh will visit upon the people because of it. The present oracle likewise refers to sin and the punishment it merits but is of special importance because it also indicates that punishment can have a medicinal rather than a destructive purpose, that it can prepare for a future redemptive act and be the condition for it. The pattern in this piece is very clear and affords an entree to Isaiah's thought in this area that can help clarify other, less clear passages. Yahweh's punishment of sin, something that Isaiah so often speaks of, does not exclude a redemptive purpose in his action, nor is it proposed merely as an alternative: punishment can be the very means by which that redemptive purpose is furthered. The original piece breaks down into two parts: vv 21-23, which characterize Jerusalem's situation, and vv 24-26, which tell what Yahweh plans to do; as the text now stands vv 27-28 are intended to be taken as the conclusion of the piece, but originally it ended at v 26.

Although the Hebrew word which opens the first part is translated *how* in English, it is frequently used in contexts which make it clear that grief and mourning are involved; it is used several times in Lamentations and is the opening word of that composition, the word which gives that book its title in Hebrew. Thus our passage opens with a strong expression of the prophet's grief, an expression that in a sense correlates with the *Ah* (*hoy* — the same word that is often translated "woe") that occurs near the beginning of the second part (v 24b). The strong sense of personal grief implied in the *how* accords with the personification of Jerusalem we find here. The only strictly personal term employed is *harlot*, but it implies that the *faithful city* is conceived in personal terms. In all probability we are dealing again with the "Daughter Zion" concept (see 1:8), here thought of as Yahweh's spouse, formerly faithful but now untrue. In spite of the apparent resemblances to Hosea, the background here is quite different; it is the city Jerusalem, not the people Israel (or Judah), which is involved, and there is no reference to the fertility cult or to idolatry. The background relates, rather, to that practice of personifying a city as a woman married to the patron deity, discussed above on v 8. If Jerusalem is thought of as the "Daughter Zion" espoused to Yahweh, then it is intelligible that infidelity can be designated as harlotry and that in her ideal condition (whether before or after) she can be designated *faithful city*, a condition that is characterized by *justice* and *righteousness*.

Although the deterioration is described mainly in terms of departure from *justice* and *righteousness* (bribes, neglect of just judgment), the reference to silver becoming dross prepares the way for the imagery of purification which will be used in the second part. The *princes* named in v 23, precisely the ones who ought to be responsible for the administration of justice (see above on 1:10), consort with thieves and accept bribes, neglecting their obligation to the weak and poor of the populace (see above on 1:17). *This* is the present situation which is being contrasted with the former, that in which *justice* and *righteousness* were present; the *but now murderers* of v 21 is not a proper contrast and is probably a later addition. Isaiah opens the second section (vv 24-26) very solemnly with a series of titles for God: *the Lord* (*'adon*), *Yahweh of hosts*, and *the Mighty One of Israel*, a title not otherwise found in the Old Testament (though cf. "the Mighty One of Jacob," Gen 49:24; Ps 132:2, 5; Isa 49:26; 60:16).

Yahweh's personal involvement in the plight of the oppressed is seen in that he speaks not of punishing evil-doers but of taking vengeance on his enemies. (The phrase *I will turn my hand against you* may be a later insertion.) The purification of Jerusalem is now promised under the imagery of the smelting away of dross (see above on v 22). The present reading *as with lye* (*kabbor*) could, with a small emendation, yield "in a furnace" (*bakkur*), a reading which perhaps suits the imagery better. This dross metaphor and the concrete steps to be taken suggest again that Jerusalem's infidelity resides primarily in the ruling class, though, as in the case of metal that needs purifying, the contamination has spread itself throughout the whole mass.

Does Isaiah, when he speaks of restoring the *judges* and *counselors*, refer to their removal and replacement by other, more worthy ones? The means for removing the incumbents would not be hard to imagine, for the deportation of the ruling class was Assyrian practice for conquered territories, a practice which underlies the threat contained in 3:1-7. Yet the verb which is used here (the hiphil or causative of *shub*, to turn or return) does not suit well the bringing in of replacements. In English we sometimes translate it "to re-store," but in Hebrew usage it is seldom if ever a question of replacing A with B but rather of returning something to its former place or condition. Since a return to Jerusalem's earliest judges and counselors (*as at first*) could hardly be what is envisoned, conversion of the present incumbents (which does suit the Hebrew usage) may be what is intended. If that is the case, the trials to come will restore not simply the city as a whole, but even those who are currently its principal problem. Isaiah's singling out of counselors has occasioned some surprise, but as a matter of fact, those who stood close to the king and influenced his decisions were of concern to Isaiah, especially because they seem often to have opposed the prophet's own views (see below on 5:12, 19; 29:13-14, 15-16). Elsewhere, too, Isaiah sees right counsel as an important element of an ideal future (9:6; 11:2). The insistence on right judgment is strong in this oracle, appearing in v 21 (*justice*), v 23 (verb "to judge," rendered *defend* in *RSV*), and v 26 (*your judges*).

The reference to restoring judges and counselors *as at first* and *as at the beginning* is usually, and no doubt rightly, taken to refer to the time of David; it was he who made Jerusalem his capital, thereby establishing the Davidic kingship there, and who brought there the Ark of the Covenant and erected the tent shrine that was later superseded by the Solomonic Temple. Yet the biblical record leads us to wonder at the reference. We are told not only that David abused his authority but even that Absalom was able to gain a following precisely by alleging great deficiencies in the judicial process that David was responsible for (2 Sam 15:2-6), either by administering it personally or by delegating his responsibility to others. Thus in Isaiah's phrase *as at first* there is perhaps an indication of his acceptance of the idealizing of David and his time that goes with the development of the dynastic oracle (2 Samuel 7) into a properly messianic complex.

The final phrase of the oracle (*Afterward you shall be called...faithful city*) both forms an evident *inclusio* with the opening line (*How the faithful city...*) and reminds us that we are dealing with a before/after time frame. Actually the oracle relates to three chronological moments, past, present, and future; however, the past is brought in only as a standard against which to judge the present and as a paradigm for the future. Thus the emphasis is upon present and future and upon the purifying judgment which will effect the transition from the present unhappy situation to the future ideal one. Jerusalem is not elsewhere referred to as "faithful" (*ne'emanah* — niphal participle of *'aman*), but the term is used of David's house (line) and of God's promise concerning it in a number of texts (2 Sam 7:16; 1 Kgs 8:26; 11:38; Isa 55:3; Ps 89:29, 38; 1 Chr 17:23, 24; 2 Chr 1:9; 6:17). There seems to have been some interrelatedness of the Zion tradition (the belief that Zion was specially chosen and specially protected by Yahweh) and the Davidic tradition (similar choice and protection of the Davidic dynasty) in their development and expression (even though historically the origins of the traditions were quite distinct). This is not surprising in view of the fact that both were celebrated in the Jerusalem Temple liturgy, that they were mutually supportive, etc. It is not impossible, therefore, that the language here has been influenced by the Davidic tradition. We should note, too, that restoration of Jerusalem's judges relates well to what is said of the qualities of the ideal king to come in 11:3-5 (and see the comment above on this same figure with reference to the counselors).

Verses 27-28 are obviously closely connected with vv 21-26, on which they can be considered either expansion or commentary. Isaiah does not elsewhere use the verb "to redeem" (*padah*), but that in itself is no argument against the authenticity of the verse. The basic sense of the verb, in its secular meaning, has to do with being ransomed, normally by substitution (said, e.g., of the first-born), but also by payment, and that which is ransomed is otherwise liable to death. Transferred to the sphere of God's activity, the verb is used of Yahweh's saving action in delivering Israel from Egypt, though this is done not by payment to the captors but by his mighty power, and thus the idea of ransom disappears. Whether the *justice* and *righteousness* referred to are Yahweh's or Zion's is not clear. Looking back to the earlier verses we would be tempted to relate these two terms to the purifying judgment spoken of there (especially since the term rendered *justice* by *RSV* — *mishpat* — more properly means judgment), a judgment which would fall most heavily upon the sinners. But since vv 27-28 contrast those redeemed with evildoers who have forsaken Yahweh, perhaps the terms refer to the qualities of the redeemed. The designation of *those in her who repent* is consonant with Isaiah's thought of repentance through purifying judgment. The verse may well be from Isaiah, but if so, it was probably brought to its present location from another context; the emphasis in vv 21-26 is on two (chronologically distinct) stages and on the process whereby an evil situation is turned into a good one, whereas in vv 27-28 the emphasis is on the distinction between two groups and the contrast of their fates.

THE WITHERING OF THE WICKED: 1:29-31

29 For you shall be ashamed of the oaks
in which you delighted;
and you shall blush for the gardens
which you have chosen.
30 For you shall be like an oak
whose leaf withers,
and like a garden without water.
31 And the strong shall become tow,
and his work a spark,
and both of them shall burn together,
with none to quench them.

Although some commentators take these verses as dating
to a period long after Isaiah, there is no compelling reason
for refusing to attribute them to him. The interpretation of
the passage is also the subject of some dispute. More generally the reference to trees and gardens is related to pagan
worship and the fertility cult; thus the imagery of a tree that
loses its leaves and the garden without water would be a case
of the punishment fitting the crime. But Georg Fohrer
argues with some cogency that it is rather a matter of the
rich and powerful coveting the properties of others (a theme
more frequent than pagan worship in Isaiah); the punishment is equally appropriate on this interpretation. The tree
and vegetation imagery — the comparison of the just with
that which flourishes, the wicked with that which withers
—is common, especially in the wisdom literature (see Job
15:30-35; Ps 1:3-4; 37:35-36; 92:12-14).

ORACLES AGAINST JUDAH AND JERUSALEM: CHAPTERS 2-12

This new collection is rather complicated in that it is itself composed of a number of smaller collections. The first of these (in its completed form) would be chaps. 2-4, with a second beginning at 5:1. This smaller second collection is itself very complex in that the "woe" of 10:1-4 belongs with the series of "woes" found in 5:8-24, and in that the long judgment oracle characterized by a refrain ("for all this his anger is not turned away and his hand is stretched out still"), contained mainly in 9:8-21, finds its completion in 5:25; these dislocations were occasioned, in turn, by the insertion into the complex of another collection, the so-called "Memoirs of Isaiah," consisting (to oversimplify a little) of 6:1-8:18. For further details see Introduction, above (p. 15), and introductions to individual sections, below.

A NEW INSCRIPTION: 2:1

2 The word which Isaiah the son of
Amoz saw concerning Judah and Jerusalem.

Since there would be no point in repeating information already contained in 1:1, it is clear that this verse originally introduced a separate collection of Isaiah's words and that the section introduced by 1:1 must have been placed before it at some later date. It seems clear that 2:1 originally introduced at least the materials contained in chaps. 2-4 (which have, in their present state, been fleshed out with some later parts, especially 4:2-6); as the book now stands; it could apply aptly to most of the material up to 13:1 (where oracles against Babylon and other foreign nations begin), and that may have been the original intention.

VISION OF JERUSALEM AND FUTURE PEACE: 2:2-4(5)

> 2 It shall come to pass in the latter days
>   that the mountain of the house of the LORD
>   shall be established as the highest of the mountains,
>   and shall be raised above the hills;
>   and all the nations shall flow to it,
> 3   and many peoples shall come, and say:
>   "Come, let us go up to the mountain of the LORD,
>   to the house of the God of Jacob;
>   that he may teach us his ways
>   and that we may walk in his paths."
>   For out of Zion shall go forth the law,
>   and the word of the LORD from Jerusalem.
> 4 He shall judge between the nations,
>   and shall decide for many peoples;
>   and they shall beat their swords into plowshares,
>   and their spears into pruning hooks;
>   nation shall not lift up sword against nation,
>   neither shall they learn war any more.
>
> 5 O house of Jacob,
>   come, let us walk
>   in the light of the LORD.

The opinion of scholars concerning the authenticity of this oracle is divided, with perhaps a greater number arguing in favor of Isaiah's authorship. None of the arguments against it are compelling. Many of the objectors seem to reject the idea that Isaiah looked forward to an ideal future of any sort and lump together such oracles as this one, 9:1-6 and 11:1-9, denying all of them to Isaiah. It is also said that the piece embodies a sort of universalism and/or eschatology which must come from a later time. It can be asserted, on the contrary, that many elements of this oracle relate well to the so-called Zion Psalms (particularly to Psalms 46; 48; 76; and 87), especially with reference to Zion as Yahweh's chosen abode (Ps 76:2; 87:1-2), as goal and place of worship for other nations (Ps 86:4-6; and cf. 76:10[11] in the *NAB* rendering of it; and in 48:2 God's "holy mountain" is called "the joy of all the earth"), and the theme of the destruction of weapons and/or the ending of warfare (Ps 46:9; 76:3). These elements of the Zion tradition antedated Isaiah and provide part of the background from which he taught. The fact that the same oracle is found in another eighth-century prophet (Mic 4:1-3) is no argument that it must come from a later time! That it should be attributed to Isaiah rather than to Micah is clear from the latter's threat against the very future of the Temple (Mic 3:12), as well as from contacts which can be seen with Isaiah's other words, e.g., the wisdom influence in the terminology used here. The emphasis that Isaiah gives to Yahweh's instruction (*torah*) corresponds well with what we find in other, surely authentic words of his (cf. above on 1:10 and below on 5:24; 8:16; and 30:9). Moreover, certain elements in this oracle accord well with those found in other passages of hope in Isaiah, including the reference to peace (cf. 9:6, 7; 11:6-9) and the destruction of the trappings of war (9:5). Although, as already mentioned, the authenticity of 9:1-7 and 11:1-9 is disputed by some, in fact these three pieces cohere very well with each other and each of them has points of contact with Isaiah's undisputed words.

Few would now argue that the expression in v 2 *in the latter days* points to a postexilic eschatology. The phrase means hardly more than "in the future" or "after this," and E. Lipiński has shown that it is found in other than postexilic texts. Nevertheless, the prophet does look beyond his own day, for reasons we will see. Bernhard Duhm may be correct in thinking of this beautiful piece as Isaiah's "swan song." The elevation of Mt. Zion (a relatively low eminence) as the highest mountain is symbolic of its dignity as Yahweh's chosen seat. In 6:1 Isaiah describes Yahweh's throne as being lofty and lifted up (*nissa'* — the same verb which is used here). Those trooping up to the mountain are a universalistic crowd (*all nations, many peoples*). It is tempting to see pilgrimage terminology in the *come, let us go up* of v 3 (cf. Jer 31:6), but the terminology is too general to be pressed. In any case, we are in the theme of the pilgrimage of the nations, one that turns up in many other OT texts (Ps 102:21-22; Isa 60:4-7, 8-14; Jer 3:17; Zeph 3:9-10; Zech 8:20-22; 14:16-19).

The purpose of the ascent is to receive instruction, a goal expressed in various terms (*teach, ways, paths*) but most especially by *torah*, which here should certainly be translated "instruction" rather than *RSV*'s "law." No human mediator is suggested by the passage, and this should occasion no surprise, for Isaiah conceives Yahweh as the imparter of wise instruction (see above on 1:10 and below on 5:24; 8:16; 28:29; and 30:9). Moreover, this was one of the important functions of the ancient oriental monarch, as can be seen in wisdom texts from Egypt, Mesopotamia, and Israel (see especially *ANET* 414-15, 418, 419; 2 Sam 14:17; 1 Kgs 3:4-14, 28; 4:29-34 [Heb. and *NAB*: 5:9-14]; 10:1-10); the wisdom of human kings was derived from God, who is therefore the ultimate source of wisdom (I. Engnell, *Studies in Divine Kingship in the Ancient Near East*, 189-191). It is clear that Isaiah vindicates the making of plans and policy for Yahweh (on *'esah* see below at 5:12,19 and W. McKane, *Prophets and Wise Men*, 70-71), but the range of meaning of that plan/policy terminology, as employed by Isaiah, was restricted, i.e., oriented towards practical, effective action, and in large part negative in content; *torah*, in his usage, on the other hand, was more apt for expressing the broader concept of "the way," the moral demands, the ethics of behavior, such as is found in the wisdom tradition.

The concept of Yahweh "judging" the earth or the nations is not foreign to Israelite thought (Ps 76:9; 96:13; 98:9), the import usually being that he will restore the right order of things by intervening against those who oppress the poor or take the offensive against Israel. Here, however, he "judges" by settling matters of dispute between the nations; since Yahweh's wisdom is perfect and his power irresistible, there can be no question about the decision he hands down being implemented. The picture of the peoples beating their weapons of war into implements of peace suggests far more than that disputes formerly settled in battle are now resolved by Yahweh's judgment. It implies, beyond this, that the nations have renounced the wars of aggression and conquest which were the norm for the powerful, including Israel in its heyday under David. Yahweh's judgment may eliminate the grounds for dispute, but it is his *torah* which teaches peace as the ideal and, indeed, the only reasonable way.

The concluding exhortation in v 5 is addressed to God's people. If even the pagan nations are going to respond so earnestly to Yahweh's guidance and with such salutary results, how much more is it incumbent upon Israel to do so! This verse, by the judgment of all, is a later addition; cf. the very different conclusion supplied at Mic 4:4.

YAHWEH'S JUDGMENT ON ALL THE EARTH: 2:6-22

6 For thou has rejected thy people,
   the house of Jacob,
because they are full of diviners from the east
   and of soothsayers like the Philistines,
   and they strike hands with foreigners.
7 Their land is filled with silver and gold,
   and there is no end to their treasures;
their land is filled with horses,
   and there is no end to their chariots.
8 Their land is filled with idols;
   they bow down to the work of their hands,
   to what their own fingers have made.
9 So man is humbled,
   and men are brought low—
   forgive them not!

10 Enter into the rock,
   and hide in the dust
from before the terror of the LORD,
   and from the glory of his majesty.
11 The haughty looks of man shall be brought low,
   and the pride of men shall be humbled;
and the LORD alone will be exalted in that day.

12 For the LORD of hosts has a day
   against all that is proud and lofty,
   against all that is lifted up and high;
13 against all the cedars of Lebanon,
   lofty and lifted up;
   and against all the oaks of Bashan;
14 against all the high mountains,
   and against all the lofty hills;
15 against every high tower,
   and against every fortified wall;
16 against all the ships of Tarshish,
   and against all the beautiful craft.
17 And the haughtiness of man shall be humbled,
   and the pride of men shall be brought low;
   and the LORD alone will be exalted in that day.
18 And the idols shall utterly pass away.
19 And men shall enter the caves of the rocks
   and the holes of the ground,
from before the terror of the LORD,
   and from the glory of his majesty,
   when he rises to terrify the earth.

20 In that day men will cast forth
   their idols of silver and their idols of gold,
which they made for themselves to worship,
   to the moles and to the bats,
21 to enter the caverns of the rocks
   and the clefts of the cliffs,
from before the terror of the LORD,
   and from the glory of his majesty,
   when he rises to terrify the earth.

²² Turn away from man
in whose nostrils is breath,
for of what account is he?

This important piece on the "day of the Lord" has suffered much in transmission; it is probable that as it stands it is incomplete and probable also that it is composed of two or more originally distinct compositions. There is a good measure of agreement that vv 10-17 (or at least vv 12-17) are fairly intact and stood as a separate oracle concerning the day of Yahweh; beyond that reconstructions vary considerably. Hans Wildberger, for example, sees the present text composed of four originally separate unities: v 6; vv 7-9a; vv 12-17; and v 19; he also judges vv 10-11 and vv 20-21 to be secondary compositions from elements of other verses; others explain the repetitions in vv 10, 19, and 21 as a refrain that is intended. It can also be argued that vv 9, 11, and 17 are intended as a refrain as the passage now stands.

It is clear from this piece that Isaiah accepted the belief in a future "day of the Lord," though the origins of the belief are obscure. It is first attested to in Amos 5:18-20, where the prophet is at pains to dash the expectation that this day of the Lord's intervention will be favorable to those who are looking forward to it. Von Rad has argued convincingly that the belief arose from Israel's Holy War tradition (*Old Testament Theology*, II, 119-25). Initially it would have related to a day in which Yahweh would win total victory over his enemies, and in popular thought God's people would have been associated with him in this victory. Like Amos, Isaiah depicts it as a day of triumph for Yahweh alone; but whereas Amos appears to see it directed against Israel, Isaiah sees it directed against the whole earth. (*OTA*, 3, #472; 4, #805.)

Isaiah's description of the day makes it seem cosmic in scope. The opening verses (vv 6-8), which probably did not relate originally to the day of the Lord poem which follows, appear to indict Judah, but the description of the day itself sees it directed against the trees, the mountains, the fortifications, the ships, and — above all — against human pride.

As regards the last named, the opening indictment fits admirably: occult knowlege, foreign alliances, wealth, military strength, and false gods are all things which can be occasions of false confidence and therefore of pride. It is to be noted that, whatever may be presupposed or implied, there is no actual word of destruction. What is quite explicit, repeatedly (vv 9, 11, 17), is the abasement of man and his pride (and of all that is *proud and lofty* — v 12); this seems to be the programmatic theme for the whole piece.

There is no suggestion here that the "day of the Lord" brings about or coincides with the end of the world or even the end of the present age; i.e., it is not here, any more than it was in Amos, an eschatological event. Of course the theme has a long development in Scripture and "the day of the Lord" does eventually come to designate the eschatological event par excellence, but there is nothing to suggest that in Isaiah it occurs otherwise than within history. Neither is there any suggestion that Yahweh's judgment is carried out by Assyria or any other human agency; Assyria itself would presumably be among those whose conduct calls for a humbling at Yahweh's hands (cf. 10:5-11, 15). The particular means of Yahweh's intervention here seems to be the storm theophany (see especially Psalm 29 and its reference to trees and mountains). In fact, the theophanic aspect of the passage is very strong; the primary source of the terror which the day occasions is *the glory of his majesty* (v 10).

If the day is not primarily destructive and does not bring an end to history, what is its purpose? Human pride is an affront to God and he reacts to it (see Isa 3:16; 5:15-16; 9:8-9; 10:7-16, 33; 28:1-4, 22). However, since it is also an obstacle to God's plan, his humbling of it can have a very positive aspect. The placing together of 2:2-5 and 2:6-22 seems to have been deliberate. The raising up of the mountain of Yahweh's house in the former stands in antithesis to the lowering of all that is exalted in the latter (this correspondence is especially striking between v 2 and v 14, where there is reference to hills and mountains being lifted up); and it stands in parallelism to the exaltation of Yahweh (alone) in the latter. The point of the juxtaposition of 2:2-5 with 2:6-22 would be that there is first a presentation of the ideal future that Yahweh plans, then what he will do about the obstacle to that plan, namely, human pride.

To the description of the uncertainties of the steps by which the piece has reached its present form, the following brief critical notes may be added. The Hebrew text of v 6 does not contain the word *diviners*, but there are good grounds for supposing that it originally stood there and is to be restored. To *strike hands with foreigners* (same verse) suggests not only commerce with them, but also the concluding of pacts or covenants; this sort of intercourse helps explain some of the pagan practices alluded to. The final words of v 9 (*forgive them not*) is one of the late expansions of the earlier, composite piece; the same can be said of v 18 and v 22 — the latter, being a plural address, is directed to the readers (not to God, as one might suppose from the English alone). In a sense, v 18 and vv 20-21 are saying the same thing about the fate of idols, but v 18 seems to be speaking from a more eschatological perspective (what God's judgment will bring to pass), whereas vv 20-21 suppose a new disposition on the part of people, impressed by God's power revealed in judgment, a power which at the same time reveals the impotence of idols. On *ships of Tarshish*, see below on 23:1.

JUDAH'S SIN AND ITS CONSEQUENCES: 3:1-12

3 For, behold, the Lord, the LORD of hosts,
    is taking away from Jerusalem and from Judah
  stay and staff,
    the whole stay of bread,
    and the whole stay of water;
2 the mighty man and the soldier,
    the judge and the prophet,
    the diviner and the elder,
3 the captain of fifty
    and the man of rank,
  the counselor and the skilful magician
    and the expert in charms.

⁴ And I will make boys their princes,
   and babes shall rule over them.
⁵ And the people will oppress one another,
   every man his fellow
   and every man his neighbor;
 the youth will be insolent to the elder,
   and the base fellow to the honorable.

⁶ When a man takes hold of his brother
   in the house of his father, saying:
 "You have a mantle;
   you shall be our leader,
 and this heap of ruins
   shall be under your rule";
⁷ in that day he will speak out, saying:
 "I will not be a healer;
   in my house there is neither bread nor mantle;
 you shall not make me
   leader of the people."
⁸ For Jerusalem has stumbled,
   and Judah has fallen;
 because their speech and their deeds
   are against the LORD,
   defying his glorious presence.

⁹ Their partiality witnesses against them;
   they proclaim their sin like Sodom,
   they do not hide it.
 Woe to them!
   For they have brought evil upon themselves.
¹⁰ Tell the righteous that it shall be well with them,
   for they shall eat the fruit of their deeds.
¹¹ Woe to the wicked! It shall be ill with him,
   for what his hands have done shall be done to him.
¹² My people — children are their oppressors,
   and women rule over them.
   O my people, your leaders mislead you,
   and confuse the course of your paths.

The original oracle here is found in vv 1-9a, but it has been expanded by some later additions. The troubles that Isaiah foresees for Judah and Jerusalem appear to be those occasioned by Assyrian oppression, so the oracle probably dates to some time after Ahaz submitted in vassalhood to Tiglath-pileser III (735 — see below on chap. 7).

More specifically, Isaiah thinks of deportation of the ruling class by Assyria. This practice of the Assyrians (and later of the Babylonians) was intended to make the revolt of subject peoples unlikely, or even impossible, by removing not the total population but precisely those elements that gave to society structure and leadership — which Isaiah here refers to as *stay and staff* (the reference to *bread* and *water* is a later, misleading, gloss). The prophet proceeds to enumerate various classes that would be removed: not only those who could protect (the military — *mighty man and soldier*) and rule them (*judge* and *elder*), but also all who might give them guidance, legitimate or not (*prophet, diviner, counselor*, and *magician*). The biblical report of the first Babylonian deportation (597) includes princes, military forces, and craftsmen and smiths (2 Kgs 24:14 — and probably also the palace officials and servants — cf. v 12), a listing which is not far removed from the present one.

Such a deportation may leave only "the poorest people of the land" (cf. 2 Kgs 24:14), who are not able to provide leadership. In Jeremiah's career we note, after the deportation of 597, a shift from princes who helped and defended Jeremiah (Jer 26:10-16) to ones who opposed and persecuted him (Jer 38:4-6). Undoubtedly the rulers Isaiah sees being removed had some claim to authority, but after Yahweh has acted, he says, the mere possession of a cloak would qualify a man for position of prince, something which would be an unwanted burden, devoid of honors. The inadequate and inexperienced leadership which results from such a situation begets, in turn, the sort of anarchy described in v 5. The store that Isaiah places in the right kind of rulers is seen in 1:23, 26, where the problem with Jerusalem can be identified with the crimes of the ruling class, and its healing with the restoration of trustworthy rulers. Both passages make reference to *ruler* or *prince, judge* and *counselor.*

Yahweh's glory, which fills the whole earth (6:3), is synonymous with his kingship, his majesty, himself; to defy that glory (v 8b) is to merit the future punishment here described. The precise nature of the crime involved in Judah's stumbling and falling is now explained. *RSV*'s reference to *partiality* (v 9) would take us to the area of unjust judgment and therefore to social crimes, but this translation is uncertain, for the Hebrew of the line is very obscure. Although Isaiah certainly threatens punishment at the hands of enemies also for social crimes (cf. 10:1-4), the threat of incursion by a foreign power more naturally suggests defiance of Yahweh in Judah's political dealings (cf. 8:5-8; 28:11-19).

Verse 12 may originally have come from a different context (it speaks of the present rather than the future) and perhaps was placed immediately after v 9a, a location later disrupted by the insertion of the two "woe" sayings of vv 9b-11. There it would have formed a transition between the preceding comments on the "instant rulers" of vv 4-7, untried and unequipped but accepted of necessity, and the indictment of the leaders contained in vv 13-15. Some read "usurers" in place of *women,* but *children* and *women* form a good sense parallel as being classes that normally did not exercise leadership in Judah. While the first half of the verse suggests oppressive leadership, the vocabulary of the second half indicates educated *leaders,* who, in misleading the people, perversely fail to provide the guidance they are capable of.

The woe-saying (*'oy,* not *hoy*) at the end of v 9 is considered by many to be a later, wisdom influenced, expansion (the evil one does falls upon oneself), though it is nothing that Isaiah could not have said. Verses 10-11 are a better candidate as a wisdom expansion, both because of its retribution doctrine and the righteous-wicked contrast (but not because of the *'oy,* which is not wisdom diction). Many would emend *tell the righteous* to "happy the righteous," thus giving a happy-woe correlation.

THE LORD, DEFENDER OF THE POOR: 3:13-15

13 The LORD has taken his place to contend,
    he stands to judge his people.
14 The LORD enters into judgment
    with the elders and princes of his people:
"It is you who have devoured the vineyard,
    the spoil of the poor is in your houses.
15 What do you mean by crushing my people,
    by grinding the faces of the poor?"
    says the Lord God of hosts.

The scene depicted here is clearly that of a legal trial (though there is nothing to justify speaking of a covenant lawsuit) in which the Lord is accuser and judge. Although the opening lines name both the people and the leaders as defendants, it is clear that the accusations are against the leaders alone (see 1:10 for a similar situation). The fact that the *elders* are named along with the *princes* indicates how badly perverted the social structures had become. The elders originally were the rulers within the tribe and its spokesmen and representatives to the larger society; as such their role would be as defenders of the common people. Here, instead, they are identified with the wealthy upperclass who are guilty of oppressing the poor. If those who should be their defenders have become their oppressors, the plight of the poor has become wretched indeed! Although the word rendered *spoil* regularly refers to stolen goods, here it may not be so much a case of out and out robbery as of seizure through legal means (foreclosure of property, etc.; see below on 5:8-10). Given the kind of justice that ought to exist among God's people, any sort of despoiling of the poor was damnable. Very possibly the "violence" of judicial corruption and bribery are involved (see 1:23; 5:7, 23; Amos 3:10; 5:11-12). No threat is levelled against these rulers, but the crime of which Yahweh here convicts them itself assures punishment to come unless the right order is restored.

FATE OF THE PROUD DAUGHTERS OF ZION: 3:16-4:1

¹⁶ The LORD said:
Because the daughters of Zion are haughty
and walk with outstretched necks,
glancing wantonly with their eyes,
mincing along as they go,
tinkling with their feet;
¹⁷ the Lord will smite with a scab
the heads of the daughters of Zion,
and the LORD will lay bare their secret parts.

¹⁸In that day the Lord will take away the finery of the anklets, the headbands, and the crescents; ¹⁹the pendants, the bracelets, and the scarfs; ²⁰the headdresses, the armlets, the sashes, the perfume boxes, and the amulets; ²¹the signet rings and nose rings; ²²the festal robes, the mantles, the cloaks, and the handbags; ²³the garments of gauze, the linen garments, the turbans, and the veils.
²⁴ Instead of perfume there will be rottenness;
and instead of a girdle, a rope;
and instead of well-set hair, baldness;
and instead of a rich robe, a girding of sackcloth;
instead of beauty, shame.
²⁵ Your men shall fall by the sword
and your mighty men in battle.
²⁶ And her gates shall lament and mourn;
ravaged, she shall sit upon the ground.
4 And seven women shall take hold of one man in that day, saying, "We will eat our own bread and wear our own clothes, only let us be called by your name; take away our reproach."

In all probability this passage is not an original unity. To begin with, most agree that the detailed listing of items of feminine finery in vv 18-23 is a later supplement to vv 16, 24. But there is also the fact that vv 25-26 abruptly address a personified Jerusalem. In addition, whereas the reversal of fortune of vv 17, 24 seems to relate to exile, the quest for husbands (4:1) would fit those women who remain in the city. Nevertheless, the passage does not hang together too badly; all parts of it suppose a defeat of the city at the hands of the Assyrians, and the concluding description of the humiliation of the women is a complete turn-around from the opening reference to their pride. Its indictment of the ruling class and the implication of an Assyrian attack fit it well to follow the preceding sections of this chapter.

Daughters of Zion here designates the women of the upperclass; Zion was the quarter of the city in which the palace was and presumably also the homes of the ruling class. Here as elsewhere Isaiah condemns pride and sees it as provoking the Lord's punishment (cf. 2:11, 17; 5:15-16; 10:5-15; 29:16). The evil here singled out is not the simple desire to be attractive, but the expensive luxuries involved (v 24), joined to a cavalier attitude toward the poor, at whose expense the wealth for such luxuries was often acquired. Like Amos, Isaiah seems to see the women as sometimes responsible for the oppression practiced by their men (Amos 4:1-3). The total reversal of fortune described in vv 17, 24 would agree well with the Assyrian practice of deportation of the upper class. In such circumstances the women, in spite of their delicacy and refined upbringing, could be treated very harshly; rape, rough and scanty clothing, and slave-concubine status were their expected lot (Lam 5:11). Those left behind in the ravaged city, personified in vv 25-26 as a desolate woman, mourning her fallen warriors, would not be much better off. Women would be willing to forego the support marriage should guarantee them (Exod 21: 10-11) in order to become a man's concubine and be delivered from what was considered to be the disgrace of being unmarried and childless. Thus pride begets humiliation and those who oppress are in turn oppressed.

FUTURE PURIFICATION AND PROTECTION OF JERUSALEM: 4:2-6

²In that day the branch of the LORD shall be beautiful and glorious, and the fruit of the land shall be the pride and glory of the survivors of Israel. ³And he who is left in

Zion and remains in Jerusalem will be called holy, every one who has been recorded for life in Jerusalem, ⁴when the Lord shall have washed away the filth of the daughters of Zion and cleansed the bloodstains of Jerusalem from its midst by a spirit of judgment and by a spirit of burning. ⁵Then the LORD will create over the whole site of Mount Zion and over her assemblies a cloud by day, and smoke and the shining of a flaming fire by night; for over all the glory there will be a canopy and a pavilion. ⁶It will be for a shade by day from the heat, and for a refuge and a shelter from the storm and rain.

This piece is widely held to be a non-Isaianic addition, though with perhaps an Isaian kernel in vv 2-4. Its insertion here is intended to mitigate the harshness of 3:16-4:1, by promising better things for the future; it concludes the collection of chaps. 2-4 on a note of promise (as it also begins; cf. 2:2-4). Possibly the purification referred to in v 4 originally spoke merely of Zion, "daughters of" being added in order to relate the piece to 3:16 (thereby impairing the Zion/Jerusalem parallelism), even though v 3 speaks of *every one.* But the concept of purifying Jerusalem through judgment is not foreign to Isaiah's thought (cf. 1:25).

These verses are complex and probably composite. Verse 2 promises God-given fertility; *the branch of the Lord* is a misleading translation if it leads us to think that we have here a reference to the ideal king of the future. Jeremiah uses the same Hebrew word (*semah*) to refer to an offspring of David (Jer 23:5; 33:15), and Zechariah applies the term to Zerubbabel (Zech 3:8; 6:12), but that meaning is ruled out here by the parallelism with *fruit of the land* and by the fact that there is no reference to David. For those who remain it is not simply a matter of having escaped destruction; they are a holy remnant, those *written down for life.* Elsewhere, too, the Old Testament speaks of those written in God's book (see Exod 32:32-33; Dan 12:1; Ps 69:28). The final verses (5-6) speak of the extraordinary protection Yahweh will afford his city and the holy remnant. The reference to *cloud* and *fire* comes from the exodus tradition (see Exod

13:21-22; 14:19, 24), where the pillar provided both guidance and protection. There the storm was part of Yahweh's theophany (Exod 19:16; cf. *Psalm 29*), but here it is one of the dangers from which this *canopy* will protect Jerusalem.

THE PARABLE OF THE VINEYARD OF THE LORD: 5:1-7

5 Let me sing for my beloved
    a love song concerning his vineyard:
My beloved had a vineyard
    on a very fertile hill.
² He digged it and cleared it of stones,
    and planted it with choice vines;
he built a watchtower in the midst of it,
    and hewed out a wine vat in it;
and he looked for it to yield grapes,
    but it yielded wild grapes.

³ And now, O inhabitants of Jerusalem
    and men of Judah,
judge, I pray you, between me
    and my vineyard.
⁴ What more was there to do for my vineyard,
    that I have not done in it?
When I looked for it to yield grapes,
    why did it yield wild grapes?

⁵ And now I will tell you
    what I will do to my vineyard.
I will remove its hedge,
    and it shall be devoured;
I will break down its wall,
    and it shall be trampled down.
⁶ I will make it a waste;
    it shall not be pruned or hoed,
    and briers and thorns shall grow up;
I will also command the clouds
    that they rain no rain upon it.

7 For the vineyard of the LORD of hosts
    is the house of Israel,
and the men of Judah
    are his pleasant planting;
and he looked for justice,
    but behold, bloodshed;
for righteousness,
    but behold, a cry!

We are inclined to think of parables as edifying religious stories, though in fact they are often weapons in a polemic. The parable calls for the hearer to render a judgment on the action described, and the judgment itself drives home the lesson the parable was intended to teach. Surprise is often part of the effectiveness of a parable, and in the instance at hand Isaiah speaks of the *vineyard* of his *beloved* (or "friend"), in order to avoid tipping his hand at the outset; to have spoken of "Yahweh's vineyard" would immediately have alerted the hearers that a parable, rather than an actual case, was in the offing. (For the similar procedure of Nathan with David, see 2 Sam 12:1-7.) The language of love enters here (the expression *dodi*, *beloved*, found in v 1, occurs frequently in the Canticle of Canticles), and so it has been suggested that the prophet, pretending to be "best man" and speaking in the name of a bridegroom, describes in metaphorical terms ("vineyard" also is used in a metaphorical sense in the Canticle of Canticles) his betrayal at the hands of a faithless bride. The meaning which is really intended, and finally revealed, suits well the allegory of Israel as Yahweh's spouse (found in Hosea, Jeremiah, Ezekiel, and Deutero-Isaiah, but not in Isaiah). This interpretation, attractive as it is, is not without its difficulties.

Isaiah's parable of the vineyard is the prototype of Jesus' parable of the wicked husbandmen (Mark 12:1-11). Elsewhere, too, Israel is depicted as Yahweh's vine (Jer 2:21; Ps 80:8-16). Isaiah speaks of Yahweh's activity in terms of an agricultural parable also in 28:23-29, though there the wisdom traits are far more prominent than here.

Isaiah's purpose in the parable is to underline Judah's

wicked behavior by contrasting it with the loving care lavished by Yahweh and the sort of grateful response which
that should have evoked; and he says that this nurturing
concern will now be replaced with destructive judgment.
Amos, too, introduces a threat of judgment by showing
Israel has repaid with sin rather than gratitude Yahweh's
elective love (described in historical rather than metaphorical terms; see Amos 2:9-16). The punishment to come (introduced after an invitation to the hearers to render a verdict)
involves the loss of the Lord's protective care; he will aban-
don his people to their enemies and allow the land to return
to its wild, uncultivated state (on the last point, cf. 7:23-25).

In the prophet's explanation of the parable (v 7), he
identifies the nation's crime as social injustice. Just as rotten
grapes might look like good grapes, so Isaiah uses words
that *sound* like the real thing: in place of *mishpat* and
sedaqah (justice and righteousness), which are the qualities
required of God's faithful (see Gen 18:19; 1 Kgs 10:9; 1 Chr
18:14; Ps 33:5; Prov 21:3; Isa 9:6; 33:5; 56:1; Ezek 18:5, 19,
21, 27; 33:14, 16, 19; 45:9), his people present him with
mispah and *se'aqah* (*bloodshed* or something similar — the
meaning is not quite certain — and outcry). The latter
expression probably ought to be understood quite literally
to mean that one heard in the land, perhaps especially in
Jerusalem, the urgent prayer for help and the bitter cry of
lamentation by the poor who lost their possessions and even
their freedom through verdicts rendered against them —
sometimes unjust verdicts rendered for bribes. Although
such dispossession was sometimes, perhaps usually,
accomplished through legal processes, this was not "justice"
in the biblical sense of the word.

A SERIES OF WOES: 10:1-4 + 5:8-24

10 Woe to those who decree iniquitous decrees,
   and the writers who keep writing oppression,
² to turn aside the needy from justice
   and to rob the poor of my people of their right,

that widows may be their spoil,
and that they may make the fatherless their prey!
3 What will you do on the day of punishment,
in the storm which will come from afar?
To whom will you flee for help,
and where will you leave your wealth?
4 Nothing remains but to crouch among the prisoners
or fall among the slain.
For all this his anger is not turned away
and his hand is stretched out still.

5 8 Woe to those who join house to house,
who add field to field,
until there is no more room,
and you are made to dwell alone
in the midst of the land.
9 The LORD of hosts has sworn in my hearing:
"Surely many houses shall be desolate,
large and beautiful houses, without inhabitant.
10 For ten acres of vineyard shall yield but one bath,
and a homer of seed shall yield but an ephah."

11 Woe to those who rise early in the morning,
that they may run after strong drink,
who tarry late into the evening
till wine inflames them!
12 They have lyre and harp,
timbrel and flute and wine at their feasts;
but they do not regard the deeds of the LORD,
or see the work of his hands.

13 Therefore my people go into exile
for want of knowledge;
their honored men are dying of hunger;
and their multitude is parched with thirst.
14 Therefore Sheol has enlarged its appetite
and opened its mouth beyond measure,
and the nobility of Jerusalem and her multitude go down,
her throng and he who exults in her.
15 Man is bowed down, and men are brought low,
and the eyes of the haughty are humbled.

16 But the LORD of hosts is exalted in justice,
   and the Holy God shows himself holy in righteousness.
17 Then shall the lambs graze as in their pasture,
   fatlings and kids shall feed among the ruins.

18 Woe to those who draw iniquity with cords of falsehood,
   who draw sin as with cart ropes,
19 who say: "Let him make haste,
   let him speed his work
   that we may see it;
   let the purpose of the Holy One of Israel draw near,
   and let it come, that we may know it!"
20 Woe to those who call evil good
   and good evil,
   who put darkness for light
   and light for darkness,
   who put bitter for sweet
   and sweet for bitter!
21 Woe to those who are wise in their own eyes,
   and shrewd in their own sight!
22 Woe to those who are heroes at drinking wine,
   and valiant men in mixing strong drink,
23 who acquit the guilty for a bribe,
   and deprive the innocent of his right!

24 Therefore, as the tongue of fire devours the stubble,
   and as dry grass sinks down in the flame,
   so their root will be as rottenness,
   and their blossom go up like dust;
   for they have rejected the law of the LORD of hosts,
   and have despised the word of the Holy One of Israel.

There is a good deal of agreement that the isolated woe-saying that begins chap. 10 belongs with the group of six that we find in 5:8-24. The combination of 10:1-4a with 5:8-24 provides us with a series to the good biblical number of seven. Moreover, 10:1-4a does not relate well to its present context but does fit very well into chap. 5 in terms of the content of the parable (vv 1-7) and the woes (vv 8-24). On the understanding that 10:1-4a originally went with 5:8-24, the refrain found in 10:4b would have been added after this woe was displaced from chap. 5 to its present location (cf. 9:12, 17, 21). The whole series (i.e., 10:1-4 and 5:8-24) may well be directed against more or less the same group, namely, the officials who, educated and in positions of authority, both advised the king on matters of state and were responsible for the administration of justice. The series very aptly follows the parable of 5:1-7, which alludes to the breakdown of justice, with consequent oppression of the poorer classes.

The woe-saying of 10:1-4 makes explicit what one can otherwise divine, that the social injustice the prophet attacks stems not simply from illegal activity, but also, perhaps in major measure, from the misuse of legal author-ity and procedures. Here it is a matter of the ruling class enacting *iniquitous decrees* which would enable them or their cronies to lay hold of the property of the poorer classes, who had little in the way of legal rights or represen-tation to defend themselves. The punishment, which will come *from afar* and involves captivity, almost certainly refers to invasion by a foreign enemy. The rich would suffer much more from such attack, would have much more to lose, and would be more apt to be led away captive (see above on 3:1-12).

In the second woe (5:8-10) Isaiah depicts with biting irony the splendid isolation which the rich acquire for themselves by taking over the holdings of the poor (aided, no doubt, by the *iniquitous decrees* of which 10:1 speaks). This latifun-dism, the heaping up of large landed estates, was part of a socio-economic revolution that took place in both Israel and Judah; it was a revolution which included the transfor-mation from a people largely of small landowners, agricul-tural, egalitarian, to a much more highly stratified society in which there was a great contrast between rich and poor, in which the latter had lost their independence and could subsist only by serving the former — perhaps often as tenant farmers on land they had formerly owned. To Isaiah and the other eighth-century prophets this was an evil situation, one made possible only because some members of Yahweh's people were willing to exploit others, forgetting what it meant to be Yahweh's people. The prophet is conscious of being privy to Yahweh's judgment on this situation and to his will and intentions (v 9: cf. Jer 23:18) and repeats the Lord's solemn oath against these oppressors: the desolation to come will not allow them to enjoy the fruit of their wickedness. (For similar sentiments, see Amos 3:15; 5:11.) The woe-oracle, unlike some other forms of prophetic speech, is not intended simply as a threat of possible future punishment, but is an assertion of what is to come to pass. Indeed, the woe-oracle may have taken its origin from the funeral lament, the *hoy* that one exclaims over the departed. In prophetic usage, however, in which *hoy* is most frequently followed by a plural participle (as is the case in the first five of this series of seven), otherwise usually by a substantive, the woe-oracle amounts to an indictment of the people (or the kind of people) specified by the participle or the substantive.

The third woe (vv 11-17) is also directed against the members of the ruling class who pursue lives of luxury, even lives of intemperance, while blandly ignoring the real state of affairs (cf. Amos 6:1-7). It was suggested above that the woes in this series are directed against more or less the same group. Thus those who here *do not regard the deeds* (more accurately, "deed") *of the Lord* and *the work of his hands* are the same as those who in v 19 taunt Isaiah concerning the *work* and the *purpose* of the Lord; the parallelism of those two terms (*work* and *purpose*) in v 19 indicates that they are more or less synonymous and throw light on the present passage: Yahweh's *deed/work* that these people do not see or regard is the bringing to pass of his plan in history. These people are so taken up with the pursuit of luxurious and wild living that they have no concern for what God wills or what he is bringing to pass. This failure to see the *work* of the Lord explains the *want of knowledge* which occasions the exile referred to in v 13. The leaders do not, will not see what Yahweh is about; since Isaiah was sent to instruct them in these things, their failure is a refusal to heed the word of Yahweh through his prophet. (See 30:8-14 for another instance of the rejection of Yahweh's instruction and consequent disaster.) Verse 13 is one of Isaiah's rare explicit references to exile.

The following verses (vv 14-17) are only loosely connected with the foregoing and perhaps all belong to different contexts. Verse 14 expands on v 13, though now the clear reference to exile has been exchanged for an imaginative description of the whole people going down to the netherworld (Sheol), here pictured as a fearful, devouring monster. Verse 15 repeats the message of 2:11, though with variant vocabulary and word order. Verse 16 now contrasts to this humbling of *man* the exaltation of *the Lord*; in this contrast we again find an echo of the "day of the Lord" oracle of chap. 2 (see especially 2:11, 17, though the verb is different than that used here). The qualities by which Yahweh is exalted, *justice* and *righteousness*, are the very ones the people are condemned for lacking in v 7; thus the contrast between *man* and *the Lord* is further underlined. Yahweh's holiness is a special concern for Isaiah (see below on 6:3). Although the context would seem to favor the idea that Yahweh *shows himself holy* by some sort of judgment, only very rarely can that meaning attach itself to *sedaqah*, which normally, when it is an attribute of Yahweh, refers to his beneficent activity (cf. the expression *sidqoth yhwh*, "the saving deeds of the Lord," in Judg 5:11; 1 Sam 12:7; Isa 51:6, 8; Dan 9:16; Mic 6:5); thus it cannot be excluded that even here salvation is somehow in view, perhaps precisely through the judgment to come (cf. 1:25-26).

It is possible that v 17 originally followed on v 10 and was misplaced in the process of transmission (cf. *NAB* arrangement); it suits the picture of desolation and unproductive agriculture of vv 9-10 (cf. also 7:23-25).

The four woes contained in vv 18-23 should perhaps be taken together as a single unit. Some of them (e.g., that in v 21) would be too brief and unspecific to stand as separate independent prophetic words, and none of them contains anything explicit as to judgment to come; the case is otherwise with the three we have just looked at. This grouping is intelligible if we recognize that all four are directed against the same group of people; the unit (which may have included v 24) could later have been combined with the three previous ones (also directed against more or less the same group) to give the present list of seven. Thus those here addressed, i.e., the royal officials, function both as advisers to the king and as administrators of justice. As men who have been educated in the school which undoubtedly existed in Jerusalem for the training of scribes for the royal court and of children of the upper classes, those who were destined for careers at court, they had been introduced into all the riches of the wisdom tradition and could lay claim to belonging to the circle of the wise. Isaiah accuses them of being poor advisers, of being corrupt judges, and of neglecting the ideals of their training, the value of which he does not question.

So constant is the iniquity of those addressed in vv 18-19 that they seem to draw it about with them, in the manner of a beast pulling a cart by stout cords. The words Isaiah attributes to them give an important insight into one of the chronic struggles of his ministry , namely, the opposition of the policy makers. Here they are depicted as taunting the prophet for the non-fulfillment of his oracles concerning Yahweh's action in history. From this passage and others (cf. 14:24-27; 28:29) we can gather that Isaiah spoke of the plan or *purpose* of Yahweh (here set in parallel to his *work* — see above on v 12). The Hebrew word here rendered "purpose," *'esah*, is a technical term to designate the advice given and the decision arrived at in council, always with a view to action (cf. 2 Sam 17:1-14). Isaiah speaks of Yahweh's "purpose" here and elsewhere (14:24-27, where its firmness is emphasized, and 28:29, where its wonderful aspect is stressed). Given Yahweh's wisdom and might, all human plans that run counter to it are doomed from the start (7:5-7; 8:10; 29:15-16; 30:1). Yahweh's "purpose" in history ought to have been the determining factor in Judah's foreign policy, and Isaiah's prophetic insight into that "purpose" should have given him the king's ear; on the basis of this insight Isaiah opposed the policy proposed or followed in 735-732, in 714-711, and in 705-701 (cf. 7; 20; 29:15-16; 30:1-5; 31:1-3). The royal counselors could accept this estimate of the situation only at the cost of compromising their own influence at the court, and it is clear from the present passage and from others that they did not, and that Isaiah condemned their short-sightedness (5:21; 29:14). Although the precise content of Yahweh's plan is not clear to us (though it certainly involved judgment — cf. 14:24-27), it was sufficiently clear to Isaiah's contemporaries for them to taunt him with the non-fulfillment of his oracles regarding it and thus to attempt to discredit him as a prophet.

In v 20 Isaiah accuses these men of the perversion of values which is manifested in unjust judgments such as acquitting the guilty (cf. v 23). The ethic imparted in their training included special concern for justice in buying and selling, protecting private property, and looking after the rights of the poor and weak members of society (cf. Prov 11:1; 14:31; 16:11; 17:5, 15, 23; 19:5, 7; 20:10; 21:13, 28; 22:16, 22-23), but they have done exactly the opposite. In fact, what is said in this woe does not at all specify the crime; this can be done only from the context — which is part of the argument that it could not originally have stood alone. The same is true of the woe of v 21, even though the diction reflects a frequent theme of the wisdom tradition (cf. Prov 3:7; 26:5, 12; 28:11). Given v 19, the *wise in their own eyes* are the counselors who give advice based on their purely secular estimate of the situation and will not take into account Yahweh's "purpose" as revealed through the prophet. On the day of Yahweh's judgment their "wisdom" will be seen for the shallow thing it is — precisely the reverse of true wisdom, in fact (cf. 29:14, 15-16).

In vv 22-23 the prophet continues to fault the responsible rulers for neglect of the wise admonitions and precepts that made up their training. The dangers of intemperate drinking are pointed out in the wisdom tradition (Prov 20:1; 21:17; 23:29-35; Sir 18:33; 19:2; 31:25-30), sometimes with a specific connection between sobriety and just judgment (Prov 31:4-5). To those passages given above that relate to just judgment (see comment on v 20) may be added others that warn against the taking of bribes (Prov 15:27; 17:23; in legislative texts, see Exod 23:6-8; Deut 16:19; but on the relevance of these legislative texts to eighth-century Judah, see Introduction). Note in particular the similarity in content of these verses with Prov 17:15: "He who justifies the wicked and he who condemns the righteous are both alike an abomination to the Lord."

As mentioned above, this series of four woes had run on without any punishment having been pronounced, but now, in v 24, Isaiah uses vegetation imagery (a frequent thing with him — cf. 9:18; 10:17, 33-34; 11:1; 17:5-6; 18:5; 28:1, 4) to supply the lack. Are these wise and wealthy rulers fresh, living, and attractive as a flower in bloom? Root and blossom (and everything in between) shall disappear as dry grass does in a fire. The second half of the verse justifies the sentence of punishment passed and at the same time sums up the content of the preceding woes: "they have rejected the instruction (*torah*) of the Lord of hosts." "Instruction" should be read rather than *RSV*'s *law* because *torah* does not occur in the singular to designate the whole law until the deuteronomic reform (seventh century), because the term it stands in parallel with, *word* (*'imrah*), does not have a legal but often has a wisdom connotation, and because the verb used with *'imrah* is never used with a legal term but is often used with wisdom terms; note especially its use in Ps 107:11, where it is used with "the counsel (or purpose — *'esah*) of the Most High" and in parallel with "the words of God" (see also Prov 1:30; 5:12; 15:5). Thus the half verse summarizes Isaiah's complaint that these leaders have rejected Yahweh's instruction, a term which here would comprehend both what pertains to Yahweh's purpose in history (as revealed through Isaiah) and those more general items of behavior, which we sum up under the rubric "social justice," that make up the riches of the wisdom tradition.

YAHWEH'S OUTSTRETCHED HAND: 5:25-29(30)

The presence in 5:25b of words that form a refrain in 9:8-21 (see 9:12, 17, 21) suggests that 5:25 originally belonged to that same composition. Indeed, it is widely held that there has been considerable shuffling around of materials that are now in chaps. 5, 9, and 10 (see above on 10:1-4 + 5:8-24); that texts originally closely joined (the series of seven woes, the poem with the "outstretched hand" refrain) came to be so widely separated is owing in part, at least, to the insertion of Isaiah's "Memoirs" (see below). It is widely held that v 25 is the remnant of what was once a strophe in a 5-strophe poem and that vv 26-29(30) form the concluding strophe. These verses will, therefore, be treated along with 9:8-21 below. It is fairly evident that the poem originally dealt with Israel (i.e., the northern kingdom), and the placing of these verses here, with their rather obvious reference to invasion by Assyria, was intended to give a concrete shape to the threats against Judah contained in the preceding parts of chap. 5.

Isaiah's Memoirs: 6:1-8:18

There is substantial agreement among scholars that the materials of this extensive passage (with the exception of some disputed verses, which will be noted as we proceed) are organically connected and chronologically ordered and that they came to form a document of some sort at an early period. Since we here frequently encounter the prophet speaking in the first person (6:1-13; 8:1-4, 5-8, 11-15, 16-18), many see in the complex the literary activity of Isaiah himself, and it is therefore often referred to as Isaiah's Memoirs (or *Denkschrift*, the term used by German scholars). Although the materials are diverse, they can all (except for the call narrative and the late insertions referred to above) be dated to the period of the Syro-Ephraimitic War (see below on chap. 7). The contents cohere in that the call narrative explains Isaiah's commission to preach and gives a hint of the import of his ministry, while the words and deeds recounted thereafter set forth his message for that crisis and the response it evoked on the part of king and people. Since that response was negative, the little booklet closes with him waiting in faith for the fulfillment of the word Yahweh had spoken through him. (It is possible to understand the "testimony" and "teaching" that Isaiah is commanded to "bind up" among his disciples in 8:16 as referring to the "Memoirs" that we are speaking of.) The whole is tied together with a literary *inclusio* in that it begins and ends with a reference to Yahweh enthroned on Zion (6:1 and 8:18).

There are not a few who extend the Memoirs to 9:7, and it can easily be conceded that the passage on the ideal king to come (9:1-7) belongs to the same historical period and coheres with what Isaiah has to say of the Davidic dynasty in chap. 7. It was the insertion of these Memoirs into the collection which stretches now from chaps. 5 to 12 that occasioned some of the disarrangement of the materials of that collection, as previously noted (see above on 5:8 and 5:25).

THE CALL NARRATIVE: 6:1-13

6 In the year that King Uzziah died I saw the Lord sitting upon a throne, high and lifted up; and his train filled the temple. ²Above him stood the seraphim; each had six wings: with two he covered his face, and with two he covered his feet, and with two he flew. ³And one called to another and said:

"Holy, holy, holy is the LORD of hosts;
the whole earth is full of his glory."

⁴And the foundations of the thresholds shook at the voice of him who called, and the house was filled with smoke. ⁵And I said: "Woe is me! For I am lost; for I am a man of unclean lips, and I dwell in the midst of a people of unclean lips; for my eyes have seen the King, the LORD of hosts!"

⁶Then flew one of the seraphim to me, having in his hand a burning coal which he had taken with tongs from the altar. ⁷And he touched my mouth, and said: "Behold, this has touched your lips, your guilt is taken away, and your sin forgiven." ⁸And I heard the voice of the Lord saying, "Whom shall I send, and who will go for us?" Then I said, "Here am I! Send me." ⁹And he said, "Go,

and say to this people:
  'Hear and hear, but do not understand;
  see and see, but do not perceive.'
[10]Make the heart of this people fat,
  and their ears heavy,
  and shut their eyes;
  lest they see with their eyes,
    and hear with their ears,
  and understand with their hearts,
    and turn and be healed."
[11]Then I said, "How long, O Lord?"
And he said:
  "Until cities lie waste
    without inhabitant,
  and houses without men,
    and the land is utterly desolate,
[12]and the LORD removes men far away,
  and the forsaken places are many in
    the midst of the land.
[13]And though a tenth remain in it,
  it will be burned again,
like a terebinth or an oak,
  whose stump remains standing
  when it is felled."
The holy seed is its stump.

One of the purposes of any prophet's call narrative is to legitimate his right to speak in the name of the Lord. Often his message was unpopular and sometimes even considered seditious; in the face of opposition the prophet's response and defense was "The Lord sent me to say this" (see Jer 26:10-19; Amos 7:12-15). Isaiah's opposition to the "party line" seems to have been denigrated as "conspiracy" (see below on 8:12), he was at odds with the royal advisers, as we have already seen (see above on 5:12, 18-19), and false prophets may have contradicted his words (see 28:7), so Isaiah had need to display his credentials. The vision is described in quite concrete terms of words and sights, but behind it would lie also a religious experience that profoundly changed his inner and outer life and would always defy description. Although the event itself lay at the beginning of his prophetic ministry, here given a precise indication of date, the account was probably formulated sometime later (though no later than shortly after the Syro-Ephraimitic War, when his memoirs were put together) and to an extent, therefore, reflects the actual experience of his ministry. The call narrative stood, as we would expect, at the beginning of the small collection just referred to; but as the Isaiah collection grew other collections of oracles were placed before it (in part, at least, because some of their content antedated the Syro-Ephraimitic War), so that this inaugural vision is found in what we now designate as chap. 6, rather than at the beginning of the book.

Isaiah's call is dated *the year that King Uzziah died*. (For a similar chronological indication by the year of a king's death, see 14:28.) The chronology of the kings of Judah is rather complicated and confused precisely for the period of which we now speak, so that a date for Uzziah's death is given only at some risk (for details, see Introduction, p. 27). Following John Bright and others, however, we would put it at 742. Uzziah's successor, Jotham, was king from 742 to 735, but because Uzziah was a leper, Jotham acted as a coregent from about 750, so that in effect he began to rule at that time. He was succeeded by Ahaz (735-715). A call in 742 would put the beginning of Isaiah's ministry very close to the beginning of the reign of the Assyrian king, Tiglath-pileser III (745-727). Isaiah's career was exercised during a period in which the might of Assyria was supreme, challenged by none but the foolhardy. Nevertheless, the King whom Isaiah sees enthroned in the Jerusalem Temple, which only faintly reflected the glory of his heavenly Temple, was the one who ruled all the earth and all of history; his *glory* fills *the whole earth* and it is his purpose which will be established. He is pictured upon a royal *throne* and in kingly garments. He is attended by angelic beings, members of his royal court, and his appearance is accompanied by earthquake and smoke (v 4), common elements of a theophany.

The term *saraph* means "burning, fiery," and *seraphim*

may function here as a substantive ("fiery beings") or possibly as an adjective, with another word, probably "cherubim," understood. A pair of gold-covered cherubim of olivewood stood in Solomon's Temple (1 Kgs 6:23-28). They imaged forth the fearful composite heavenly creatures who were thought to protect Yahweh's throne and to make up part of his royal court (cf. Akkadian *karabu*, from which the concept is derived). Commentators have sometimes identified the seraphim with the saraph-serpents of the desert (see Num 21:6; Deut 8:15), called "fiery" because of their bite, especially since Isaiah refers elsewhere to flying saraphs (14:29; 30:6), which are apparently snakes. But this view is to be rejected. In spite of the wings, the creatures have hands, faces, and sexual parts that need covering (the *feet* of v 2 is a euphemism — cf. Exod 4:25; Isa 7:20) and so are basically human in form. Ezekiel (1:5-14) also describes composite celestial creatures, whom he later (9:3; 10:1-22) identifies as cherubim, which are human in form (1:5), and which have hands, faces, and wings; they also use one pair of wings for flight and another to cover their bodies (1:11). Isaiah's creatures use a third pair to veil their faces out of reverence for the divine presence (cf. 1 Kgs 19:13); Ezekiel may have thought this rather reckless for creatures in flight, and his have only four wings.

The cry of the seraphim emphasizes the holiness of Yahweh, obviously his predominant quality for Isaiah; one of his favorite titles for the Lord is "the Holy One of Israel," a title used approximately a dozen times in the first thirty-nine chapters of Isaiah, about the same number of times in the rest of the Isaiah collection, and but rarely in the rest of the Old Testament. Moral perfection is included in the concept, but it doesn't exhaust it. More basic is the quality of separateness, apartness; in God this relates especially to his transcendence, but Israel can also be holy through its participation in the Lord (see Exod 19:6; Lev 19:2; Deut 7:6).

The cry of the seraphim (v 3) probably reflects a venerable liturgical acclamation. The title *Yahweh of hosts* means originally "he who brings the (heavenly?) hosts into being" (*yahweh* being the causative of an older form of the verb "to be"), a title specially connected with the Ark of the Covenant and probably relating to Israel's holy war tradition.

The Hebrew word rendered *glory* (*kabod*) is sometimes used as a technical term to express the visible fiery splendor which marked the Lord's presence on Sinai, in the Tabernacle, and in the Temple (Exod 24:16-17; 40:34-35; 1 Kgs 8:11; cf. Ezek 10:18-19; 43:2-5). But that usage may be later than Isaiah, and, in any case, it could hardly have the whole earth as its scope in this text because ordinary mortals could not endure its presence (Exod 40:35; 1 Kgs 8:11). Since Isaiah conceives Yahweh as having a plan that comprehends all the earth (14:26-27) and of being the power that has all nations at his beck and call (5:26-29; 7:18-19; 10:5-6), his *glory* may be primarily the kingly majesty and divine power which he holds and exercises through *the whole earth*, though a visible component is not excluded. Immediately after the call narrative Isaiah's Memoirs concern themselves with a crisis involving Judah, Israel, Syria, and Assyria (chaps. 7-8).

The theophany is a shattering experience for Isaiah; his first reaction is an awareness of his own and of his people's sinfulness. The proximity of sin to the holiness of God is a dangerous situation, and this is what prompts Isaiah's *Woe is me!* It was, in fact, dangerous to see God in any circumstances, there being a common Old Testament conviction that "no one can see God and live" (Exod 33:20; Judg 13:22). The fact that Isaiah does has important implications not only in terms of his belonging to an exclusive circle of those who have seen God and live, but also in terms of his role as God's spokesman and agent of his will. The reference to unclean *lips* (v 5) somewhat surprises, but Hebrew thought tends to be quite concrete; in any case, this opens the way for the cleansing of Isaiah's lips, an act which prepares him for the mission to which he is soon to be invited. Isaiah's confession has expressed his solidarity in guilt with the rest of the people; now he is set apart from them both by having seen God and by his cleansing.

The Lord now speaks (v 8), and his question indicates that

a messenger is needed. This and other elements have suggested to many that Yahweh's council has been in session and that a course of action has been determined upon. This conviction is strengthened by the plural (*who will go for us?*); cf. also what was said above about Yahweh's policy (*'esah* — 5:12, 19). There is here a strong parallel to the vision of Micaiah ben Imlah in 1 Kgs 22:19-22, which tells of Yahweh enthroned, of deliberation with his heavenly court, of decision, and of a commissioning. It is not said here that Isaiah was privy to the deliberations, it is true, but Jeremiah marks the true prophet off from the false on the basis of being present in his council or not (Jer 23:18, 22), and Isaiah can claim "The Lord of hosts has sworn in my hearing. . ." (5:9). Certainly Isaiah's being privy to what Yahweh intends to do is an important ingredient of his message and also a point on which he set himself above the circle of advisers of Judah's kings. The Lord's question *Whom shall I send?* constitutes an invitation, and Isaiah accepts it with alacrity. This alone is enough to make him a rather unique prophet (cf. the reluctance of Moses, whose call anticipates that of the classical prophets, Exod 3:11-4:16; and of Jeremiah, Jer 1:6; and the reaction of Ezekiel, Ezek 3:14).

The words of Yahweh's commissioning (vv 9-10) are some of the most difficult to understand in the Old Testament. If taken literally they would mean that Isaiah was sent in order that the people would be rendered deaf, blind, and so obtuse that they would not understand, be converted, and be healed. Some commentators have in fact gone that route, asserting that what we have here is not an indictment but a "word of power"; Isaiah's mission was to make it possible for the punishment already determined to come, though sometimes this is seen as a necessary condition for some more positive work on the part of the Lord. Although it would be an oversimplification to think these difficult words do nothing more than suggest one outcome of his ministry, namely, that his preaching occasioned a hard-hearted rejection that opened the door for greater punishment, it is nevertheless difficult to suppose that it was the

Lord's intention to block out the conversion that would have occasioned a healing.

What is expressed in vv 9-10 in a negative way allows us to reconstruct what should be the positive process: seeing and hearing should lead to understanding, understanding to conversion, and conversion to healing. In this is seen the evil of the lack of perception and understanding that blocks out the desired result. Furthermore, it is clear that Isaiah made every effort not only to make his message intelligible, but also to make it appealing and effective, now presenting Yahweh as a provident father (1:2-3), now reminding Jerusalem of her former state as faithful bride (1:21), now offering the alternatives of prosperity and the sword (1:19-20). We should recall that the call narrative most probably reflects some of the circumstances of his ministry. If his ministry was characterized by opposition to the policies adopted by the kings under whom he prophesied and by opposition to the counsel of the circle of the kings' royal advisers, those who were held in esteem by all for their wisdom, prudence, and insight, this would call for some justification. Does Isaiah think he alone is wise? The response to the question is found in the reference to the blinding and hardening: it is precisely those who should most especially perceive and understand, the counselors who surround the king and the king himself, whom Isaiah thinks of as having been blinded and hardened and made unperceiving. The command to harden, then, reflects the opposition of "the wise," an opposition already apparent in Isaiah's encounters with Ahaz and the counselors whose advice Ahaz is bent on following (7:1-17), and with the people who follow them (8:1-8). Thus the connection between the vocation narrative and the rest of the Memoirs is apparent.

Isaiah's concern for his people is revealed in his poignant cry, *How long?* (v 11). More than a question, it is a prayer for a limited duration to the baneful kind of ministry involved in the "hardening," and we are reminded that an important aspect of the prophet's work is that of intercession. The phrase "How long?" is encountered in a number of the psalms of supplication (e.g., 13:2; 74:10; 79:5; 80:4; 89:46; 90:13; 94:3), where it is an urgent cry for pity and relief, but at the same time an expression of confidence. We are not to suppose that here the pattern is so completely broken that this plaintive cry goes unheard and unanswered. Thus, although the response refers to devastation of the land, such devastation as would be occasioned by war and invasion, the possibility of something better beyond this is not excluded: *until* is not the same as "forever," and the Lord's response does not rule out the pattern of restoration after destruction found elsewhere in Isaiah.

The authenticity of vv 12-13 is disputed. Most commentators take these verses to be a later addition occasioned by the Assyrian deportation (or even the Babylonian captivity). Although the arguments for this are not overwhelming, it is true that v 11 can easily be read as a conclusion that needs no further completion. These verses may have belonged originally to another context; the (probable) reference to deportation would not be unsuitable to Isaiah's time. And if the reference to *a tenth* is intended to suggest a Judah that remains after an Israel that has been destroyed (cf. 1 Sam 11:8; 2 Sam 19:43; 1 Kgs 11:31), the background would be the events of 722: preserved from the destruction which overtook the northern kingdom, Judah would in turn be *burned*, though the Hebrew here is uncertain and has given rise to quite diverse interpretations. The concluding words of v 13, *the holy seed is its stump*, are also somewhat mangled. They are apparently intended to relate to the remnant concept, suggesting that from the stump of the felled tree a new growth can arise. The remnant concept is indeed found in Isaiah, but here the words seem patently built upon an image which was intended to speak of destruction.

FIRST ENCOUNTER WITH AHAZ: 7:1-9

7 In the days of Ahaz the son of Jotham, son of Uzziah, king of Judah, Rezin the king of Syria and Pekah the son

of Remaliah the king of Israel came up to Jerusalem to wage war against it, but they could not conquer it. ²When the house of David was told, "Syria is in league with Ephraim," his heart and the heart of his people shook as the trees of the forest shake before the wind.

³And the LORD said to Isaiah, "Go forth to meet Ahaz, you and Shear-jashub your son, at the end of the conduit of the upper pool on the highway to the Fuller's Field, ⁴and say to him, 'Take heed, be quiet, do not fear, and do not let your heart be faint because of these two smoldering stumps of firebrands, at the fierce anger of Rezin and Syria and the son of Remaliah. ⁵Because Syria, with Ephraim and the son of Remaliah, has devised evil against you, saying, ⁶"Let us go up against Judah and terrify it, and let us conquer it for ourselves, and set up the son of Tabeel as king in the midst of it," ⁷thus says the Lord GOD:

It shall not stand,
    and it shall not come to pass.
⁸For the head of Syria is Damascus,
    and the head of Damascus is Rezin.

(Within sixty-five years Ephraim will be broken to pieces so that it will no longer be a people.)

⁹And the head of Ephraim is Samaria,
    and the head of Samaria is the son of Remaliah.
If you will not believe,
    surely you shall not be established.'"

Whereas the call narrative (chap. 6) can be considered part of the framework of Isaiah's Memoirs (along with 8:16-18 — though some would include 9:1-7 as part of the framework), the encounter(s) with Ahaz bring(s) us directly into the substance of it. The events contained therein relate closely to the Syro-Ephraimitic War, which is to be dated to 735-732. ("Syro-Ephraimitic" is the traditional terminology for this conflict. The biblical sources speak of Aram, the ancient name for what we call Syria, and Ephraim, the principal tribe of Israel, often used, as here, to designate the whole of the northern kingdom. "Syro-Israelite" would perhaps be less confusing.) On Tiglath-pileser III's accession (745), his attempt to reimpose Assyrian rule on former vassals, and the response of subject peoples, see Introduction, p. 22. Pekah, the usurper who overthrew Menahem's son Pekahiah to take the throne in Israel, cast his lot with the anti-Assyrian coalition, of which Rezin, king of Syria (740—732) was the leading member. Judah, under Jotham (750-735), did not join the coalition, and the Syro-Ephraimitic War was an attempt to force Judah into it, or at least to neutralize it in the event of an Assyrian attack; 2 Kgs 15:37 seems to indicate that Syria and Israel initiated hostilities against Judah already in the days of Jotham, though 2 Kgs 16:5-9 and Isa 7:1 speak only of Ahaz. Ahaz, apparently urged on by his royal advisers, thought his wisest course was to send tribute to Assyria and voluntaily submit as a vassal, a course he eventually followed (2 Kgs 16:7-8). This was a policy bitterly opposed by Isaiah, and his Memoirs detail his attempts in the course of this crisis to dissuade Ahaz from it.

The opening verse of this section (7:1) is taken, with some small changes, from 2 Kgs 16:5. This is a later editor's attempt to put the events of the chapter into their historical context, but it may give a misleading impression. Verse 2 speaks only of Syria and Israel being in league (if that is what the text means — the Hebrew is problematical), so it is not certain that Jerusalem was actually under siege at the time of Isaiah's encounter(s) with Ahaz. The expression *house of David* to refer to an individual king, as it does here (see also v 13), is unusual, but it calls attention to the fact that Ahaz is, for the time, the embodiment of the dynasty. Since the fate of the dynasty is a factor in the intentions of the enemy leaders (v 6) and the fate of Ahaz as embodiment of the dynasty is at issue in the mind of Isaiah (v 9), the expression is of some importance for the interpretation of the chapter.

Isaiah is bidden by Yahweh himself to meet Ahaz and to take with him his son *Shear-jashub* ("a remnant will return"), though in fact the child is not mentioned in the subsequent narrative nor, in fact, anywhere else in Isaiah's oracles (but see below on 8:18); but the phrase does recur in

10:21, in a context which indicates the reference is to moral conversion rather than return from battle. On Isaiah's penchant for consigning his teaching through names, see also 7:14; 8:1-4; and 9:6. The *conduit* referred to in v 3 brought water from the spring Gihon into the *upper pool*; Ahaz was undoubtedly inspecting the adequacy of Jerusalem's water supply for a siege. Later Isaiah will use this spring as a symbol of the saving power of Yahweh in which the people would not trust (8:6-8).

The message Isaiah delivers to Ahaz is that the threat now posed by Syria and Israel will quickly melt and that these nations therefore are not to be feared (v 4); *be quiet* means, above all, that Ahaz is not to seek help from Assyria by submitting to vassalhood, the solution urged upon him by his advisers. From v 6 we learn that part of the strategy of the coalition was to depose Ahaz and to set up another king in his stead, probably one not of David's line, and obviously one who would fall in with their plans for Judah. Although we cannot be sure who this replacement was to be, it has been argued that the Tabeel in question was the son of Hiram, king of Tyre; if this is correct, it would suggest that Tyre was also a member of the coalition. On what basis could Isaiah assert so boldly *It shall not stand and it shall not come to pass* (v 7)? It is safe to say that at least three elements enter here: God's promises concerning the house of David, the holy war tradition, and the fact that Yahweh's "purpose," not Syria's or Israel's, would be established. On the last point, compare the *it shall not stand* of v 7 with what is said of the counsel (=purpose, *'esah*) of "you peoples" in 8:10, namely, "it will not stand"; and contrast it with Yahweh's words in 14:24: "as I have purposed, so shall it stand."

Allusions to the Davidic dynasty and, by implication, to God's promises to it, run through this section. We have already referred to the unusual use of *house of David* in v 2 (and in v 13), and there is the stated intention of the coalition to depose Ahaz and replace him with another. In all likelihood we can list here also the difficult and probably elliptical reference to the *heads* in vv 8-9. This is usually taken as an implied contrast between the capitals and kings of the two attackers, on the one hand, and Jerusalem and its king, on the other. Since both Jerusalem (especially under "Zion" terminology) and the Davidic monarchy were celebrated in the liturgy as specially chosen by Yahweh and as enjoying his special protection, the point of the implied contrast would be clear. Even Isaiah's warning in v 9, *if you will not believe, surely you shall not be established*, may relate to this theme. The demand for faith in Yahweh is characteristic of Isaiah's teaching (though sometimes expressed in other terminology, e.g., to lean on, to wait for, to be still) and an important aspect of it. This verse features a play on words in that *believe* and *be established* are two different forms of the same verb (*'aman*, whose basic sense has to do with being firm, steady, and from which our word "Amen" comes); the *NAB* renders it "unless your faith is firm you shall not be firm." In fact this verb is used rather frequently to refer to the firmness of David's house because of God's promises concerning it (see 2 Sam 7:16; 1 Kgs 8:26; 11:38; Isa 55:3; Ps 89:28, 37; 1 Chr 17:23, 24; 2 Chr 1:9; 6:17). Isaiah may here be saying that the promise cuts both ways: it has indeed been spoken but it requires Ahaz's faith to be effective. Faith for Isaiah, therefore, has very practical implications: to turn to Assyria for help to sustain that which has been guaranteed by Yahweh is to turn faith into unacceptable lip-service and to threaten the viability of the promise itself.

Additional background for Isaiah's assurance that the purpose of the coalition *shall not stand* may perhaps be found in Israel's holy war tradition. The exhortation *be quiet, do not fear* (v 4) relates very well to this tradition (cf. Deut 20:3-4), according to which victory comes from the Lord, not from human means. In this case there would be no prohibition of self-defense, but rather the insistence that victory would come from the Lord — but again with the proviso that no other help be sought. (The reference to *sixty-five years* in v 8 is in all probability a later insertion, for action at so far a remove would have been of no use to Ahaz; in addition, it interrupts the connection that should obviously exist between v 8a and v 9a. A lapse of sixty-five years from the events of 735 would bring us to the time of

Esarhaddon [680-669], an Assyrian king who settled a foreign population in Samaria [see Ezra 4:2], a sort of crown-
ing blow to the erstwhile kingdom of Israel, which the
glossator sees as a final fulfillment of Isaiah's words concerning its demise.)

THE SIGN OF IMMANUEL: 7:10-17

> ¹⁰Again the LORD spoke to Ahaz, ¹¹"Ask a sign of the
> LORD your God; let it be deep as Sheol or high as
> heaven." ¹²But Ahaz said, "I will not ask, and I will not
> put the LORD to the test." ¹³And he said, "Hear then, O
> house of David! Is it too little for you to weary men, that
> you weary my God also? ¹⁴Therefore the Lord himself
> will give you a sign. Behold, a young woman shall con-
> ceive and bear a son, and shall call his name Immanuel.
> He shall eat curds and honey when he knows how to
> refuse the evil and choose the good. ¹⁶For before the child
> knows how to refuse the evil and choose the good, the
> land before whose two kings you are in dread will be
> deserted. ¹⁷The LORD will bring upon you and upon
> your people and upon your father's house such days as
> have not come since the day that Ephraim departed from
> Judah — the king of Assyria."

This passage is closely connected with the preceding and
could even be part of the same encounter between Isaiah
and Ahaz, though the words *again the Lord spoke to Ahaz*
would suggest some interval. There is no difficulty understanding why Isaiah bids Ahaz to ask for a sign. The king is
confronted with a fearful situation and a difficult decision:
on the one hand there is the temptation to turn to Assyria
for help, a course apparently urged upon him by his advisers, while on the other hand there is the prophet who speaks
an oracle to him in the name of the Lord denouncing such a
course of action. The strategists can present arguments
based on tangible realities, such as the number of Assyrian
chariots, the might and success they have demonstrated,

etc., the kind of arguments the prophet cannot present. Yet if the word he speaks really does come from the Lord it should override all other considerations; and so the prophet tells Ahaz to *ask a sign* as a way of demonstrating that he does indeed speak the word of the Lord. Ahaz's refusal to do so probably means that his mind is already made up, that he will appeal to Assyria for help; if the sign were given, especially if this encounter were at all public, he would have little choice except to act on the prophet's word.

To the king who refuses to ask for a sign, Isaiah now gives, unbidden, the sign of Immanuel (vv 14-15). The nature of the Immanuel sign has been the subject of much debate and has been explained in quite diverse ways. The sign does not consist merely in the birth and naming of the child, but refers also to his diet (*curds and honey*) in relation to knowing to *refuse the evil and choose the good*. And the prophet goes on to renew his promise of the rapid demise of Syria and Israel but adds also the threat of horrendous days to come; a later gloss identifies this, quite accurately, as *the king of Assyria*, i.e., Assyrian invasion.

There is hardly an element of this Immanuel sign that has not been disputed. The name, of course, means "God with us" (Heb.: *'imma-nu'el*), but who is the young woman and what does the name mean in the circumstances? Is *curds and honey* food of abundance or of penury? And how does it relate to the knowledge of good and evil?

In spite of the citation of Isa 7:14 in Matt 1:23, the verse cannot be understood, in its historical context, as a prediction of the virginal conception of Jesus. (*OTA*, 1, #800.) The term translated *young woman* (more accurately, "*the* young woman": *ha-'almah*) is not the technical term for a virgin, nor could an event that took place only some seven centuries later in any sense be a "sign" for Ahaz; furthermore, although we accept the virginal conception of Jesus as an object of faith, it is in no sense a visible *sign* to confirm the truth of what has been said. Not a few scholars have seen the *young woman* used in a generalizing sense to mean "any young woman"; i.e., any new mother could name her child "God with us" because the threat of Syria and Israel will have disappeared. Others see here a reference to the prophet's wife, the child being either the same as that named Maher-shalal-hash-baz in 8:1-4 or another sign fulfilling much the same function (see below on 8:1-4). The greater number, however, and with better reason, understand the *'almah* to be a wife of Ahaz and the child to be a son born to Ahaz himself. As such he would be a guarantee of the continuation of the dynasty, the vehicle of God's messianic promises; for this reason the child can be called "God with us." But more than this is involved.

It is important to note the change in the import of the sign because of Ahaz's refusal to ask. Initially the nature of the sign was immaterial: the king was invited to ask for *any* sign (*deep as Sheol or high as heaven* is a way of saying it can be anything in the vast extent between the realm of the dead [see 14:11-15 on "Sheol"], considered to lie below the earth, and the sky above). But since the king's refusal to ask for a sign apparently indicates he has already determined to reject the course urged by the prophet (note Isaiah's exasperated response — v 13), there is no longer need for a sign for confirmation. The new sign does not concern itelf with a time-frame for the evaporation of the Syria-Israel threat but relates to broader matters of the prophet's message. A new son of David will be born and the present threat will indeed disappear, but the advent of Assyria will mean a devastated land in which agriculture will be impossible (see below on vv 23-25) and in which the only food available will be that which can be obtained from flocks (curds from milk) or found in the fields (wild honey — v 15; see below on vv 21-22). It is in such circumstances that Immanuel will grow to maturity and, because of these privations, will learn to *refuse the evil and choose the good* (and so become the very antithesis of Ahaz!); the Hebrew expression in v 15 is more easily understood to mean "so that he may know to reject evil and choose good" than the "when he knows..." of *RSV* (or the more common "by the time he knows..."). It is incorrect to see here a chronological indication of when the Syria-Israel threat will end. We know that Isaiah expected this within a relatively brief time (see v 4 and below on

8:1-4), but the age required for "knowing good and evil" in the Old Testament, whenever it can be determined from the context, is always that of adult discernment (around twenty years of age when specified). Therefore what Isaiah has to say about Immanuel carries far beyond the immediate crisis; we have to suppose that he thinks of Immanuel, a faithful king, as the replacement for the faithless Ahaz (cf. v 9b). In Isaiah's thought the devastation to come (here seen as the result of Ahaz's foolish course of action, of his disobedience and lack of faith) was neither merely punitive nor finally destructive, but was to be a preparation for and a means to the future restoration. (See further on vv 21-22, and see 1:21-26, where the same pattern of judgment and restoration is found.)

This tells us that the son of David Isaiah expects was not to be merely a continuator of the dynasty, but the prince of God's restored people, a Davidid purified and perfected through affliction, in whom the name "God with us" would find its meaning (*OTA* 2, #738). The same picture emerges from the portrait in 9:1-7, which probably stems from this same period. That the oracle did not find satisfactory fulfillment in Ahaz's immediate successor simply means that it had to await future fulfillment (see below on 8:17 and 30:8).

A SERIES OF FRAGMENTS: 7:18-25

[18]In that day the LORD will whistle for the fly which is at the sources of the streams of Egypt, and for the bee which is in the land of Assyria. [19]And they will all come and settle in the steep ravines, and in the clefts of the rocks, and on all the thornbushes, and on all the pastures.

[20]In that day the Lord will shave with a razor which is hired beyond the River — with the king of Assyria — the head and the hair of the feet, and it will sweep away the beard also.

[21]In that day a man will keep alive a young cow and two sheep; [22]and because of the abundance of milk which they give, he will eat curds; for every one that is left in the land will eat curds and honey.

²³In that day every place where there used to be a thousand vines, worth a thousand shekels of silver, will become briers and thorns. ²⁴With bow and arrows men will come there, for all the land will be briers and thorns; ²⁵and as for all the hills which used to be hoed with a hoe, you will not come there for fear of briers and thorns; but they will become a place where cattle are let loose and where sheep tread.

The concluding part of this chapter is composed of a series of brief, sometimes fragmentary, oracles which probably date from this same period, i.e., 735-732. The phrase *in that day*, which we find at the beginning of each of the four pieces (at vv 18, 20, 21, and 23), relates them to what precedes. This may have been the work of an editor, but since Isaiah may have originally spoken them and then wished to incorporate them into his Memoirs, it cannot be excluded that the transitions were his own work. In any case, these passages help specify the nature of the threat formulated so briefly and cryptically at the end of v 17 (i.e., that the calamity foretold would be foreign invasion) and detail the circumstances.

That Yahweh is able to summon foreign nations to do his bidding (merely by whistling!) agrees with other Isaiah passages (cf. 5:26-30; 10:5-6, 15). The reference to both Egypt and Assyria in vv 18-19 is unexpected and certainly hinders the passage from being an unambiguous reference to danger from Assyria. Although the double reference could have been simply for the sake of poetic parallelism (cf. Hos 11:5, 11), there are not a few scholars who would see the mention of the fly from Egypt as a later expansion, dating perhaps to the time when Hezekiah began negotiating with Egypt for help against the Assyrians (see below on chap. 18). The text would then originally have referred merely to Yahweh whistling for the bee (Assyria); this makes better sense, for some ancient sources do speak of bees responding to the whistling of the beekeeper, but whistling for a fly has very little meaning.

Although *with the king of Assyria* is a later gloss to

explain Isaiah's more poetic expression, v 20 repeats more or less the same message of Yahweh's use of Assyria in order to punish Judah, but here the metaphor is different. Yahweh's instrument (cf. 10:5-6) is now *a razor*; "*the* river" without further specification in the Old Testament is regularly the Euphrates, and the country beyond it is here certainly Assyria. *The hair of the feet* is a euphemism for genital hair (cf. "feet" in 6:2; Exod 4:25). The shaving off of all the hair from head to foot marks a degrading, insulting sort of treatment (as was the shaving off even of the beard — cf. 2 Sam 10:4). On another level (and this may also be intended) Assyria would denude Judah of all it had — a process already begun in the huge tribute sent to Tiglath-pileser III by Ahaz (see 2 Kgs 16:8).

The two concluding oracles (vv 21-22, 23-25) tell, in more realistic terms, of this denuding and devastation of the land, first in pastoral and then in agricultural terms. The typical flock will be very small, consisting of a cow and two sheep, and even these will not be easy to raise. The Hebrew behind *RSV*'s "keep alive" (the piel of *hayah*) means precisely that, to sustain in life under difficult or threatening circumstances (see Gen 7:3; 19:32, 34; Exod 1:17, 18, 22; Num 31:15; Jos 9:15; Jgs 21:14; for its use with domestic animals, see 1 Kgs 18:5). This verb indicates very clearly that the scene depicted is not an idyllic one, as some would have it, taking *curds and honey* to be the equivalent of the standard cliché, "milk and honey" (though it may well be that an editor took it in this sense and compounded confusion by adding the reference to *abundance of milk* in v 22). The impossibility of raising crops leaves as the only sustenance the milk products that can be obtained from scanty flocks and the wild honey available in the fields. The reference to Immanuel's fare in v 15 must be understood in the same way.

The heavy-handed, repetitive, and somewhat contradictory description of the land overgrown with briars and thorns in vv 23-25 comes from later hands, though the trampling down of farm lands and its reversion to pasture is found elsewhere in Isaiah (5:5, 17).

MAHER-SHALAL-HASH-BAZ: 8:1-4

8 Then the LORD said to me, "Take a large tablet and write upon it common characters, 'Belonging to Maher-shalal-hash-baz.'" ²And I got reliable witnesses, Uriah the priest and Zechariah the son of Jeberechiah, to attest for me. ³And I went to the prophetess, and she conceived and bore a son. Then the LORD said to me, "Call his name Maher-shalal-hash-baz; ⁴for before the child knows how to cry 'My father' or 'My mother,' the wealth of Damascus and the spoil of Samaria will be carried away before the king of Assyria."

Although Isaiah's encounters with Ahaz produced no fruit by way of influencing his policy, he continues to present his message, this time with a prophetic act and another symbolic name. Since the passage is immediately followed by a reference to "this people" (v 5), it may be that it was intended more for the larger public than for the king. This sign is described as consisting of three parts: the writing out of a name before witnesses, the conception and birth of a child, and the giving of the name to the child and an explanation of its prophetic meaning. Since Isaiah fathers the infant, the prophetess who bears it is presumably his wife and possibly is called "prophetess" for that reason; nothing else is known of her. The name imposed on the child, *Maher-shalal-hash-baz*, means something like "speedy spoil, hasty prey" and is explained to signify that before the child can say "Mama" and "Daddy" the capital cities of Syria and Israel will be plundered by the Assyrians. Thus Isaiah puts himself on public record as saying that the defeat of Syria and Israel will come within a specific time — two years as the outer limit from the time of conception. We don't know how long after the Immanuel oracle this new event occurred, though, since Isaiah was no doubt still attempting to influence Ahaz's policy, it could not have been long. We do know that Ahaz was not deterred, and so the written record and the witnesses stood as testimony that the step, with all the consequences it entailed, could have been avoided.

THE WATERS OF SHILOAH: 8:5-8

> [5]The LORD spoke to me again: [6]"Because this people
> have refused the waters of Shiloah that flow gently, and
> melt in fear before Rezin and the son of Remaliah; [7]there-
> fore, behold, the Lord is bringing up against them the
> waters of the River, mighty and many, the king of Assyria
> and all his glory; and it will rise over all its channels and
> go over all its banks; [8]and it will sweep on into Judah, it
> will overflow and pass on, reaching even to the neck; and
> its out-spread wings will fill the breadth of your land, O
> Immanuel."

These verses suppose that Ahaz has now certainly decided
to turn for help to Assyria (perhaps has already done so) and
that in so doing he enjoys considerable support from the
people: Isaiah, speaking in Yahweh's name, refers to them
as *this people*, an expression substituted for "my people"
when reproach is intended (cf. 6:9; 8:11). Again Isaiah
speaks in symbolic terms, using *the waters of Shiloah* as a
symbol of Yahweh and his quiet strength, *the River* (the
Euphrates — see above on 7:20) as a symbol of the might of
Assyria. By choosing the one (Assyria) they have rejected
the other (Yahweh). Shiloah apparently was the name for
the channel which brought water from the spring Gihon into
a pool in the city, where it would be available for use. If this
is where the encounter with Ahaz referred to in 7:3 took
place, the two passages are nicely tied together. Gihon was a
perennial source and therefore a fitting symbol of the constant, reliable strength of Yahweh, especially if one were to
think in terms of a siege. But this they had rejected in favor
of the awesome might of Assyria. Very well, they would
have Assyria, and like a stream in spate it would overflow all
barriers, inundating the land and sweeping all before it.
From the time of Ahaz's appeal, Judah would no longer
know freedom or independence, and the attempt to shake
off Assyria's yoke (under Hezekiah) would bring precisely
the sort of flood Isaiah here speaks of.

The exact meaning of the second part of v 8 is disputed.
Even if it is intended to continue the same message, there is

an abrupt and unexpected change in imagery, from a river to a huge bird. But "wings" are usually a symbol of protection, not threat (cf. Deut 32:11; Ps 17:8; 36:7; 57:1; etc.), and thus its wings (better: "his wings") would have to refer to Yahweh and the sense would have changed from threat to promise of protection. For this reason this final half-verse is often taken for a later addition. However, if the interpretation of Immanuel given above is correct, this half-verse can perhaps be attributed to Isaiah and to this context: whatever trials the Assyrian "flood" may bring, this isn't the end. Since it is in this devastated land that Immanuel grows to maturity, even the address to him (deleted by most of those who don't delete the whole half-verse), is perhaps not unexpected.

THE COUNSEL OF THE NATIONS
WILL COME TO NOUGHT: 8:9-10

⁹ Be broken, you peoples, and be dismayed;
  give ear, all you far countries;
 gird yourselves and be dismayed;
  gird yourselves and be dismayed.
¹⁰ Take counsel together, but it will come to nought;
  speak a word, but it will not stand,
  for God is with us.

These two verses probably come from this same period, but they could not originally have followed Isaiah's promise of Judah's inundation by Assyria. The nations from whom Judah has nothing to fear, whose counsel will come to nought (v 10), cannot be a reference to Assyria (the only nation mentioned in the immediately preceding context). The oracle does suit what Isaiah says concerning Syria and Israel in 7:4-8, however. It could have been drawn to its present location because of the "God with us" (=Immanuel) with which it ends — which here is a statement of fact, the reason for Judah's security, but at the same time a play on the name. The *all you far countries* is a rather expansive term that surprises, if only Syria and Israel are intended, but it is probable that the language of the Zion psalms, from which this passage draws its themes (cf. especially Pss 46; 48; 76), has had an influence here. The assertion that the counsels or purposes of others than Yahweh will not stand is a thought we have previously encountered in Isaiah (cf. 5:12, 19).

ISAIAH AND YAHWEH, CO-CONSPIRATORS: 8:11-15

> [11]For the LORD spoke thus to me with his strong hand upon me, and warned me not to walk in the way of this people, saying: [12]"Do not call conspiracy all that this people call conspiracy, and do not fear what they fear, nor be in dread. [13]But the LORD of hosts, him you shall regard as holy; let him be your fear, and let him be your dread. [14]And he will become a sanctuary, and a stone of offense, and a rock of stumbling to both houses of Israel, a trap and a snare to the inhabitants of Jerusalem. [15]And many shall stumble thereon; they shall fall and be broken; they shall be snared and taken."

This material is again in the first-person form and no doubt brings us back to the prophet's Memoirs after the insertion of vv 9-10. But these words seem to be addressed to him for his own sake, rather than as a message for the people (again referred to as *this people* as a sign of disfavor — see v 5). Now that it is clear that Ahaz has determined to reject Yahweh's word with reference to the Syro-Ephraimite crisis (apparently following his advisors and with broad support from the people), Isaiah and those with him form a little remnant of faith (though the term is not used here), and the Lord encourages them to stand fast ("them" because the verbs and personal suffixes in vv 12-13 are second-person *plural*). The Lord exhorts them not to be swayed by the fact that the many have gone off on a different course, and the reference to *conspiracy* (v 12) indicates that Isaiah has been branded as disloyal or worse. At least one commentator thinks this charge arises from the fact that while Ahaz still reigned, Isaiah had proclaimed a different successor to David, i.e., Immanuel. It is more likely that Isaiah's rejection of what had been determined upon as official policy was enough to mark him as a traitor to the state. Americans witnessed a similar phenomenon during the 1960s, when opposition to the administration's policy in Vietnam was branded by some as disloyalty.

It is clear that v 13 needs a small emendation (as also does v 14). Verse 12 had used together *conspiracy*, *fear*, and *dread*, and it seems the same was intended in v 13. Rather than *RSV*'s *him you shall regard as holy*, we should read "with him make your conspiracy"; the present text was either the result of a copyist's error or (more likely) a deliberate change by one who did not want to see the Lord involved in conspiracy. But the Lord's way is the right way, the loyal way, and the way which shall prevail (therefore *let him be your fear . . . your dread*), and there is some obvious irony in accepting the charge of conspiracy and then associating the Lord with it. Similarly, a very small change in v 14 would give us "snare" in place of *sanctuary*, which fits far better with *stone of offense* and *rock of stumbling* and with the threatening tone of this and the following verse. The expression *both houses of Israel* (v 14) refers to Israel and Judah and indicates the extent to which Isaiah still regarded the two as one people. To him the separation into two kingdoms was an example of the worst sort of tragedy (see 7:17), and the fact that Ahaz's appeal to Assyria was calculated to direct the force of that mighty nation against Israel could only worsen the split and would have provided Isaiah with an additional reason for opposing that course. Isaiah had previously indicated that Israel was not to be feared and that turning to Assyria would, in the end, be a disastrous step for Judah; here he speaks with great emphasis of the total inversion that was taking place: Yahweh's protective strength becomes a destructive force to those who reject it.

WAITING FOR YAHWEH: 8:16-18

> [16]Bind up the testimony, seal the teaching among my
> disciples. [17]I will wait for the LORD, who is hiding his
> face from the house of Jacob, and I will hope in him.
> [18]Behold, I and the children whom the LORD has given
> me are signs and portents in Israel from the LORD of
> hosts, who dwells on Mount Zion.

With this passage we come to the end of Isaiah's
Memoirs. Isaiah's message has been rejected and he, with
his intimates, has withdrawn from the public scene. But that
is not the end of the story: Yahweh's word has been spoken
and will attain its goal (cf. 55:10-11); what is needed now is
an explicit attestation of what has been transacted so that
when fulfillment comes it will not be possible to gainsay it.
That is the meaning of the Lord's command concerning the
testimony and *teaching* which was to be kept among the
prophet's disciples. Although we cannot know for sure, it is
probable that it is this command which prompted the putting together of what we have been calling Isaiah's Memoirs
and that they are coterminous with the *testimony* here
referred to (aside from the additions we have had occasion
to note).

Having completed this lasting witness of what Yahweh
has spoken, it remains only to *wait* for Yahweh to act, as he
surely will. At a later point Isaiah speaks of writing something down so that it may be as "a witness forever" (30:8),
but in the present circumstances he seems to be waiting for
the Lord to act within a more measurable time. To *wait* in
these circumstances, as elsewhere in Isaiah, is actually a very
positive concept and, in fact, part of the terminology of faith
(see also the reference to *hope* in v 17). The Isaiah collection
nowhere else refers to his disciples, so this text would be
precious if for no other reason. Clearly they, along with
Isaiah and his children, are "waiting" in faith. That Yahweh
is hiding his face from the house of Jacob means that the
people are not experiencing his saving help, the answer to
their prayers (cf. Ps 13:1; 27:9; 44:24). The reason for this is

obvious, consisting as it does of their refusal to respond in faith.

But the expression suggests a temporary rather than a definitive state of affairs (Yahweh does not hide his face forever). What Isaiah waits for is the fulfillment of Yahweh's word, but the content of the *testimony* is not wholly negative. Isaiah and his children are designated as *signs and portents in Israel from the Lord of hosts* (v 18). This designation is justified, no doubt, because of their names, and it is to these names that we must look for an explanation of what Isaiah expects. One of these names, Maher-shalal-hash-baz, has been explained in detail (8:1-4), and it indicates that the period of waiting should see an end to the Syria-Israel threat.

The name of the other son, Shear-jashub, was mentioned in 7:3, and nowhere else. If 7:1-8:15 be taken as the extent of Isaiah's Memoirs (chap. 6 and 8:16-18 functioning as its framework), then Shear-jashub is introduced at the earliest possible point in the narrative section; he appears again, unnamed, at the very end of the piece, among Isaiah's sons in 8:18. This leads us to suspect that he is named in 7:3 simply so he will be known as one of Isaiah's sons in 8:18— especially since his presence in 7:3 is given no explanation at all. The name itself, as all recognize, is a two-edged thing: to speak of "remnant" has an unfavorable connotation, for this implies the loss of a very substantial part of the whole; on the other hand, the assurance that there *will be* a remnant means that at least some will be spared. Where there is life, there is hope; where there is a remnant there is existence, continuity, and future possibilities.

The meaning of "return" in this name is ambiguous. If it were taken in the physical sense, the return would be from exile or from battle, but that does not seem to suit the present context (i.e., the context of the events of 735-732); Isaiah sees Assyria (not Syria-Israel) as the threat, but he expresses this in terms of a devastation of the land rather than exile. (Only once in his oracles does Isaiah speak of exile — in 5:13 — though the idea may be implied in other

passages that speak of removal of leaders or of depopula-
tion, such as 3:1-5 and 6:11-12). But the Hebrew term (*shub*)
can equally well mean "return" in a moral sense, i.e., with
reference to repentance, conversion (cf. Amos 4:6, 8, 9, 10,
11; Jer 3:12; 4:1; 31:18). Isaiah uses it in this sense in his
programmatic call narrative (6:10). There it is explained why
the people as a whole will not "turn and be healed," and the
way is opened for us when, only shortly later, we encounter
"a remnant shall return," to understand this in a moral
sense. No doubt the "turning" involved is closely connected
with Isaiah's demand for faith, so to speak of "a remnant of
faith" is not unwarranted. But perhaps we ought not to
restrict this "remnant" simply to Isaiah, his sons, and his
disciples. If the explanation of Immanuel given above is
correct, the implication would be that those survivors who
with him were to undergo the purifying trials of the aftermath of invasion also fall under the term. The child's name
is also a reminder of the possibility of repentance which still
remains for others. (Note that the attempt to explain the
name should be tied to the Memoirs and the events of
735-732; the Hebrew phrase behind the name is used twice in
contradictory senses in 10:21-22, where there are doubts
about authenticity. We cannot know what prompted Isaiah
to give his son this name — he was probably born and
named a couple of years before his introduction during
Isaiah's crisis with Ahaz — but the present context gives the
best indication of how we are to understand it.)

Can we ignore the fact that Isaiah is listed along with his
sons as a sign and portent? Exactly what is the import of this
is difficult to know. However, if the significance of the sons
lies in their names, it is at least worth recalling that Isaiah's
name says something like "Yahweh saves" or "Yahweh is
salvation." His inclusion among the signs and portents can
again be an indication of something positive for those who
are waiting in faith. The closing words of Isaiah's Memoirs,
the Lord of Hosts, who dwells on Mount Zion, recall to us
the opening of the call narrative and its vision of Yahweh
enthroned in the Temple (6:1).

The import of the "testimony" of which this section speaks should remind us that there is a predictive element in prophecy. It would be wrong to overemphasize this, as has been done so often in the past; but to totally neglect it, as is sometimes done now, would be to misunderstand an important aspect of prophecy.

TWO BRIEF ADDITIONS: 8:19-22

> [19]And when they say to you, "Consult the mediums and the wizards who chirp and mutter," should not a people consult their God? Should they consult the dead on behalf of the living? [20]To the teaching and to the testimony! Surely for this word which they speak there is no dawn. [21]They will pass through the land, greatly distressed and hungry; and when they are hungry, they will be enraged and will curse their king and their God, and turn their faces upward; [22]and they will look to the earth, but behold, distress and darkness, the gloom of anguish; and they will be thrust into thick darkness.

Although the Isaian authenticity of these verses is sometimes defended, it seems that vv 19-20, at least, are a later addition and that if vv 21-22 are Isaian, they come from another context. The reference to *teaching* and *testimony* in v 20 harks back to the same terms in v 16; but the purpose of the document provided by Isaiah has been made abundantly clear, and it is unlikely that Isaiah would now present it as an antidote for necromancy (i.e., the consulting of the dead). It is far more likely that a late hand used the reference to counter a sin which was condemned in Israel (Deut 18:9-14; 1 Sam 28:3, 9) but which was a perennial temptation. The Hebrew of v 20 is difficult and probably corrupt, and therefore the meaning is doubtful. The same is true of vv 21-22, which do not render very good sense. The *NAB* has transferred them, with some emendations, into the middle of 14:25; this arrangement supposes that they originally formed part of the description in 14:24-27 of how Yahweh would (finally) deal with the Assyrians.

FOR TO US A CHILD IS BORN:
9:1-7 (Heb. 8:23-9:6)

9 But there will be no gloom for her that was in anguish. In the former time he brought into contempt the land of Zebulun and the land of Naphtali, but in the latter time he will make glorious the way of the sea, the land beyond the Jordan, Galilee of the nations.

² The people who walked in darkness
  have seen a great light;
those who dwelt in a land of deep darkness,
  on them has light shined.

³ Thou hast multiplied the nation,
  thou hast increased its joy;
they rejoice before thee
  as with joy at the harvest,
  as men rejoice when they divide the spoil.

⁴ For the yoke of his burden,
  and the staff for his shoulder,
  the rod of his oppressor,
  thou hast broken as on the day of Midian.

⁵ For every boot of the tramping warrior in battle tumult
  and every garment rolled in blood
  will be burned as fuel for the fire.

⁶ For to us a child is born,
  to us a son is given;
and the government will be upon his shoulder,
  and his name will be called
"Wonderful Counselor, Mighty God,
  Everlasting Father, Prince of Peace."

⁷ Of the increase of his government and of peace
   there will be no end,
upon the throne of David, and over his kingdom,
  to establish it, and to uphold it
with justice and with righteousness
  from this time forth and for evermore.
The zeal of the LORD of hosts will do this.

As was pointed out above, some commentators consider this, rather than 8:16-18, to be the conclusion of Isaiah's

Memoirs, some designating the passage, along with the call narrative, as the framework for the central section, 7:1-8:18. Although that is not the position adopted here, the passage is from about the same time and relates importantly to the contents of the Memoirs. That explains very well why the editor responsible for the present order placed it where it is. The Isaian authorship of the passage has often been questioned, but more on the basis of theories of the development of royal messianism or preconceptions about what Isaiah taught (or, more usually, what he did not teach) concerning future salvation. In fact, there is a far heavier concentration of oracles relating to hopes of an ideal Davidid in the eighth and seventh-century prophets (Isa 7:14-15; 9:1-7; 11:1-9; Jer 23:5-6; 30:8-9; Ezek 17:22-23; 34:23-24; 37:24-25; Mic 5:2-4) than in those of the later periods (where they appear less often, and then in dependence on earlier texts — e.g. Zech 9:9-10), so there is little basis for arguing that such hopes arose only in exilic and postexilic times. In fact, several elements of this oracle (along with 2:2-4 and 11:1-9) are more easily explicable in terms of Isaiah's ministry than from any other context.

If the argumentation given concerning the Immanuel oracle is correct (see above on 7:10-17), it would follow that the *Prince of Peace* described here is the same figure: Isaiah would hardly have spoken of two separate Davidic heirs in such idyllic terms. The present passage would thus exhibit in clearer lines what is hinted at inn of David is to take the throne to rule *with justice and with righteousness* (9:2-7). If Immanuel is in fact a royal child, he ought probably to be identified with the "child" of this present oracle. (A legitimate objection could be raised to this suggestion in that Immanuel, on the argument proposed above, would be experiencing a period of affliction while he grows to maturity, while 9:1-7 would have the deliverance from Assyria take place already in his infancy; on this see below on v 6.)

The first part of 9:1 is the addition of an editor who wanted to ease the transition from the darkness of the closing lines of chap. 8 to the radiant light which is now to be described. If we date the oracle shortly after Tiglath-pileser

III overran Israel and incorporated her northern territories into the Assyrian provincial system, it is these events that are meant in the reference to the northernmost tribes of Zebulun and Naphtali. The unexpressed subject of the verbs *brought* and *will make* is Yahweh, who is understood to have himself brought to pass Israel's subjugation through Assyria; he will also be Israel's deliverer. The changed situation is described first of all as the inbursting of new light, so apt a symbol for divine deliverance. The greatness of the joy soon to be known by them is described by comparing it to that experienced on the most festive of occasions (reaping the harvest, gathering the spoils of a defeated enemy). (The opening words of v 3 probably do not speak of "multiplying the nation" but should be emended to give better parallelism; cf. *NAB*'s "you have brought them abundant joy.")

After the joyfilled comparisons, the *reasons* for the joy are explained. Three closely related reasons are given, each introduced by the word *for* (Hebrew *ki* — vv 4 , 5, and 6). The *yoke*, *rod*, and *staff* are all symbols that related to Assyria's oppressive domination, which had indeed already been experienced in the north, and it is from this that deliverance is now proclaimed. In *the day of Midian* we see a reference to the defeat of the Midianites under Gideon (Judg 7:15-25); this brings us into the sphere of Israel's holy war tradition. The holy war tradition is also at hand in the description of the destruction of boots and garments of the defeated enemy (v 5); in normal circumstances these might be considered booty to be plundered, but when the victory is the Lord's, plunder was sometimes forbidden.

These first two reasons (deliverance from oppression and destruction of the trappings of warfare) are closely related to and dependent upon the third reason, the "birth" of the wonderful child now described (v 6). In all probability this poem looks forward not to a physical birth but to the accession to the throne of a new king; Ps 2:7 instructs us that birth terminology could be used for such an occasion, most especially because Yahweh adopts the new king as his son (cf. 2 Sam 7:14; Ps 89:26-27). There is also the fact that in Egypt there was the custom of bestowing a five-part name on the new king at the time of his coronation, similar to the four-part name given here. (For this reason some scholars assume that v 6 originally provided five names and that one has been lost.)

Isaiah's penchant for consigning his teaching in names is already well attested through the examples of Shear-jashub, Immanuel, and Maher-shalal-hash-baz; in the present case the names tell us what he expected of this new king. *Wonderful Counselor* signifies not so much that he would in fact counsel others as that he would be able to devise wonderful plans (cf. what is said of the ideal king of the future in 11:2 and of Yahweh in 28:29) — and we are reminded that Ahaz's dependence on advisers who offered poor counsel led to what, in Isaiah's eyes, was his failure and downfall. To be a *wonderful counselor* also implies the ability to give effect to the plans conceived. For the Old Testament to call any human *Mighty God* ('*el gibbor* — sometimes rendered "God-Hero," or even "a god of a warrior") surprises us, though in fact such terminology can be used in an attenuated sense (cf. 1 Sam 28:13; Ps 45:6; 82:6). Here it expresses the wonderful nature of the king and his God-like character. The idea of might also indicates that he is able to do whatever is required for the salvation of his people; this would not make him primarily a warrior, for v 7 says his reign will be one of endless peace. "Father-Forever" (rather than *Everlasting Father*) stresses his faithful care for his people (cf. 11:4). In a sense the last title, *Prince of Peace*, is the result and climax of the first three, as we remember that the Hebrew *shalom* means far more than simply the absence of conflict, including as it does the concept of fulness and completeness.

It is v 7, with its reference to the throne of David and his kingdom, that makes it certain the *child* in question is a royal figure; the succession to David's throne is secure, and much, much more. For all the wonderful things that are said of the child, he is presented not so much as one who effects deliverance as one who accompanies the deliverance effected by Yahweh: *the zeal of the Lord of hosts will do this*. If Isaiah expected all these things to be verified in the one who succeeded Ahaz, as it seems he did, he was certainly disappointed. Ahaz's successor was Hezekiah, and although the deuteronomic editors of 2 Kings gave him high marks (2 Kgs 18:5), Isaiah found reason to be gravely disappointed in him (see below on chaps. 28-31). In addition, the northern territories were not delivered from the rule of Assyria until its power was crushed by a rising Babylon late in the seventh century. This does not mean that Isaiah abandoned his hope of an ideal king of David's line who would fulfill all the expectations he had expressed. The indications are that during his own lifetime he came to project them into a much more distant future (see below on 11:1-9).

Oracles Against Judah and Jerusalem Resumed

After the Isaiah Memoirs and the pieces tacked onto them, evidently inserted into the long collection marked by the inscription at 2:1, that collection resumes. The insertion of the Memoirs helps explain the wide separation of some pieces that go together, as has already been noted, and may have occasioned their dislocation.

YAHWEH'S OUTSTRETCHED HAND: 9:8-21 (Heb. 9:7-20) + 5:25-29(30)

9 8 The Lord has sent a word against Jacob,
    and it will light upon Israel;
 9 and all the people will know,
    Ephraim and the inhabitants of Samaria,
  who say in pride and in arrogance of heart:
10 "The bricks have fallen,
    but we will build with dressed stones;
  the sycamores have been cut down,
    but we will put cedars in their place."
11 So the LORD raises adversaries against them,
    and stirs up their enemies.
12 The Syrians on the east and the Philistines on the west
    devour Israel with open mouth.

For all this his anger is not turned away
and his hand is stretched out still.

13 The people did not turn to him who smote them,
nor seek the LORD of hosts.

14 So the LORD cut off from Israel head and tail,
palm branch and reed in one day—

15 the elder and honored man is the head,
and the prophet who teaches lies is the tail;

16 for those who lead this people lead them astray,
and those who are led by them are swallowed up.

17 Therefore the Lord does not rejoice over their young men,
and has no compassion on their fatherless and widows;
for every one is godless and an evildoer,
and every mouth speaks folly.
For all this his anger is not turned away
and his hand is stretched out still.

18 For wickedness burns like a fire,
it consumes briers and thorns;
it kindles the thickets of the forest,
and they roll upward in a column of smoke.

19 Through the wrath of the LORD of hosts
the land is burned,
and the people are like fuel for the fire;
no man spares his brother.

20 They snatch on the right, but are still hungry,
and they devour on the left, but are not satisfied;
each devours his neighbor's flesh,

21 Manasseh Ephraim, and Ephraim Manasseh,
and together they are against Judah.
For all this his anger is not turned away
and his hand is stretched out still.

5 25 Therefore the anger of the LORD was
kindled against his people,
and he stretched out his hand against
them and smote them,
and the mountains quaked;
and their corpses were as refuse
in the midst of the streets.

For all this his anger is not turned away
and his hand is stretched out still.

26 He will raise a signal for a nation afar off,
and whistle for it from the ends of the earth;
and lo, swiftly, speedily it comes!
27 None is weary, none stumbles,
none slumbers or sleeps,
not a waistcloth is loose,
not a sandal-thong broken;
28 their arrows are sharp,
all their bows bent,
their horses' hoofs seem like flint,
and their wheels like the whirlwind.
29 Their roaring is like a lion,
like young lions they roar;
they growl and seize their prey,
they carry it off, and none can rescue.
30 They will growl over it on that day,
like the roaring of the sea.
And if one look to the land,
behold, darkness and distress;
and the light is darkened by its clouds.

It has already been suggested above (see on 5:25-29) that these two passages taken together form a five-strophe poem, each strophe possibly originally of seven lines each. The units are: 9:8-12, 13-17, 18-21; 5:25 (fragmentary), and 26-29. (The verse numbers of chap. 9 are given according to the *RSV*; Hebrew text enumeration is one less.) The refrain *for all this his anger . . .* clearly marks the end of each of the first four strophes. The fact that this refrain is found also at 10:4 has led some to designate 10:1-4 as the fifth of six strophes, but this passage is a woe-oracle and simply does not fit the pattern; the refrain was added to it, once it had reached its present location, under the mistaken notion that it formed part of the poem.

The reference to *the inhabitants of Samaria* (9:9) and the manner of reference to Ephraim and Manasseh (vv 9 and 21) make it clear that it is the northern kingdom of Israel that is spoken of, not Judah and not Judah and Israel together. While it is evident that the destruction promised in 5:26-29 is future, there is no little disagreement concerning the import of 9:8-21, for the verbal forms are a mixture of perfect and future which seem to point in both directions. Some commentators find here a series of calamities which Isaiah foresees, all of which will find their climax in the Assyrian invasion proclaimed in 5:26-29; in this interpretation the perfect tenses are read as the "prophetic perfect," a usage which is indeed well-attested. Others, however, interpret the first four strophes as recounting specific events of the past, punishments already sent by the Lord in order to bring about conversion; these have been ignored and so the refrain speaks of the Lord's continued anger and of his outstretched hand until (in the last strophe) final punishment is promised. A close parallel for this procedure is found in Amos 4:6-12. This is the better of the two interpretations. It makes sense to foretell disaster after warning shots have been ignored; it makes less sense to insist that warning blows are going to be ignored so that disaster will follow. The refrain is most easily understood if Yahweh's unabated anger and outstretched hand find their explanation in the rejection of the conversion which past punishments were intended to call forth; and the general themes of acts of Yahweh in history whose significance his people do not grasp is thoroughly Isaian. Since Isaiah depicts the Assyrians as being summoned from afar and describes (as though to those who had not experienced it) their deadly military efficiency, the composition must certainly be dated sometime before the events of 732 (*HI*, 272n.)

First strophe (9:8-12). The word Yahweh has sent is that which proclaims the coming punishment. If the view presented above is correct, that the events in vv 9-21 are past calamities, then the *word* in question here looks forward to. the final strophe (5:26-29) and to the Assyrian invasion there foretold; the intervening material doesn't explain *why* that punishment is to come, this being understood from the broader content of the prophet's teaching; but it explains that the rejection of Yahweh's corrective blows has made it inevitable. The Old Testament recognized that the word, once spoken, had a power of its own (see Gen 27:18-37); this was particularly true of Yahweh's word, which was understood to be supremely efficacious and the determining force in history (see Isa 40:6-8; 55:10-11). *Ephraim* here stands for the northern kingdom (it is otherwise in v 21), which is named along with its capital. The determination to rebuild with better materials would not in the normal course of events be blameworthy, but in this case it represents a failure to discern Yahweh's purpose in some blow which has fallen. Some specific event must lie behind v 10, but it is not clear what it is. The naming of the destructive enemies in v 12, on the other hand, may be quite general. Even though specific mention is made of *the Syrians* and *the Philistines*, this may be by way of example (as even *on the east and...on the west* may suggest). Both the Philistines and the Syrians were inveterate enemies of Israel (see 1 Kings 20; 22; 2 Kgs 6:8-24; 8:12, 28-29; 10:32-33; 13:3-4; Amos 1:3-5, 6-8), though occasionally they could unite in common purpose against the danger from Assyria (see above on chap. 7). The refrain in v 12 brings the strophe to an end but indicates that there is more to follow.

Second strophe (9:13-17). The opening line of this strophe expresses explicitly the lack of conversion that is the subject of the successive parts of the poem. The cutting off of *head and tail, palm branch and reed* refers, under two types of imagery, to the leaders and common people, both of which fall under Yahweh's judgment. The explanation given in v 15 is provided by a glossator who feared the imagery would not be understood, though his identification of the *tail* with the prophet who teaches lies does not suit the context. Elsewhere, too, in speaking of Judah, Isaiah refers to the baneful effects of poor leadership (3:12; 5:13-14). In fact, the words *those who lead* and *those who are led* in v 16 make clear what is intended by *head and tail* in v 14. It is an unfortunate fact that those who are ruled can be swept to destruction by the wickedness and the foolishness of their leaders, but here Isaiah's accusation is that *everyone is godless and an evildoer* (v 17). That indictment helps to explain the assertion that even to the widow and orphan Yahweh shows no compassion — those helpless members of society who normally are to be treated with the greatest consideration (Isa 1:17, 23). The indictment of the society as a whole, in all its members, is not without parallel in the prophetic literature (cf. Jer 5:1-5; 6:11; 7:17-18; 15:8; 18:21; Ezek 9:6 mentions young and old, women and children, though it also distinguishes between those who have committed idolatry and those who have not). Rather than *does not rejoice* at the beginning of v 17 we should probably translate "does not spare"; cf. *NAB*. Again the refrain indicates there is more to come. It is difficult to relate this strophe to specific historical events. A number of commentators have asserted that it refers to Jehu's bloody purge and its aftermath (2 Kings 9-10), and this possibility cannot be ruled out.

Third strophe (9:18-21). The third strophe utilizes very effectively the imagery of fire. Just as the second strophe began with a reference to lack of conversion to explain the Lord's continued wrath, so this one speaks of wickedness burning like *a fire.* This aptly portrays not only sin's destructiveness, but also its rapid spread (as fire in highly flammable thorn bushes) and progessive nature (as fire ignites and consumes whole forests). The fire imagery is further extended to the punishment for sin, as the people are said to be *fuel* for the conflagration (v 19b). *RSV*'s *the land is burned* in the first half of the verse makes very good parallelism, but the Hebrew verb (niph. of *'tm*) is otherwise unattested, so the meaning is somewhat doubtful; other translations prefer other solutions. The word translated *fuel* means literally "food" (from a verb meaning "to eat") and so, in turn, leads into the new theme of a mutual destruction that is likened to cannibalism. The abysmal depths to which Israel had sunk is revealed in this violent language of brother devouring brother's flesh. As covenant people their relations should have been characterized by fulness of peace (*shalom*) and justice (*sedaqah*), but destructive violence was the rule instead. This description need not relate to any particular event but simply to the anarchical times of the final years of the northern kingdom. From 746 to 724 six different kings reigned in Israel, four of them attaining the throne through the assassination of his predecessor. These changes in command were largely motivated by opposing strategies for dealing with the Assyrian threat; but no sooner had one party established itself in power than the other sought to replace it. Israel made war on Judah at various times during the period of the divided monarchy (922-722), so there is no need to see a reference to the Syro-Ephraimitic War (see above on chap. 7) in v 21. The repetition of the refrain again suggests more to come, and this is one of the grounds for arguing for the insertion here of 5:25-29.

Fourth strophe (5:25). It was pointed out above (see on 5:25-29, p. 81) that the refrain found in this verse marks it as part of the poem we have been discussing, though it represents only a fragment of what was once the fourth strophe. Originally something preceded the *therefore* to explain it. Some commentators have seen here a reference to an actual earthquake (or even to the one mentioned in Amos 1:1), but this is far from certain. Such descriptions of the trembling of nature is the language of theophany (cf. Amos 8:8; Ps 18:7; 77:16, 18), and any visitation by God, even by way of plague (Hab 3:5) or enemy invasion, could be considered a theophany. Although the text is too incomplete to indicate the nature of the visitation, the dead were many and their bodies lay unburied. Since burial of the dead was an act of piety (2 Sam 21:10-14; Tobit, *passim*) and necessary for their repose in the nether world, the lack of it points up the magnitude of the calamity. Again the refrain indicates that there is more to come.

Fifth strophe (5:26-29). The continuation postulated by the refrain of the preceding verse is found in this fifth strophe. Since it refers to future chastisement and brings the poem to an end, the refrain is not used at the close; instead, all the previous blows having brought no amendment and the opportunities for repentance having been exhausted, we are given a preview of final destruction in the form of an invasion by the Assyrians. Since Yahweh is Lord of all the earth, even the mightiest of the nations exist only to do his will; he has ony to whistle and they come to do his bidding (cf. 7:18-19); elsewhere Isaiah likens Assyria to an instrument in Yahweh's hand (7:20; 10:5, 15). From 745 to 727 Assyria was ruled by Tiglath-pileser III, a very capable and vigorous king who had brought Assyrian arms far to the west. Israel, under Menahem, submitted and paid tribute to him at least by 738. But under Pekah (736-732) Israel became an important member of the anti-Assyrian coalition, even to the point of invading Judah in concert with Syria in an attempt to force them into the coalition (see above on chap. 7). In response to rebellion the Assyrians overran Israel, deported some of the population, and took away much of her territory. This poem, which speaks of bringing Assyria from afar and describes their military prowess, almost certainly antedates these events. Israel, now ruled by Hoshea, her last king, revolted again at the death of Tiglath-pileser III, but his successor, Shalmaneser V, retaliated by capturing Hoshea and ultimately conquering what was left. Samaria fell in 722/721 and much of the population (more than 27,000 according to Assyrian sources) was deported, and no more is heard of them; the territory was organized into an Assyrian province. Indeed, the lion had carried off its prey, and there was no one to rescue it.

5:30. This verse is a later expansion built upon v 29, though the glossator has altered the imagery from that of a beast of prey to that of a cosmic upheaval. The reference to the sea brings to mind the chaos monster (see below on 27:1; 30:7) and the departure of light suggests the undoing of creation.

WOE AGAINST DESPOILERS OF THE POOR: 10:1-4: (see above, with 5:8-24, p. 73).

WOE AGAINST ASSYRIA, YAHWEH'S SCOURGE: 10:5-15

⁵ Ah, Assyria, the rod of my anger,
 the staff of my fury!
⁶ Against a godless nation I send him,
 and against the people of my wrath I command him,
to take spoil and seize plunder,
 and to tread them down like the mire of the streets.
⁷ But he does not so intend,
 and his mind does not so think;
but it is in his mind to destroy,
 and to cut off nations not a few;
⁸ for he says:
 "Are not my commanders all kings?
⁹ Is not Calno like Carchemish?
 Is not Hamath like Arpad?
 Is not Samaria like Damascus?
¹⁰ As my hand has reached to the kingdoms of the idols
 whose graven images were greater than those of
  Jerusalem and Samaria,
¹¹ shall I not do to Jerusalem and her idols
 as I have done to Samaria and her images?"

¹²When the Lord has finished all his work on Mount Zion and on Jerusalem he will punish the arrogant boasting of the king of Assyria and his haughty pride. ¹³For he says:
 "By the strength of my hand I have done it,
  and by my wisdom, for I have understanding;
 I have removed the boundaries of peoples,
  and have plundered their treasures;
  like a bull I have brought down those who
   sat on thrones.
¹⁴ My hand has found like a nest the wealth of the peoples;

and as men gather eggs that have been forsaken
  so I have gathered all the earth;
and there was none that moved a wing,
  or opened the mouth, or chirped."
¹⁵ Shall the axe vaunt itself over him who hews with it,
  or the saw magnify itself against him who wields it?
As if a rod should wield him who lifts it,
  or as if a staff should lift him who is not wood!

Although here treated in several sections, most of the rest of chap. 10 (i.e., vv 5-27) would appear to be intended by the final editor to hang together as a statement on Assyria's offense and punishment. The basic Isaian oracle here is vv 5-15, to which has later been added a number of other pieces, some possibly from Isaiah, others not. Although vv 5-15 indict Assyria, no punishment is proclaimed; and this may have occasioned the insertion here (with an introductory "therefore") of a passage (vv 16-19) which originally pertained to a different context. Many authors believe that the original conclusion to vv 5-15 is found in 14:24-27, a passage which describes Assyria's fate. Whether this solution is adopted or not, it is to be noted that our present passage begins with *woe* (*hoy*), and that alone suggests that dire things will happen to Assyria, whether the punishment is described or not. Since none of the conquests referred to in v 9 came later than 717 and since Isaiah condemned as folly Hezekiah's revolt against Assyria in 705 (and therefore would not be proclaiming that Assyria was ripe for a fall at that time), this oracle is usually dated between those two limits.

Elsewhere Isaiah had designated the earth's powerful nations, Assyria included, as being at Yahweh's beck and call (5:26-30; 7:18-19), sometimes designating them as his instrument (7:20). Here we find the same relationship of Yahweh to Assyria, but the main theme is not his use of this most powerful nation on earth to punish Judah (although it is mentioned), but rather Assyria's failure to recognize that it is simply Yahweh's agent, its arrogant boasting, and its intention of exceeding the mission committed to it. Human pride is an obstacle to God's plan, and he punishes it wherever it is found (2:7-9, 11-17; 3:16-4:1; 9:8-9; 28:1-4). Verses 5-7 are important in that they indicate that, in Isaiah's understanding, Yahweh sends Assyria against Judah not for destruction but for chastisement. This is seen not only in the divergent intentions of Yahweh and Assyria (cf. vv 6 and 7), but also in the *rod* and *staff* imagery. These are frequently instruments of correction (and as such their use is commended by the wisdom tradition — cf. Prov 10:13; 13:24; 22:15; 23:13, 14; 26:3; 29:15), but not of destruction (cf. Ezek 21:10, 13 [Heb 21:15, 18], where the sword for destruction replaces the rod because Judah has spurned correction); in Isa 1:4-9 Judah is depicted as an individual unrepentant though beaten from head to foot, and since the description probably reflects the Assyrian invasion of 701, the agreement with our present text is quite good.

The cities mentioned in v 9, Carchemish, Calno (Calneh), Arpad, Hamath, Damascus, and Samaria, are given in geographical order, north to south, to emphasize the threat to Judah, which would be next in line of march; these cities were all taken by Assyria between 738 and 717, Carchemish in punishment for rebellion. Verse 13 (minus the *for he says*) would seem to be the natural continuation of v 9, and vv 10-12 may be later insertions, though v 12's reference to Yahweh's *work* accords well with Isaiah's use of the term (see above on 5:12, 19) and may come from another context. Samaria is depicted as having presented no more problem to the Assyrians than Damascus, even though its God was Yahweh; why then should Jerusalem be any more trouble than Samaria (v 11)? Assyria is made to speak of the idols of Jerusalem and Samaria as though in ignorance of the imageless nature of Israel's worship (vv 10-11); the reader knows better and is also expected to know how false is the equation of Yahweh, divine king of all the earth, with the idols of these pagan nations, behind which stood no gods at all.

Assyria's boasting, interrupted by vv 10-12, continues in vv 13-14: all objectives have been attained, thanks to Assyria's own power and wisdom, with none able to withstand.

The commentary on this overweening pride and self-confidence comes in v 15; through a rhetorical question and an exclamation it stresses the point made at the very outset, namely, that Assyria is merely an instrument in the hand of Yahweh; how ridiculous to think that an instrument could act independently of or contrary to the intentions of the one who employs it! Although there is here no specific reference to Yahweh's plan or counsel, the thought of it as a limiting factor on all human plans is not far below the surface.

A SERIES OF COMPLETIONS:
10:16-19, 20-23, 24-27a

16 Therefore the Lord, the LORD of hosts,
 will send wasting sickness among his stout warriors,
and under his glory a burning will be kindled,
 like the burning of fire.
17 The light of Israel will become a fire,
 and his Holy One a flame;
and it will burn and devour
 his thorns and briers in one day.
18 The glory of his forest and of his fruitful land
 the LORD will destroy, both soul and body,
 and it will be as when a sick man wastes away.
19 The remnant of the trees of his forest will be so few
 that a child can write them down.

20In that day the remnant of Israel and the survivors of the house of Jacob will no more lean upon him that smote them, but will lean upon the LORD, the Holy One of Israel, in truth. 21A remnant will return, the remnant of Jacob, to the mighty God. 22For though your people Israel be as the sand of the sea, only a remnant of them will return. Destruction is decreed, overflowing with righteousness. 23For the Lord, the LORD of hosts, will make a full end, as decreed, in the midst of all the earth.

24Therefore thus says the Lord, the LORD of hosts: "O my people, who dwell in Zion, be not afraid of the Assyrians when they smite with the rod and lift up their staff against you as the Egyptians did. ²⁵For in a very little while my indignation will come to an end, and my anger will be directed to their destruction. ²⁶And the LORD of hosts will wield against them a scourge, as when he smote Midian at the rock of Oreb; and his rod will be over the sea, and he will lift it as he did in Egypt. ²⁷And in that day his burden will depart from your shoulder, and his yoke will be destroyed from your neck."

There are good reasons for holding that these verses were supplied either from another context or were composed by an editor (they seem to reflect terminology and concepts from other Isaian passages, especially 9:17-18 and 17:3-4); if they do indeed come from another context, they may originally have been directed against Judah. Their purpose here is to provide an explicit judgment against Assyria, for though punishment is implied in the "woe" of v 5 and called for in the evils attributed to Assyria, nothing is spelled out in the present context. There are tensions within the passage, such as the shift from sickness to fire as the means of destruction, and that from warriors to forest and land as the object to be destroyed; and while action against attacking warriors would be a suitable consequence of vv 5-15, that against the forest and trees in the distant land is unexpected.

It may have been the reference to the "remnant (of the trees)" in v 19 that occasioned the addition of vv 20-23, another passage whose Isaian authorship is contested. Difficulties have been raised because Assyria's blow against Judah (701) was the result of Hezekiah's revolt against Assyria, and therefore the reference to *leaning upon* is not explained. No historical situation seems to provide a good background for the oracle, and it is not even certain whether *remnant of Israel* in v 20 originally referred to those of the northern kingdom or of Judah. But the teaching and the language are very consonant with Isaiah, with the implicit call for faith, the contrast between faith in Yahweh and in worldly powers, and the use of "to lean upon" (*sa'an*) to express this (cf. 30:12; 31:1). And it can be pointed out that the historical occasion for vv 5-6 (where Assyria is designated "rod" and "staff" and therefore as one that smote them, as in v 20) is no easier to find, at least if vv 5-15 are dated between 717 and 705, as is usually done.

It has already been pointed out that the remnant concept is a two-edged thing and that the verbal part of the name of Isaiah's son Shear-jashub is subject to various interpretations (see above on 8:18), and in vv 21-22 this name (or at least the same Hebrew words) is utilized in conflicting ways. Verse 21 speaks in a positive manner of the *return* to *the mighty God* (*'el gibbor*, one of the names found in 9:6), and therefore in the moral sense of "conversion." But v 22 uses the phrase in a negative way, with its specific reference to destruction (and cf. v 23), and speaks of *return* in a physical sense, as from battle or exile. Verses 22-23 appear, therefore, to have been built on to v 21 by someone who wanted to utilize the remnant concept to emphasize God's judgment and its destructive aspect. As has been pointed out above (on 8:18), Shear-jashub, in the context of Isaiah's Memoirs, relates to "return" in the moral sense, and v 21 agrees more closely with this.

The Isaian authorship of the third completion, vv 24-27, is also contested. It picks up again the "rod" and the "staff" from v 5, but also the "smiter" from v 20 and the reference to the removal of Assyria's yoke and to Midian from 9:4. Furthermore, there is an echo of the exodus tradition (v 26), which otherwise is hardly found in Isaiah (see Introduction p. 20). As consoling as these words might seem to be, they come from a later redactor. Isaiah did, however, foretell the destruction of Assyria (14:24-27), though this did not come to pass until late in the seventh century.

THE ASSYRIAN (?) ADVANCE: 10:27b-34

27b He has gone up from Rimmon,
28   he has come to Aiath;
he has passed through Migron,
    at Michmash he stores his baggage;
29 they have crossed over the pass,

> at Geba they lodge for the night;
> Ramah trembles,
>   Gibeah of Saul has fled.
> 30 Cry aloud, O daughter of Gallim!
>   Hearken, O Laishah!
>   Answer her, O Anathoth!
> 31 Madmenah is in flight,
>   the inhabitants of Gebim flee for safety.
> 32 This very day he will halt at Nob,
>   he will shake his fist
>   at the mount of the daughter of Zion,
>   the hill of Jerusalem.
> 33 Behold, the Lord, the LORD of hosts
>   will lop the boughs with terrifying power;
> the great in height will be hewn down,
>   and the lofty will be brought low.
> 34 He will cut down the thickets of the
>   forest with an axe,
>   and Lebanon with its majestic trees
>   will fall.

This passage does not identify the advancing enemy, but in view of its present context, a chapter that relates to the Assyrians, it seems certain that the editor who placed it here understood it to refer to them. But whereas the rest of the materials in the chapter speak of Assyria only to explain how they have provoked Yahweh's anger and will fall under his punishment, the campaign here described is full of threat for Judah. Although its authenticity is not usually questioned, the historical background is unclear. Assyrian invasion of Judah that took place during Isaiah's career, that of Seenacherib in 701, came up from the south, whereas the route described in the present passage is from the north (see Map 1). It has been argued that the route here described is that taken by the Assyrians in 711 when they put down the rebellion of Ashdod (see below on chap. 20), and that they came down through the former territory of Israel to Judah as a warning to Hezekiah not to join the revolt; since such a tactic is conceivable, that possibility cannot be excluded. On the other hand, it is perhaps more likely that we have here not a decription of an actual campaign but rather a prophetic threat of one, fleshed out with the details of how this would be likely to take place. The approach an enemy from Mesopotamia would almost invariably take would be from the north; this is so much the case that Jeremiah, in oracles closely akin to this one, speaks in vivid, though probably visionary, terms of "the foe from the north" (Jer 4:5-31; 5:15-17; 6:1-5). If this is the case, the present oracle would be part of Isaiah's attempt to dissuade Hezekiah from revolting against Assyria after the death of Sargon II in 705 (see below on chaps. 28-31). An editor may have thought this a good place for the passage because the shaking of the fist at Jerusalem (v 32) seemed to him an arrogant gesture that exemplified the sort of pride and resistance depicted in vv 5-15.

The concluding verses (vv 33-34) are sometimes denied to Isaiah, but in fact they now direct the threat expressed in this oracle against Judah's rulers (*the great, the lofty*), those who would have been primarily responsible for the policies that bring the Assyrians against the city. The theme of bringing low that which is lifted up is found in 2:6-19 (and some of the same terminology), as well as elsewhere in Isaiah. For some these verses describe Yahweh's destruction of the Assyrians, while others see them as belonging with 11:1-9 and forming an introduction for it (see below). Mount *Lebanon* was famous for its luxuriant forests (see below on 29:17; 33:9; 35:2).

THE SHOOT FROM THE STUMP OF JESSE: 11:1-9

11 There shall come forth a shoot from the stump of Jesse,
and a branch shall grow out of his roots.
2 And the Spirit of the LORD shall rest upon him,
the spirit of wisdom and understanding,
the spirit of counsel and might,
the spirit of knowledge and the fear of the LORD.
3 And his delight shall be in the fear of the Lord.

> He shall not judge by what his eyes see,
>   or decide by what his ears hear;
> 4 but with righteousness he shall judge the poor,
>   and decide with equity for the meek of the earth;
> and he shall smite the earth with the rod of his mouth.
>   and with the breath of his lips he shall slay the wicked.
> 5 Righteousness shall be the girdle of his waist,
>   and faithfulness the girdle of his loins.
>
> 6 The wolf shall dwell with the lamb,
>   and the leopard shall lie down with the kid,
> and the calf and the lion and the fatling together,
>   and a little child shall lead them.
> 7 The cow and the bear shall feed;
>   their young shall lie down together;
>   and the lion shall eat straw like the ox.
> 8 The sucking child shall play over the hole of the asp,
>   and the weaned child shall put his hand on the adder's den.
> 9 They shall not hurt or destroy
>   in all my holy mountain;
> for the earth shall be full of the knowledge of the LORD
>   as the waters cover the sea.

This is one of the Old Testament's best-known descriptions of the ideal king of the future, whom later Judaism and Christianity call the "Messiah," a term not found in this sense in the Old Testament. Many scholars reject the Isaian authorship of this piece for much the same reasons they reject 9:1-7 (as well as 2:2-4, on both of which, see above), but it is quite consonant with the teaching and background of his ministry; in fact, it would not be an exaggeration to say that it fits better into Isaiah's context than into any other.

Some argue that in the opening reference to *a shoot from the stump of Jesse* a new beginning from the line of Jesse (David's father) is required because the monarchy has come to an end and therefore the oracle must be late. (Note that the Hebrew term employed here for shoot is not *semah*, the one which is sometimes seen to function as a technical term for the future messianic ruler — see above on 4:2.) If one were to follow the opinion of those who see 10:33-34 as the beginning of this oracle, the reference to the new *shoot* is easily explained by the description in these verses of the end of Judah's rulers under the image of trees being felled. What is perhaps more likely is that our passage has been attracted to its present context by those verses, which now form a good introduction to the *shoot* imagery.

Even without this expedient, however, the text does not postulate that the monarchy has come to an end. David's line, which was of importance because of the messianic expectations connected with it (from 2 Samuel 7 and the developments sprung from it), did not come to an end with the destruction of the monarchy in 687 but continued with King Jehoiachin in exile and in Sheshbazzar, Zerubbabel, and their descendants, after the exile. What is expressed here, rather, is the moral bankruptcy of the historical kings as Isaiah saw them, and the resultant need to look for hope in one who would spring from the pure sources of the dynasty rather than in these kings or their descendants (who, in the tree imagery employed, would be the boughs and branches). A very similar procedure is found in Micah (5:1-4; Hebrew, 4:14-5:3), where that prophet looks forward to an ideal Davidic ruler to appear from David's place of origin, Bethlehem Ephrathah, rather than from Jerusalem, where the contemporary kings held sway.

This oracle is probably to be dated late in Isaiah's ministry. If Isaiah had expected Ahaz's son and immediate successor to be "Immanuel" and the fulfiller of the glorious hopes expressed in 9:1-7, he was certainly bitterly disappointed, for Hezekiah's response to God's word through Isaiah in the crisis of 705-701 was little better than that of Ahaz in 735. Isaiah, the prophet who demanded faith of others, did not cease to "wait for" all the Lord had revealed (8:17-18), but in this oracle its fulfillment is looked for in a far more distant future.

The ideal future king is described as the recipient of Yahweh's *spirit* (v 2) and therefore as a charismatic figure, and in this he is placed in the line of Israel's great leaders of old, such as Moses, Joshua, the Judges, Saul, and David

(Num 11:17; Deut 34:9; Judg 3:10; 6:34; 11:29; 1 Sam 10:10; 11:6; 16:13). The particular gifts listed here, while relating importantly to the king's role in maintaining the public order by rendering just judgment and protecting the rights of the poor, also set him off from Ahaz and Hezekiah, as Isaiah experienced them. Gifts of *wisdom* and *counsel* render him independent of the sort of counselors who led Ahaz and Hezekiah into bad policies and insure that he will formulate right plans (see above on 9:6), while the gift of *might* insures that he will be able to put them into effect. It is interesting to note that the gifts of *wisdom and understanding* (*hokmah* and *binah*) here attributed to the king are precisely the qualities which "the wise" claimed for themselves (5:21) and which Isaiah says will disappear from them at the time of Yahweh's judgment (29:14). It can be argued that, for Isaiah, true wisdom resides in Yahweh alone and that it comes to humans only by his gift, as here it comes to the messianic king through Yahweh's spirit. The wisdom tradition, which, especially in its origins, was empirically oriented, came to the position that true wisdom came from God (Prov 8:1-9:11; Sir 1:1, 5-7), and in this pilgrimage Isaiah seems to have played an important role.

There is considerable overlap in the six gifts listed in v 2, but also some differentiation. *Counsel* is obviously closely related to *wisdom and understanding*, though also distinct from them; *might*, as pointed out above, enables *counsel* to be put into effect. *Knowledge* here is probably to be understood as "knowledge of God" (in parallel with *fear of the Lord*), which elsewhere functions virtually as a synonym for "true religion," in the sense of true worship and service of God (cf. Hos 2:20; 6:6; Jer 22:15-16). *Fear of the Lord* is an expression at home in the wisdom tradition, where it functions as the wellspring of wisdom (Job 28:28; Prov 1:7; Sir 1:12). It is the last named of the gifts here and probably is understood to be the root of them all. Thus Isaiah denies wisdom and understanding to "the wise" of his time, against whom he waged a polemic, attributes them to the ideal king to come, and sees them rooted in the religious quality of *fear of the Lord*.

The repetition of *fear of the Lord* at the beginning of v 3 is an insertion by a later editor, but the Greek translation of the Old Testament (the Septuagint) avoided the repetition by translating the first *fear of the Lord* as "reverence" (*eusebeia*); thus it provided seven terms instead of the six (in three pairs) of the Hebrew, and from this derives the list of the traditional seven gifts of the Holy Spirit.

The gifts attributed to the messianic king in v 2 are in part traditional qualities of the ideal king in Israel and elsewhere (this is particularly true of wisdom — see 2 Sam 14:17; 1 Kings 3:4-14, 28; 4:29-34 [Heb.: 5:9-14]; 10:1-10), though no echo of them is found in Israel's royal psalms. Psalm 72, on the other hand, gives prominent attention to the king's responsibility for justice in the land, for that kind of generous "justice," in particular, that looks to the defense of the poor and the helpless. In vv 3-5 of our Isaiah passage this duty of the king is given prominent attention. This charismatic figure, however, does not simply judge as others do, on the basis of evidence seen and testimony heard (v 3); the wisdom which is God's gift enables him to see the inner nature of things; the power that operates in him cuts down without delay those who are guilty of imposing on the defenseless. This sort of concern for just judgment for the weaker members of society finds frequent expression in Isaiah's oracles (1:17, 23; 5:23; 10:1-4), and the restoration of right judgment was part of his vision for the future (1:26).

The "rightness" of things in the days of this king are depicted in vv 6-9 as extending to the elimination of every kind of violence (and we are reminded of the essential connection between justice and peace). We encounter dangerous animals, usually, only in the secure environment of the zoo, but in ancient Israel they were far more of an immediate reality (see Hos 13:7-9; Amos 3:4, 8). But here they are depicted as having abandoned their violent and destructive ways so that they are no longer a threat to one another or even to the most tender of human infants. Something similar is found in Hosea's promise of an all-encompassing "covenant" which would eliminate both animal violence and the human violence of war (Hos 2:18).

But Isaiah's picture is much more idyllic and portrays the conditions of a paradise where violence was unknown. Although the expression *in all my holy mountain* in v 9 would seem to limit this peace to Jerusalem, this apparently is not intended; the reason for this blessed condition, namely, the presence of *the knowledge of God*, extends to all the earth. The connection between the presence of *the knowledge of God* and the idyllic conditions which result is very much in harmony with Isaiah's thought, for elsewhere he indicates the absence of such knowledge to be the reason for Judah's estrangement and the punishments that follow from it (cf. 1:3; 5:13; 6:10).

SOME LATER EXPANSIONS: 11:10-16

10In that day the root of Jesse shall stand as an ensign to the peoples; him shall the nations seek, and his dwellings shall be glorious.

11In that day the Lord will extend his hand yet a second time to recover the remnant which is left of his people, from Assyria, from Egypt, from Pathros, from Ethiopia, from Elam, from Shinar, from Hamath, and from the coastlands of the sea.

12 He will raise an ensign for the nations,
    and will assemble the outcasts of Israel,
and gather the dispersed of Judah
    from the four corners of the earth.

13 The jealousy of Ephraim shall depart,
    and those who harass Judah shall be cut off;
Ephraim shall not be jealous of Judah,
    and Judah shall not harass Ephraim.

14 But they shall swoop down upon the shoulder of the Philistines in the west,
    and together they shall plunder the people of the east.
They shall put forth their hand against Edom and Moab,
    and the Ammonites shall obey them.

15 And the LORD will utterly destroy
    the tongue of the sea of Egypt;

and will wave his hand over the River
   with his scorching wind,
and smite it into seven channels
   that men may cross dryshod.
16 And there will be a highway from Assyria
   for the remnant which is left of his people,
as there was for Israel
   when they came up from the land of Egypt.

The reference to a remnant of God's people in widely scattered lands in v 11 dates this passage to a much later period; the expression *the root of Jesse* of v 10 no longer refers to the origin of the messianic king, as in v 1, but is a title for the king himself. These two verses (vv 10-11) are in fact a late composition intended to provide a transition to the somewhat earlier vv 12-16; they provide a universalistic note (*him shall the nations seek*) that is not found in the verses they build on. The *yet a second time* of v 11 alludes to the Lord's earlier saving work in delivering Israel from Egypt. In all probability v 11 referred originally only to Assyria and Egypt (cf. vv 15-16), but a late expansion makes it relevant to a situation in which the Jews now knew a widespread Diaspora (Dispersion).

The *he* of v 12 is Yahweh, who is to give some signal, here unspecified, for the reassembly of his people from wherever they have been scattered. The reference to the *jealousy* between *Ephraim* and *Judah* (v 13) probably points to a time after the exile and to the alienation of the Jews and Samaritans detailed in Ezra-Nehemiah (Ezr 4:1-3; Neh 4:1-5) and reflected in many texts thereafter (Luke 9:52; John 4:9). The hostility had its roots in the initial separation of Israel from Judah, a situation which was deplored by Isaiah (7:17) and to which the prophets promised a remedy (Jer 3:11-14; 31:1-6, 10-14; Ezek 37:15-28). The *shoulder of the Philistines* (v 14) is the strip of southern coastal plain occupied by that people (see Map 1). The warlike stance of v 14 is in marked contrast to the universalism of v 10; it aims at subjecting anew to a united Israel-Judah those peoples first conquered by David.

With vv 15-16 attention returns to the remnant which was
the concern of the opening vv 11-12. Just as Yahweh had
once brought the enslaved Israelites out of Egypt by means
of a miraculous passage through the sea (Exodus 14), so
again will he provide passage through the waters for the
returning remnant; here, however, the same sort of miracle
is worked also for those who must come from Assyria (*the
River*, as elsewhere in the Old Testament is the Euphrates;
see above on 8:7). The exodus tradition does not, in fact, tell
of a *highway* (v 16) for those who left Egypt, but Deutero-
Isaiah speaks of one for those who are to return from
Babylon (40:3-5). Even though Assyria had passed from the
scene long before vv 11-16 were written, Egypt and Assyria
continued to be the foreign powers which Israel's poets most
frequently used to typify the pagan nations —Egypt, no
doubt, because it had been the land of bondage, Assyria
because it was the first to conquer Israel on her own land
and continued as the dominant power so long. For other
late passages in the Isaiah collection that deal with these
two, see 19:23-25; 27:12-13.

THE CONCLUSION OF THE COLLECTION: 12:1-6

12 You will say in that day:
>   "I will give thanks to thee, O Lord,
>   for though thou wast angry with me,
>   thy anger turned away,
>   and thou didst comfort me.

>   2   "Behold, God is my salvation;
>   I will trust, and will not be afraid;
>   for the LORD God is my strength and my song,
>   and he has become my salvation."

>   ³With joy you will draw water from the wells of salvation.
>   ⁴And you will say in that day:
>   "Give thanks to the LORD,
>   call upon his name;
>   make known his deeds among the nations,
>   proclaim that his name is exalted.

5 "Sing praises to the LORD, for he has done gloriously;
let this be known in all the earth.
6 Shout, and sing for joy, O inhabitant of Zion,
for great in your midst is the Holy One of Israel."

The collection of oracles which began in chap. 2 is now completed by a hymn of thanksgiving. This hymn is constructed very much like many of those in the psalter but is unique in that it does not relate to past favors but rather anticipates the realization of those which are promised in the preceding chapters. *You will say in that day* is an introduction which may very well reflect the "in that day" which is encountered so many times in the preceding chapters. From this one can conclude that the time of trial had not yet passed away. The composition is certainly later than Isaiah and draws on many parts of Scripture, especially the Psalms. The repetition of *and you will say in that day* in v 4 may mark a new beginning, a suggestion which is strengthened by the shift from the first person (*I will give thanks* —v 1) to the second person plural (already in v 3: *you will draw water*). But the two parts are closely related in style of composition and aim. The first emphasizes deliverance from punishment visited for sin; the second proclaims God's praise in more general terms. The reference to *the nations* (v 4) is a reminder of the universalistic passages in the preceding chapters (2:2-4; 11:11), while the address to the *inhabitant of Zion* (v 6) accords well with the attention paid to Jerusalem (and the threats leveled!), as does the closing exaltation of *the Holy One of Israel*, Isaiah's characteristic title for Yahweh.

ORACLES AGAINST THE NATIONS: CHAPTERS 13-23

The editors of the Isaian writings have provided a collection of oracles against the pagan nations not unlike the collections found also in Jeremiah 46-51 and Ezekiel 25-32. This collection is not the simple result of a gathering together here of all Isaiah's oracles against countries other than Judah; we have already encountered some against Assyria (not to mention Syria, though in passages in which it is closely connected with Israel), and indeed some of those in 13-23 are related to these. If the editors did incorporate a substantial amount of Isaian material, which is indeed the case, it has been incorporated into material from other sources, most of it from a much later time. (On the formation of this collection, see introduction, p. 16). In some cases it is possible that originally Isaian material has been adapted to suit the situation of a later time. Therefore the matter of authenticity comes down to dealing with individual passages, and in many cases a firm judgment will be difficult or impossible to make.

Whatever their source, such oracles make clear that Yahweh is Lord of all the earth, not simply of a certain chosen people, and that he holds all accountable and subject to his judgment. In some cases, it must be admitted, the judgment on other nations is made not so much in defense of Yahweh's prerogatives (as when, e.g., Isaiah threatens Assyria in 10:5-15 for vaunting itself against Yahweh) as in a spirit of ardent Jewish nationalism.

This collection is set off from all that precedes it by a new inscription at 13:1 which introduces the prophet anew. The meaning of the word translated *oracle* (*massa'*) in that verse derives from a verb which means "to lift up" and can mean "burden," and that is the meaning commentators often give it here, understanding it as the introduction to an announcement of doom. More likely, however, our *massa'* relates to "lifting up (the voice)," and in that sense means *oracle*. But it seems always to refer to an oracle of doom and is used frequently in our present collection to introduce a new passage, regularly with the name of the country or other object against which it is directed: 13:1; 15:1; 17:1; 19:1; 21:1, 11, 13; 22:1; 23:1 (see also 14:28; 30:6).

ORACLE AGAINST BABYLON: 13:1-22

13 The oracle concerning Babylon which Isaiah the son of
   Amoz saw.
   ² On a bare hill raise a signal,
        cry aloud to them;
      wave the hand for them to enter
        the gates of the nobles.
   ³ I myself have commanded my consecrated ones,
        have summoned my mighty men to execute my anger,
      my proudly exulting ones.

   ⁴ Hark, a tumult on the mountains
        as of a great multitude!
      Hark, an uproar of kingdoms,
        of nations gathering together!
      The LORD of hosts is mustering
        a host for battle.
   ⁵ They come from a distant land,
        from the end of the heavens,
      the LORD and the weapons of his indignation,
        to destroy the whole earth.

⁶ Wail, for the day of the LORD is near;
    as destruction from the Almighty it will come!
⁷ Therefore all hands will be feeble,
    and every man's heart will melt,
⁸   and they will be dismayed.
  Pangs and agony will seize them;
    they will be in anguish like a woman in travail.
  They will look aghast at one another;
    their faces will be aflame.

⁹ Behold, the day of the LORD comes,
    cruel, with wrath and fierce anger,
  to make the earth a desolation
    and to destroy its sinners from it.
¹⁰ For the stars of the heavens and their constellations
    will not give their light;
  the sun will be dark at its rising
    and the moon will not shed its light.
¹¹ I will punish the world for its evil,
    and the wicked for their iniquity;
  I will put an end to the pride of the arrogant,
    and lay low the haughtiness of the ruthless.
¹² I will make men more rare than fine gold,
    and mankind than the gold of Ophir.
¹³ Therefore I will make the heavens tremble,
    and the earth will be shaken out of its place,
  at the wrath of the LORD of hosts
    in the day of his fierce anger.
¹⁴ And like a hunted gazelle,
    or like sheep with none to gather them,
  every man will turn to his own people,
    and every man will flee to his own land.

¹⁵ Whoever is found will be thrust through,
    and whoever is caught will fall by the sword.
¹⁶ Their infants will be dashed in pieces before their eyes;
    their houses will be plundered
      and their wives ravished.
¹⁷ Behold, I am stirring up the Medes against them,

who have no regard for silver
and do not delight in gold.

18 Their bows will slaughter the young men;
they will have no mercy on the fruit of the womb;
their eyes will not pity children.

19 And Babylon, the glory of kingdoms,
the splendor and pride of the Chaldeans,
will be like Sodom and Gomorrah
when God overthrew them.

20 It will never be inhabited
or dwelt in for all generations;
no Arab will pitch his tent there,
no shepherds will make their flocks lie down there.

21 But wild beasts will lie down there,
and its houses will be full of howling creatures;
there ostriches will dwell,
and there satyrs will dance.

22 Hyenas will cry in its towers,
and jackals in the pleasant palaces;
its time is close at hand
and its days will not be prolonged.

Chap. 13, after the inscription (on which see above), falls into three parts: the first (vv 2-5) speaks of the summoning of a mighty army to execute Yahweh's judgment against an unnamed city; the second (vv 6-16) takes occasion from this foreshadowing of violence to introduce a lengthy description of the "day of the Lord"; and the third (vv 17-22) finally identifies the city as Babylon and the attackers as the Medes and describes the destruction in detail.

Although the editor's inscription had identified this as an oracle against Babylon, the poet creates some tension by refraining from any clear identification of those involved; note that terms such as *my consecrated ones* and *my mighty men* (v 3) give no hint except that the ones so designated are considered to be summoned by Yahweh to carry out his purpose. Babylon was not a matter of concern to Judah in the days of Isaiah, coming back into world prominence only late in the seventh century. If the present oracle really does look to the end of the Babylonian empire (Babylon fell to Cyrus in 539), a date around the middle of the sixth century is indicated. However, Babylon (much like Egypt and Assyria) could function as the model of the wicked nation against whom Yahweh's wrath was turned, so a much later date is possible.

Although *the whole earth* (*'eres*) in v 5 may have meant only, in the context of those verses, "the whole land (of Babylonia)," the expression gives occasion for the introduction of a detailed description of the "day of the Lord." This description differs in many respects from that of Isaiah's in 2:6-21. Comparison of the future distress to birth pangs (v 8) and references to cosmic disturbance (vv 10, 13) occur in later texts and become common in apocalyptic, but are not found in Isaiah's text. The present passage also speaks uncompromisingly of a fairly universal destruction (vv 9, 12, 15), whereas Isaiah referred primarily to the humbling of human pride, a theme which is not absent from the present composition (v 11), though naming specifically *the arrogant* and *the ruthless*. This second section, then, represents the very important biblical theme of judgment day with a universal reference, though not yet strictly eschatological in nature (i.e., there is no indication that it occurs outside of history or that it brings history to an end). In its present context, however, it appears to have been pressed into service to describe the utter annihilation of the Babylonians.

It is only with the third section (vv 17-22) that the tension created at the beginning is resolved by the naming of the protagonists. The reference to *the Medes* (v 17) would lead us into historical difficulties if we insist on a precise understanding of the term. The Medes and the Babylonians (see Map 2) were allies in bringing the mighty Assyrian empire to an end (Nineveh, the Assyrian capital, fell to the Medes in 612, and the Babylonians wiped out the remnant of the Assyrian army at Haran in 609), and although there was later suspicion and hostility between the two, the Medes did not threaten Babylon. However, Cyrus, the king of Anshan (a territory of Persia and part of the empire of the Medes), who was a vassal of the Medes until his revolt in 556, did bring about the downfall of the Babylonian empire (though without destruction to Babylon); someone writing at a great distance in time and place might easily refer to Medes instead of Persians. The book of Daniel refers to "Darius the Mede" succeeding to the Chaldean (= Babylonian) rule (5:30), regularly joins the Medes and Persians together (6:8, 12, 15; 8:3, 7), and even associates "Darius (the Mede)" and "Cyrus the Persian" (6:28). Babylon's destruction is portrayed in fearful terms, as befits the city which then and later (Jonah 1:2; Rev 17:5-6) stood as the very symbol of wickedness: its fate will be like that of Sodom and Gomorrah (v 19) and none shall live in its desolate ruins except creatures of the wilderness (vv 20-22).

PROMISE OF RESTORATION: 14:1-2

14 The LORD will have compassion on Jacob and will again choose Israel, and will set them in their own land, and aliens will join them and will cleave to the house of Jacob. ²And the peoples will take them and bring them to their place, and the house of Israel will possess them in the LORD's land as male and female slaves; they will take captive those who were their captors, and rule over those who oppressed them.

These two verses, almost certainly from exilic times, look forward to a reversal of Israel's fortunes through the Lord's merciful power. The suggestion that he *will again choose Israel* betrays the thought that the destruction of the monarchy and subsequent exile amounted to a rejection of Israel; Jeremiah had in like fashion spoken of the end of the old covenant and had, at the same time, promised a new one (Jer 31:31-34). Here the return to the land will be a sign of election renewed. There seems to be some tension between v 1b and v 2 in that *join* and *cleave to* suggest pagan conversion and a positive relationship of the *aliens* to Israel: Israel's enslavement of them would then be an "adjustment" added later by a less broad-minded zealot. This is not necessarily the case, however; the text may be reflecting, in a somewhat summary and confused way, a theme found in Deutero- and Trito-Isaiah of the nations assisting God's people in their return to their own land in a spirit both of good will and of service (45:14-17; 49:22-23; 60:8-14; 61:5-7). The theme of conversion also occurs in a number of texts (cf. 18:7; 19:19-22; 56:3, 6; Zech 8:22-23).

TAUNT-SONG OVER THE KING OF BABYLON: 14:3-23

[3]When the LORD has given you rest from your pain and turmoil and the hard service with which you were made to serve, [4]you will take up this taunt against the king of Babylon:
"How the oppressor has ceased,
    the insolent fury ceased!
[5] The LORD has broken the staff of the wicked,
    the scepter of rulers,
[6] that smote the peoples in wrath
    with unceasing blows,
that ruled the nations in anger
    with unrelenting persecution.
[7] The whole earth is at rest and quiet;
    they break forth into singing.
[8] The cypresses rejoice at you ,
    the cedars of Lebanon, saying,
'Since you were laid low,
    no hewer comes up against us.'
[9] Sheol beneath is stirred up
    to meet you when you come,
it rouses the shades to greet you,
    all who were leaders of the earth;
it raises from their thrones
    all who were kings of the nations.
[10] All of them will speak
    and say to you:
'You too have become as weak as we!
    You have become like us!'
[11] Your pomp is brought down to Sheol,

the sound of your harps;
  maggots are the bed beneath you,
    and worms are your covering.

12 "How you are fallen from heaven,
    O Day Star, son of Dawn!
  How you are cut down to the ground,
    you who laid the nations low!
13 You said in your heart,
    'I will ascend to heaven;
  above the stars of God
    I will set my throne on high:
  I will sit on the mount of assembly
    in the far north;
14 I will ascend above heights of the clouds,
    I will make myself like the Most High.'
15 But you are brought down to Sheol,
    to the depths of the Pit.
16 Those who see you will stare at you,
    and ponder over you:
  'Is this the man who made the earth tremble,
    who shook kingdoms,
17 who made the world like a desert
    and overthrew its cities,
    who did not let his prisoners go home?'

18 All the kings of the nations lie in glory,
    each in his own tomb;
19 but you are cast out, away from your sepulchre,
    like a loathed untimely birth,
  clothed with the slain, those pierced by the sword,
    who go down to the stones of the Pit,
    like a dead body trodden underfoot.
20 You will not be joined with them in burial,
    because you have destroyed your land,
    you have slain your people.
  "May the descendants of evildoers
    nevermore be named!

21 Prepare slaughter for his sons
   because of the guilt of their fathers,
lest they rise and possess the earth,
   and fill the face of the world with cities."

22"I will rise up against them," says the LORD of hosts, "and will cut off from Babylon name and remnant, offspring and posterity, says the LORD. 23And I will make it a possession of the hedgehog, and pools of water, and I will sweep it with the broom of destruction, says the LORD of hosts."

The taunt-song or satire proper is found in vv 4b to 21 and has been fitted with a prose introduction and conclusion. These prose sections are from a later hand and, since it is here only that the tyrant is identified as Babylonian, it has been suggested that the poem itself, cast ironically in the form of a funeral lament, originally referred to an Assyrian king (Sargon II or Sennacherib). This hypothesis would make Isaian authorship possible, and the poem is, indeed, a magnificent composition, not unworthy of Isaiah's great poetic skill. On this hypothesis it would have been given its present setting (i.e., directed against a Babylonian King) to make it applicable to a new situation under Babylonian oppression. Yet this suggestion seems less probable than the more obvious explanation that it was composed much later than Isaiah and was, from the beginning, directed against a Babylonian king (possibly against Nebuchadnezzar, under whom the second deportation and the destruction of Jerusalem took place, or Nabonidus, the last king of Babylon). Again, the Babylonian king against whom the taunt-song is directed may not have been a specific individual (he is unnamed in this piece) but may function as a type of the wicked tyrant.

Verses 4b-8 have the earth rejoicing in the new-found peace, now that the violent oppressor is removed from the scene. The cedars of Lebanon (v 8) were much in demand for the construction of magnificent buildings from Egypt to Mesopotamia (see 1 Kgs 5:5-9 for the acquisition of cedars from Lebanon for the building of Solomon's Temple), and during the ascendancy of Babylon the principal demand would have come from there.

With fine irony the poet describes the welcome with which those who have preceded the king to Sheol now greet him. There is no evidence of belief in a satisfactory life after death in Israel until late in the Old Testament period; Job (14:7-12) and Ecclesiastes (3:18-21) still do not expect it. And when it does appear, it comes, in accord with Hebrew anthropology, in terms of bodily resurrection (see Dan 12:2; 2 Macc 7:9, 11, 14, 22-23, 29). The Hebrew Sheol spoken of in the present composition is the abode of the dead, where existence cannot be called "life" in any sense; it is characterized by weakness (v 10), maggots (v 11), and darkness (Job 10:22). It has much in common with the Hades of the Greeks except that most of the mythological elements are lacking — though some passages, such as the present one, can describe it in highly imaginative terms; here it is even personified. However powerful the king may have been in his lifetime, he is now no better off than the others in Sheol, where death, the great leveler, has carried him.

With another *How!* (v 12; cf. v 4b) the poet begins a dramatic contrast between the king's present situation and his former state — or, more accurately, his former pretensions, for he is presented as having aspired to divine prerogatives (ascending to heaven, equalling *the Most High* —vv 13-14). It is widely held that this section utilizes an old pagan myth concerning the presumption of a lesser god and his punishment. The *Most High* whom he attempts to unseat (v 14) is 'Elyon in Hebrew, a frequent title of Yahweh in the Old Testament (Gen 14:22; Num 24:16; Deut 32:8; Ps 7:17; 9:2; 18:13; etc.), but one in earlier and wider use and often given to Baal. The reference to *the mount of assembly in the far north* is an allusion to the concept in pagan mythology of Mt. Zaphon (i.e., the mountain of the north, identified as Mt. Cassius) as the mountain of the gods (cf. Ps 48:2 for the application of the concept to Jerusalem/Mount Zion). The author could have found no starker contrast, no better way of expressing the sudden reversal of the king's lot than this descent from the mountain of the gods to Sheol (v 15). The title which stands behind *Day Star* (v 12) probably alludes to a Canaanite deity, but the Latin for "Venus, the morning star" is *lucifer,* and the Church Fathers saw in this description an account of Satan's fall from heaven, and from the Latin rendering of the passage comes our use of Lucifer as a name for the devil. (For another example of the utilization of an old myth for the death of a foreign ruler—this time the king of Tyre—with some points of contact with this one, see Ezek 28:11-19.)

The concluding verses of the poem (vv 16-20a, taking vv 20b-21 as a later addition) continue to treat the theme of the fall and humiliation of the monarch, but now in more prosaic terms that regard the corpse and its disposition by those on the earth above. The very sight of it impresses the viewers with just how mortal this mighty conqueror was (vv 16-17). So great is the dishonor to which he has now fallen that he is not even accorded burial (cf. Jeremiah's prediction of a similar dishonor for the wicked King Jehoiakim, Jer 22:18-19), without which, the ancients believed, not even the minimal peace of Sheol could be known. The addition in vv 20b-21 would save the world from falling into the hands of sons of such a man by having them put to death. The practice of putting a ruler's son to death is well attested (1 Kgs 16:10-11; 2 Kgs 10:1-11), though this was usually to prevent rivals to the new king's throne rather than, in this case, as a punishment for evil and a remedy against its perpetuation (but see also 2 Kgs 25:6-7).

The prose conclusion provided to the poem in vv 22-23 turns from king to the wicked empire and sees it totally brought to an end. As in 13:20-22, it will henceforth be devoid of human population but will be abandoned to the wild creatures.

YAHWEH'S PURPOSE FOR ASSYRIA: 14:24-27

24 The LORD of hosts has sworn:
"As I have planned,
    so shall it be,

and as I have purposed,
so shall it stand,
25 that I will break the Assyrian in my land,
and upon my mountains trample him under foot;
and his yoke shall depart from them,
and his burden from their shoulder."
26 This is the purpose that is purposed
concerning the whole earth;
and this is the hand that is stretched out
over all the nations.
27 For the LORD of hosts has purposed,
and who will annul it?
His hand is stretched out,
and who will turn it back?

Assuming the authenticity of these verses, we are back to Isaiah's own ministry and to the time of the Assyrian domination. There is a division on the question of authorship, with excellent scholars on both sides. Yet it can be argued that what is said here agrees well with what Isaiah teaches elsewhere concerning Yahweh's plan/purpose, and for this and other reasons his authorship is to be affirmed. It is to be conceded, though, that v 25b (concerning the *yoke* and *burden* which is to be lifted) is probably a later addition taken from 9:4.

The passage in its present form does not appear to be complete, and this is understandable in the view, mentioned above, of those authors who see these verses as the original ending for 10:5-15. Other authors see in this piece a change in Isaiah's attitude toward Assyria (from seeing it as Yahweh's instrument to seeing it as an object of his wrath), sometimes dating it to the time of the Assyrian invasion of 701. Yet it is to be denied that the prophet who opposed Hezekiah's rebellion and insisted it would bring disaster suddenly changed his mind about the outcome of the foolish adventure (see further below on chaps. 36-37). Furthermore, Isaiah's solemn language about Yahweh's *purpose* (see below) is hardly compatible with the sudden reversal in position postulated by this view; the diction does not suit an *ad hoc* response to Assyria's arrogance (already castigated in 10:5-15) or Hezekiah's (unreported) repentance. Rather, since Assyria, as Yahweh's instrument, was sent for the punishment of Judah, its domination was, from the first, destined to pass away; Assyria's failure to recognize its place in Yahweh's plan and the limits of its mission (10:5-10) could only hasten the end and render it more terrible. The reference to Yahweh's plan/ purpose (which, in verb or substantive, appears in three out of these four verses) accords well with other passages we have seen (5:19; 8:10). To say that Yahweh's purpose *stands* (v 24) means that it will be carried into effect; plan or purpose (*'esah*) is always formed with a view to action, and when it is Yahweh's, there is no lack of power to put it into effect. On this point the contrast between the outcome of what "the peoples" have planned in 8:9-10 and the outcome of what Yahweh has planned in this passage is instructive; see also 7:5-7.

The passage is not primarily one of promise for Judah, though the assurance that Assyria's power would be broken could not but be comforting; but basically it is a question of what Yahweh has purposed *concerning the whole earth* (v 26). The fact that the Assyrians are to meet their fate *in my land* and *upon my mountains* (v 25) does not imply an invasion already in progress but does suggest the centrality of Judah in the prophet's thought concerning Yahweh's purpose. Here the Lord's hand, previously stretched out against Israel (5:25; 9:12, 17, 21), is said to be *stretched out* (vv 26-27) *over all the nations* (v 26). Thus the control and governance that Yahweh exercises over his own people also extends to all nations, though without the overtones of election, in this instance to Assyria.

B. S. Childs has seen in v 26 an example of the "summary-appraisal" form, a form which is at home in the wisdom tradition (cf. Job 8:13; 18:21; 20:29; 27:13; Ps 49:13; Prov 1:19). For other instances of this procedure in Isaiah, see 17:14b and 28:29. Thus we have here another link between Isaiah and wisdom.

REJOICE NOT, O PHILISTIA: 14:28-32

²⁸ In the year that King Ahaz died came this oracle:
²⁹ "Rejoice not, O Philistia, all of you,
    that the rod which smote you is broken,
  for from the serpent's root will come forth an adder,
    and its fruit will be a flying serpent.
³⁰ And the first-born of the poor will feed,
    and the needy lie down in safety;
  but I will kill your root with famine,
    and your remnant I will slay.
³¹ Wail, O gate; cry, O city;
    melt in fear, O Philistia, all of you!
  For smoke comes out of the north,
    and there is no straggler in his ranks."

³² What will one answer the messengers of the nation?
  "The LORD has founded Zion,
    and in her the afflicted of his people find refuge."

The occasion for this oracle is the death of an Assyrian king, the hope for freedom from Assyria that this gave rise to in Philistia, and the temptation to revolt against Assyria that must have been experienced also in Judah. To the Philistines Isaiah gives the warning that an even stronger Assyrian king will replace the dead one and to Judah the assurance that their safety is in the protection Yahweh affords them in Jerusalem, the city of his choice. It can be assumed that v 30a is out of place and should follow v 32.

The death of a great king was a favored time for subject peoples to revolt, but the historical situation of these verses is difficult to pinpoint since the king in question is not named. The oracle is dated *in the year that King Ahaz died* (for a similar dating procedure, see 6:1), which, on the chronology followed in this commentary, would be 715, and no Assyrian king died around that time. However, there are serious problems surrounding the Ahaz-Hezekiah chronology (see Introduction, p. 27), so no firm argument can be built around it. It is conceivable that the editor who supplied the notice was mistaken, or even that the Hebrew text should be emended slightly and read "in the year of the king's death I saw in vision. . . " Thus the Assyrian king in question could be any one of three, namely, Tiglath-pileser III (died in 727), Shalmaneser V (died in 722), or Sargon II (died in 705); Shalmaneser V's son, Sargon II, might be the best candidate since he did "smite" the Philistines during the revolt of 714-711 (see below on chap. 20; *HI*, 281, 292).

Isaiah combines diverse imagery in depicting the succession of Assyrian kings, speaking now of a *rod*, now of a *serpent's root*, now even of the mythological *flying serpent* (v 29). The death of one Assyrian king, the prophet is saying, will not make that much difference; and, in fact, Assyria was blessed with an extraordinary succession of very able and vigorous rulers. More important than anything he might say to the Philistines, however, was Isaiah's word to Judah in these circumstances. The *messengers* to whom a response was to be given (v 32) would be the emissaries of the Philistines coming to solicit Judah's cooperation in a scheme to revolt against Assyria; the reply to be given was that Judah's security lay not in alliances with other nations but in the protection afforded by Yahweh. In this Isaiah is consistent with the advice he gave Hezekiah during the events of 705-701 and also with that given Ahaz in 735: trust in Yahweh's promises, unlike that reposed in foreign powers, is never misplaced. In the present case we have a clear indication that the basis for this confidence is Yahweh's election of Zion/Jerusalem. This is a long way from an affirmation that Zion was inviolable, which came to be the popular belief, and it is to be noted the emphasis is on the protection of the poor, needy, and afflicted (vv 30a, 32b). In this, as in other elements of the Zion tradition, Isaiah shares a broad Old Testament background; see the Zion Psalms in general (Psalms 46; 48; 76; 87; and 132). On Yahweh's founding of Zion, see Ps 87:1, and on the special place of the afflicted, see Ps 76:9; 132:14. (On the Zion tradition see further below on 17:12-14.)

LAMENT OVER MOAB: 15:1-16:14

15 An oracle concerning Moab.
  Because Ar is laid waste in a night
    Moab is undone;
  because Kir is laid waste in a night
    Moab is undone.
2 The daughter of Dibon has gone up
    to the high places to weep;
  over Nebo and over Medeba
    Moab wails.
  On every head is baldness,
    every beard is shorn;
3 In the streets they gird on sackcloth;
    on the housetops and in the squares
    every one wails and melts in tears.
4 Heshbon and Elealeh cry out,
    their voice is heard as far as Jahaz;
  therefore the armed men of Moab cry aloud;
    his soul trembles.
5 My heart cries out for Moab;
    his fugitives flee to Zoar,
    to Eglath-shelishiyah.
  For at the ascent of Luhith
    they go up weeping;
  on the road to Horonaim
    they raise a cry of destruction;
6 the waters of Nimrim
    are a desolation;
  the grass is withered, the new growth fails,
    the verdure is no more.
7 Therefore the abundance they have gained
    and what they have laid up
  they carry away
    over the Brook of the Willows.
8 For a cry has gone
    round the land of Moab;
  the wailing reaches to Eglaim,
    the wailing reaches to Beerelim.
9 For the waters of Dibon are full of blood;

> yet I will bring upon Dibon even more,
> a lion for those of Moab who escape,
>   for the remnant of the land.

16 They have sent lambs
>   to the ruler of the land,
> from Sela, by way of the desert,
>   to the mount of the daughter of Zion.
> ² Like fluttering birds,
>   like scattered nestlings,
> so are the daughters of Moab
>   at the fords of the Arnon.
> ³ "Give counsel,
>   grant justice;
> make your shade like night
>   at the height of noon;
> hide the outcasts,
>   betray not the fugitive;
> ⁴ let the outcasts of Moab
>   sojourn among you;
> be a refuge to them
>   from the destroyer.
> When the oppressor is no more,
>   and destruction has ceased,
> and he who tramples under foot
>   has vanished from the land,
> ⁵ then a throne will be established in steadfast love
>   and on it will sit in faithfulness
>   in the tent of David
> one who judges and seeks justice
>   and is swift to do righteousness."

> ⁶ We have heard of the pride of Moab,
>   how proud he was;
> of his arrogance, his pride, and his insolence—
>   his boasts are false.
> ⁷ Therefore let Moab wail,
>   let every one wail for Moab.
> Mourn, utterly stricken,
>   for the raisin-cakes of Kir-hareseth.

8 For the fields of Heshbon languish,
    and the vine of Sibmah;
  the lords of the nations
    have struck down its branches,
  which reached to Jazer
    and strayed to the desert;
  its shoots spread abroad
    and passed over the sea.
9 Therefore I weep with the weeping of Jazer
    for the vine of Sibmah;
  I drench you with my tears,
    O Heshbon and Elealeh;
  for upon your fruit and your harvest
    the battle shout has fallen.
10 And joy and gladness are taken away
    from the fruitful field;
  and in the vineyards no songs are sung,
    no shouts are raised;
  no treader treads out wine in the presses;
    the vintage shout is hushed.
11 Therefore my soul moans like a lyre for Moab,
    and my heart for Kirheres.
    12And when Moab presents himself, when he wearies himself upon the high place, when he comes to his sanctuary to pray, he will not prevail.
    13This is the word which the LORD spoke concerning Moab in the past. 14But now the LORD says, "In three years, like the years of a hireling, the glory of Moab will be brought into contempt, in spite of all his great multitude, and those who survive will be very few and feeble."

Although the content of these two chapters are now intended to be taken as a single unit, it appears to have been composed of three originally distinct parts, with some editorial additions at various points: 15:1-9 is a lament over a severe devastation of Moab by an unnamed attacker; 16:1-5 speaks of the fate of the fugitives; and 16:6-11 is a further lament, perhaps reflecting deliberately on the first part. (16:13-14 is a later addition, in prose.) There is no agreement as to whether the devastation referred to describes a past event or is a prophecy of a future event (and on this point some put the first part in a different category than the third part). While it is probable that at least the first part refers to something that has already happened, no basis is given for identifying the event described, i.e., when it happened and who the attacker was. Parts of the poem appear, in somewhat altered form, in Jer 48:29-38. There is little basis for either affirming or denying Isaiah's authorship of these chapters.

Moab was a kingdom located east of the Dead Sea, with Ammon to the north and Edom to the south (see Map 1). Gen 19:30-38 tells of the birth of Moab and Ben-ammi, the eponymous ancestors of the Moabites and the Ammonites, through the incestuous relations of Lot (Abraham's nephew) with his two daughters; the story expresses, in a disparaging way, Israel's recognition of kinship with these peoples. When David fled from Saul he left his parents in the keeping of the king of Moab (1 Sam 22:3-5), but later, as king of a united Israel and Judah, David conquered Moab and treated the population with some cruelty (2 Sam 8:2). Moab seems to have become independent after the death of Solomon, though later kings of Israel sometimes succeeded in making them again subject. The famous stele of Mesha, king of Moab in the ninth century, tells of success, at least for the time, in shaking off Israel's yoke (*ANET*, 320-21); see also in 2 Kgs 3:1-27. This text also tells us that as vassal Mesha had to pay tribute of 100,000 lambs to Israel each year (see below on 16:1).

The first part (15:1-9) vividly depicts a situation of widespread destruction, of terror, flight, and confusion. *Ar* and *Kir* do not necessarily designate specific places, but may be terms to indicate Moab and its cities in general. If they are to be taken as cities, they are south of the Arnon, approximately west of the tongue (Lisan) of the Dead Sea. The places named in vv 2-4 (*Dibon, Nebo, Medeba, Heshbon,* and *Elealeh*), on the other hand, are to the north of the Arnon, some even beyond the northern end of the Dead Sea. In these places we hear of weeping, prayer (the high places of v 2 are sanctuaries), and signs of mourning (shaving of head and beard, sackcloth — vv 2-3). Flight by way of *Zoar* (at the south end of Dead Sea — v 5) and escape into Edom, with whatever possessions they can manage to carry (v 7), is compatible with the possible reference to Petra/ Sela, a royal city of Edom, in 16:1 and with the hope of eventual escape to Judah (16:1-5); it also suggests that the enemy comes from the north. The theme of general lament is taken up again in vv 8-9a, where the locations, to the extent they are known, seem to be in the north; the Hebrew has "dimon" rather than *Dibon*, but this may be a deliberate alteration for the sake of the play on the Hebrew word for "blood" (*dam*). The first-person threat (probably in the name of Yahweh) in v 9b is at odds with the tone of the preceding and is probably a later addition.

The second part (16:1-5) abounds with problems, which are relieved only in small measure by removing the intrusive v 2 to after 15:9a. If 16:1 speaks of sending lambs (whether in the indicative — as the *RSV* has — or the imperative) it is a matter of tribute to the Judean king, an acknowledgment of vassalhood, as in the days of David, who first conquered Moab (2 Sam 8:2). But the Septuagint appears to have divided the same Hebrew letters into words that describe the refugees hugging the earth like reptiles (see *NAB*). Petra/ Sela is far to the south of the borders of Moab (see Map 2), but a temporary refuge there has been suggested; however, since the Hebrew *sela'* means first of all "rock" or "cliff," it is not certain that a proper name is intended here. What is clear (v 1b, 3-5) is that sanctuary for the escapees is being sought in Jerusalem until a time of safety. Since v 5 sounds as though the Davidic kingship has ceased, it is probably a later addition to this earlier piece.

While the second part seemed to treat the plight of the Moabites, with whom the people of Judah acknowledged kinship, with some sympathy, the third part (vv 6-12) indicates a rejection of the plea for sanctuary: Moab's arrogance and pride supply the reason (v 6). Therefore the theme of lamentation is taken up again, with mention of many of the same place names found in the first part. Now, however,

reference is made almost exclusively to the splendid vineyards of Moab, where the battle cry has replaced the glad
shouts of vintage time (vv 9-10), and to their products of
wine and raisin-cakes (vv. 7,10). And here the suspicion
arises that the lamentation masks a taunt for what is considered a well-deserved come-down. Verses 13-14 were added
at some later time; they take the preceding composition to
be a prophecy of the future and attempt to assign a definite
time of *three years* for its fulfillment. The reference to
hireling characterizes the period as tiring and troublesome.

ORACLE AGAINST SYRIA AND ISRAEL: 17:1-11

17 An oracle concerning Damascus.
Behold, Damascus will cease to be a city,
and will become a heap of ruins.
² Her cities will be deserted for ever;
they will be for flocks,
which will lie down, and none will make them afraid.
³ The fortress will disappear from Ephraim,
and the kingdom from Damascus;
and the remnant of Syria will be
like the glory of the children of Israel,
says the LORD of hosts.

⁴ And in that day
the glory of Jacob will be brought low,
and the fat of his flesh will grow lean.
⁵ And it shall be as when the reaper gathers standing grain
and his arm harvests the ears
and as when one gleans the ears of grain
in the Valley of Rephaim.
⁶ Gleanings will be left in it,
as when an olive tree is beaten—
two or three berries
in the top of the highest bough,
four or five
on the branches of a fruit tree,
says the LORD God of Israel.

⁷In that day men will regard their Maker , and their eyes will look to the Holy One of Israel; ⁸they will not have regard for the altars, the work of their hands, and they will not look to what their own fingers have made, either the Asherim or the altars of incense.

⁹In that day their strong cities will be like the deserted places of the Hivites and the Amorites, which they deserted because of the children of Israel, and there will be desolation.

10 For you have forgotten the God of your salvation,
       and have not remembered the Rock of your refuge;
   therefore, though you plant pleasant plants
       and set out slips of an alien god,
11 though you make them grow on the day that you plant them,
       and make them blossom in the morning that you sow;
   yet the harvest will flee away
       in a day of grief and incurable pain.

The nucleus of the composition, vv 1-6, couples Syria and Israel and foretells an end to both of them in a manner that corresponds with what Isaiah had to say about these two kingdoms in the days of the Syro-Ephraimitic crisis (see above on 7:1); there is no reason to deny these verses to Isaiah or to doubt that they date to this period. But the original nucleus has been later expanded by vv 7-8 and possibly by v 9, while vv 10-11 are an independent composition.

Damascus, the capital of Syria, is the primary focus in vv 1-3, Israel in vv 4-6, and these were probably originally separate compositions (note the *and in that day* of v 4). Although Damascus was taken and ravaged by Tiglath-pileser III in 732, it was not destroyed and left desolate in the manner here expected. (For another Isaian reference to flocks taking over human habitations, see above on 5:17.) Ezekiel 27 treats Damascus as a prosperous city. But the Assyrian attack did bring to an end Damascus' position as leader of the Syrian forces; Rezin, its king, was executed, large numbers of the Syrian population were deported, and the territories were organized into the Assyrian provincial system. The fate of the *remnant of Syria* (v 3) becomes intelligible in the light of v 4.

It is obvious that when vv 4-6 were uttered the northern kingdom was still in prosperous circumstances (see also below on 28:1-4). Pictured here, however, is a reversal of that situation: fatness would turn into a wasted leanness, and from a rich harvest, only a few stray ears of grain or a couple of olives would remain; thus of Israel, as of Syria (v 3), only *a remnant* would survive. The *Valley of Rephaim* (v 5) was southwest of Jerusalem; it was not part of Israel's territory and Isaiah must have mentioned it because reaping grain there was a familiar sight to him.

In the original historical context the reason for the destruction threatened against Syria and Israel would have been apparent; this is not the case with the present literary context of vv 1-6, however, and it is probably for that reason that vv 7-8 were added. These verses suggest that the offense was idolatry and that the punishment inflicted would lead to a conversion to God. The thought applies more aptly to Israel than to Syria. The *Asherim* of v 8 are sacred pillars or trees that relate to the worship of Asherah, the goddess of fertility.

Verse 9 is often treated as a gloss, but it could in substance be the conclusion to vv 4-6 on Israel; just as Yahweh's power once emptied cities of their former pagan inhabitants in favor of the Israelites whom he brought into the land, so is he now able to empty them of Israelites who enter into league with pagans against their brother Judah. The Hebrew text is disordered, and *RSV* takes the reference to *the Hivites and the Amorites* from the Septuagint.

But v 9 can also be taken as an introduction to vv 10-11; these three verses are in prose. That vv 10-11 stand apart from v 9 is evident in that v 9 refers to those threatened in third-person plural, while vv 10-11 address someone (no doubt a personification of a people) in second-person, singular, feminine. Verses 10-11 refer to pagan practice, apparently that of Adonis, the god who was thought to die at the first coming of the summer heat; cultic and visual representation was given this by the growing of plants in small vessels so that they sprouted rapidly and withered away early. The point made here is that the worship of foreign gods is as unproductive as this practice and, in fact, merits a punishment (v 11). These verses could be from Isaiah, brought here because of the reference to harvest in vv 5-6, though they could more easily have been addressed originally to Judah than to Israel.

ATTACK (ON JERUSALEM) AND DELIVERANCE (BY YAHWEH): 17:12-14

12 Ah, the thunder of many peoples,
   they thunder like the thundering of the sea!
Ah, the roar of nations,
   they roar like the roaring of mighty waters!
13 The nations roar like the roaring of many waters,
   but he will rebuke them, and they will flee far away,
chased like chaff on the mountains before the wind
   and whirling dust before the storm.
14 At evening time, behold, terror!
   Before morning, they are no more!
This is the portion of those who despoil us,
   and the lot of those who plunder us.

This short piece is remarkable in its failure to name the attacking enemy, the city or country attacked and delivered, and the agent of deliverance. The latter two of these can be supplied from the background into which the piece fits, i.e., the so-called Zion tradition. The Zion Psalms (see above on 14:32) point to a background scenario in which foreign attackers come up against Jerusalem (Zion), the city of Yahweh's choice; through Yahweh's own intervention the enemy is crushed and routed. The overall plan is seen most clearly in Psalms 46, 48, and 76, and even some close parallels as to detail: thus there is a description of the foreign enemies under the imagery of "waters (that) roar and foam" (Ps 46:3) and it is "at thy rebuke" (Ps 76:6) that the enemy is routed. These psalms do not refer to any specific enemy, but speak in a general way and in the plural ("the nations rage,"

Ps 46:6; "the kings assembled," Ps 48:4) either because they
see Yahweh's protection as present in all circumstances or
because they look to a final and definitive attack in some
vague and distant future (the sea imagery suggests chaotic,
primal forces). The failure of the tradition to identify a
specific enemy was no doubt what led Isaiah to speak in the
same vague terms, even though he may have had Assyria in
mind; in fact, the verbs and pronouns in vv 13b-14a are
grammatically singular, in spite of *RSV*'s plurals.

If this is the correct explanation, the passage could be
fitted in with others that speak of Yahweh's intention to
bring Assyrian power to an end (see above on 10:5-15;
14:24-27) in a general sense. Some authors would date the
piece to the events of 705-701, but since Isaiah then ada-
mantly opposed rebellion against Assyria and foretold disaster for Judah at their hands, it seems unlikely he would at
that time have spoken words which, indirectly at least,
would be so reassuring to Judah with reference to the Assyrian threat. Another possibility is that the passage dates to
the events of 735 and was spoken with the intention of
reassuring Judah in the face of the Syro-Ephraimitic invasion. This explanation would require casting Israel among
the pagan nations, but vv 1-6 of this chapter already join
Israel to Syria and v 9 (which may conceivably come from
Isaiah) likens Israel to their pagan predecessors in the land.
A third view would relate this reassuring oracle to chap. 18:
the promise of Yahweh's protection obliterates any need to
seek help through pacts with other nations.

Verse 14b is again one of those that Childs classifies as a
"summary-appraisal" form (see above on 14:26). The delivery described is understood, then, not as an isolated inci-
dent, but as one instance of the manner in which those who
enjoy Yahweh's special protection are defended.

ORACLE AGAINST EGYPT/ETHIOPIA: 18:1-7

> **18** Ah, land of whirring wings
>   which is beyond the rivers of Ethiopia;
>   ² which sends ambassadors by the Nile,

in vessels of papyrus upon the waters!
Go, you swift messengers,
   to a nation, tall and smooth,
to a people feared near and far,
   a nation mighty and conquering,
   whose land the rivers divide.

3 All you inhabitants of the world,
   you who dwell on the earth,
when a signal is raised on the mountains, look!
   When a trumpet is blown, hear!
4 For thus the LORD said to me:
  "I will quietly look from my dwelling
   like clear heat in sunshine,
   like a cloud of dew in the heat of harvest."
5 For before the harvest, when the blossom is over,
   and the flower becomes a ripening grape,
he will cut off the shoots with pruning hooks,
   and the spreading branches he will hew away.
6 They shall all of them be left
   to the birds of prey of the mountains
   and to the beasts of the earth.
And the birds of prey will summer upon them,
   and all the beasts of the earth will winter upon them.

   7At that time gifts will be brought to the LORD of hosts
from a people tall and smooth,
   from a people feared near and far,
a nation mighty and conquering,
   whose land the rivers divide,
to Mount Zion, the place of the name of the LORD of hosts.

Egypt, so often the abettor of revolts against the Assyrian empire on the part of the smaller vassal state, had been suffering from internal weakness from a little before the middle of the eighth century. Ethiopia (the biblical Cush) lay far to the south of Egypt (see Map 2) and around 716 the Ethiopian king Piankhi was able to subject Egypt to his rule;

he founded the 25th (Ethiopian) dynasty, which endured until around 663 (*HI*, 281). Piankhi and his successors again attempted to counter the Assyrians by trying to persuade revolt against them on the part of subject peoples. (See also chap. 20, which may relate to the same events as this chapter; in 20:3, 5 the names of Egypt and Ethiopia are used together.)

The present chapter relates to an embassy from the Egyptians/Ethiopians to Judah to persuade their cooperation in a broader uprising of vassals against Assyria. Such revolts occurred in 714 and 705, Egypt promising major support in each case; the present chapter could relate to either instance, though more probably to the former, in which Hezekiah refused to join (see below on chap. 20). The embassy seems to have made a large part of the journey — as far as the Nile Delta or possibly even as far as the Judean coast — in *vessels of papyrus*, i.e., boats constructed of bundles of papyrus reed, very light and capable of rapid travel. The arrival of these emissaries in Jerusalem appears to have created quite a stir.

That Isaiah indicated that an unfavorable reply was to be given to them is abundantly clear (especially on the basis of what he has to say elsewhere), though there are not a few obscurities and vv 4-6 are susceptible of more than one interpretation. Verse 7 is without doubt a later addtion and in all probability v 3 and v 6b are also later additions.

Although Ethiopia might be characterized as a land of *whirring wings* (v 1) because of insects or some other reason, the Hebrew probably refers simply to the swiftness of their boats. Isaiah's *go, you swift messengers* is an invitation for them to return home with a message of refusal. Allusion is made to the handsome appearance of the Ethiopians, a point well-attested in other ancient sources. (As indicated above, v 3 is a later interpolation; it is a tissue of expressions found in late passages in Isaiah and adds little that is intelligible to the present one.)

Verses 4-6, as has been suggested, are open to more than one interpretation. Verse 4 indicates that Yahweh will not act immediately (i.e., in the revolt now being plotted) because the time is not yet ripe. Like a patient farmer he will wait until the proper season and then harvest the crops. That this *harvest* signifies the destruction of a powerful nation is indicated not only by the cutting and hewing terminology (v 5), but especially by the reference to the leaving of them (probably the bodies of the slain) to the *birds of prey* and the *beasts of the earth* (v 6a; v 6b, added later, builds upon this imagery in a somewhat confused manner). These verses (vv 4-6) mean that Judah is not to join with the Egyptians because Yahweh holds aloof and will not act at this time; they may also say that at the proper time Yahweh will himself bring an end to the power of Assyria without help from Egypt or any other nation. Assyria is not mentioned in the piece, but it is without doubt the occasion for the embassy, and this interpretation would accord with other passages in which Isaiah speaks of the future destruction by Yahweh of the Assyrians (10:5-15; 14:24-27); this would be especially apt if it is understood that 17:12-14, which also no doubt refers to the destruction of the Assyrians, was placed immediately before this passage for that reason. However, the threat is more probably directed against the Ethiopians. Isaiah would be saying that their plotting against Assyria will ultimately bring grave peril upon themselves; this would agree with the message delivered by him in chap. 20.

Verse 7 is a later addition. It uses the very expressions found in v 2 to describe the Egyptians, but now speaks of their conversion to the Lord. While this is out of harmony with the context of the preceding verses, it accords well with other late additions (see below on 19:18-25).

JUDGMENT ON EGYPT: 19:1-15

19 An oracle concerning Egypt.
Behold, the LORD is riding on a swift cloud
and comes to Egypt;
and the idols of Egypt will tremble at his presence,
and the heart of the Egyptians will melt within them.
2 And I will stir up Egyptians against Egyptians,
and they will fight, every man against his brother

and every man against his neighbor,
city against city, kingdom against kingdom;
3 and the spirit of the Egyptians within them will be
emptied out,
and I will confound their plans;
and they will consult the idols and the sorcerers,
and the mediums and the wizards;
4 and I will give over the Egyptians
into the hand of a hard master;
and a fierce king will rule over them,
says the Lord, the LORD of hosts.

5 And the waters of the Nile will be dried up,
and the river will be parched and dry;
6 and its canals will become foul,
and the branches of Egypt's Nile will diminish and dry up,
reeds and rushes will rot away.
7 There will be bare places by the Nile,
on the brink of the Nile,
and all that is sown by the Nile will dry up,
be driven away, and be no more.
8 The fishermen will mourn and lament,
all who cast hook in the Nile;
and they will languish
who spread nets upon the water.
9 The workers in combed flax will be in despair,
and the weavers of white cotton.
10 Those who are the pillars of the land will be crushed,
and all who work for hire will be grieved.

11 The princes of Zoan are utterly foolish;
the wise counselors of Pharaoh give stupid counsel.
How can you say to Pharaoh,
"I am a son of the wise,
a son of ancient kings"?
12 Where then are your wise men?
Let them tell you and make known
what the LORD of hosts has purposed against Egypt.
13 The princes of Zoan have become fools,
and the princes of Memphis are deluded;
those who are the cornerstones of her tribes

have led Egypt astray.

14 The LORD has mingled within her
   a spirit of confusion;
   and they have made Egypt stagger in all her doings
   as a drunken man staggers in his vomit.

15 And there will be nothing for Egypt
   which head or tail, palm branch or reed, may do.

Commentators are divided on whether or not to attribute this oracle to Isaiah. No final answer can be given, though there is nothing in it that couldn't have come from Isaiah; the criticism of the Egyptian counselors and their plans seems to echo things he said of Judah's wise men. The poem falls into three parts: vv 1-4 describe civil turmoil in Egypt; vv 5-10 speak of the drying up of the Nile and the impact of this on Egypt; and vv 11-14 inveigh against the stupidity of Egyptian policy. Verse 15 is summarizing addition.

If this oracle is to be attributed to Isaiah or to his time, the period of civil strife in Egypt (vv 1-4) would be that before the take-over of Piankhi. During the time the Twenty-second Dynasty still claimed to rule (ca. 935-725), the Twenty-third Dynasty established itself (ca. 759-715); and before the Twenty-third had run its course, the Twenty-fourth Dynasty (ca. 725-709) claimed power. Thus the Twenty-third Dynasty had to contend with one or another rival dynasty throughout the forty-five years of its existence. Piankhi the Ethiopian, founder of the Twenty-fifth Dynasty (see above on chap. 18), having earlier conquered Upper Egypt (i.e., along the Nile valley, south of Memphis — see Map 2), invaded and took over Lower Egypt (i.e., the Delta region), thus bringing the Twenty-third Dynasty to an end; the last king of the Twenty-fourth Dynasty was allowed to rule as his vassal. Yahweh is seen in this first section as the Lord of history who disposes of Egyptian affairs with sovereign power; he enters the land and causes the Egyptians and their idols to tremble with fear, he provokes civil war, confounds their plans, and hands them over to a *hard master*. It is conceivable that this is a reference to Piankhi, but since his vigorous action which finally unified Egypt was more a blessing than a curse, it might better refer to conquest by the Assyrians. If this passage relates at all to the third section, vv 11-15, this seems the more likely solution, for those verses decry the sort of short-sighted Egyptian policy of abetting revolt that ultimately brought the Assyrians against them. The period here in question would be that of Osorkon IV (730-715). Only under Esarhaddon (680-669), however, did Assyria begin the conquest of Egypt (see Map 3).

The central section, vv 5-10, does not relate to what precedes and follows except in the most general sense, and it is possible that it comes from a separate source and was later inserted here. The Egyptian year knew three seasons, and they related to the annual flooding of the Nile rather than to the solar cycle. Egypt has, indeed, been called "the gift of the Nile," so much did farming and other industries depend on this very predictable source. Verses 5-10 thus introduce a rather shocking theme by speaking of its drying up; in some detail the consequences are described for agriculture and the fishing and textile industries. (This theme is carried on into v 10, where "spinners" rather than *pillars* should be read; cf. *NAB.*)

If vv 5-10 are intrusive, as is probably the case, the final section, vv 11-14(15) would originally have followed directly on vv 1-4; the threat of Assyria which may be contained in vv 1-4 would then be explained very well by the wrongheaded planning derided in vv 11-14. Here we meet ideas very similar to those encountered in Isaiah's criticism of Judah's policy and its royal counselors. Just as Judah's circle of advisers were "wise" only in their own eyes (5:21) and their wisdom was destined to perish (29:14), and just as Judah failed to seek Yahweh's counsel (30:1-2), so too are the Egyptian royal counselors guilty of giving stupid counsel and being without wisdom (vv 11-12a) and of failing to know what Yahweh has purposed against Egypt (v 12b). Even this stupidity is attributed to Yahweh's activity (v 14 —cf. 6:10), no doubt so that what he has *purposed against*

Egypt can come to pass. These similarities suggest that the Egyptian policy here so strongly condemned is that of fomenting revolt against Assyria among her vassals. In this sense the passage is as much a warning to Judah to stay clear of such entanglements as it is a warning to Egypt itself.

LATER ADDITIONS CONCERNING EGYPT: 19:16-25

[16]In that day the Egyptians will be like women, and tremble with fear before the hand which the LORD of hosts shakes over them. [17]And the land of Judah will become a terror to the Egyptians; every one to whom it is mentioned will fear because of the purpose which the LORD of hosts has purposed against them.

[18]In that day there will be five cities in the land of Egypt which speak the language of Canaan and swear allegiance to the LORD of hosts. One of these will be called the City of the Sun.

[19]In that day there will be an altar to the LORD in the midst of the land of Egypt, and a pillar to the LORD at its border. [20]It will be a sign and a witness to the LORD of hosts in the land of Egypt; when they cry to the LORD because of oppressors he will send them a savior, and will defend and deliver them. [21]And the LORD will make himself known to the Egyptians; and the Egyptians will know the LORD in that day and worship with sacrifice and burnt offering, and they will make vows to the LORD and perform them. [22]And the LORD will smite Egypt, smiting and healing, and they will return to the LORD, and he will heed their supplications and heal them.

[23]In that day there will be a highway from Egypt to Assyria, and the Assyrian will come into Egypt, and the Egyptian into Assyria, and the Egyptians will worship with the Assyrians.

[24]In that day Israel will be the third with Egypt and Assyria, a blessing in the midst of the earth, [25]whom the LORD of hosts has blessed, saying, "Blessed be Egypt my people, and Assyria the work of my hands, and Israel my heritage."

The preceding verses on the fate of Egypt have occasioned the addition of new reflections which in turn generated further additions, all of which come long after the time of Isaiah. The phrase *in that day* often signals a new beginning, and it may be that we have a new development each time the words recur (vv 16, 18, 19, 23, 24). They range from expressing a hostile attitude toward Egypt to some of the most beautiful and universalist passages in the Old Testament. There are not a few problems in these verses, however, some of them perhaps unresolvable.

Verses 16-17 build on the preceding (cf. especially the reference to Yahweh's *purpose* in v 17 with that in v 12), but allusions to fear, Yahweh's hand, and trembling like women may reflect the exodus and holy war traditions (cf. Exod 15:14-16; 23:27; Deut 11:25). Here Judah is exalted at the expense of Egypt.

The author of v 18 now speaks of the worship of Yahweh in Egypt and presumably the reference is not to Egyptian conversion but to the Jewish Diaspora there. "Five cities" could be intended as a round figure, but more likely the author has five locations in mind with a considerable Jewish population so that they *speak the language of Canaan*, i.e., Hebrew. *City of the Sun*, if that is to be read, would be Heliopolis, but the standard Hebrew text has "city of destruction." The Septuagint calls it "city of righteousness," a term applied to Jerusalem by Isaiah (1:26) and that may well be the original import; a later copyist, shocked to see an Egyptian city so designated, changed it to "city of destruction," which was later still misread (or deliberately softened) to *City of the Sun* (ḥeres for heres).

Verses 19-22 now take the much larger step to Egyptian conversion to Yahweh. The cult objects (*altar* and sacred *pillar*), presumably the work of the Jewish Diaspora, are a reminder to the Egyptians of Yahweh's presence and power — a power the author knows the Egyptians experienced to their sorrow in a previous age. As in the days of the Judges, those who are oppressed cry out to Yahweh and he sends them a savior to deliver them (cf. Judg 3:9, 15; 4:3; 6:7-14). The apparently obvious meaning of the text is that it is the Egyptians who are oppressed and cry out to Yahweh, but because Hebrew is notoriously slow to repeat the antecedents of pronouns, the opinion of those who think it is the Jews in their midst who are oppressed (perhaps even by the Egyptians!) cannot be ruled out. At any rate, the marvelous deliverance constitutes a revelation of Yahweh to the Egyptians (a far more positive one than that expressed in Exod 14:4, 18), who now turn to worship him. For Egypt to *know the Lord* is a very positive statement which goes far beyond intellectual knowledge (see above on 5:13).

A still greater universalism is brought in in v 23 with the introduction of the Assyrians. Those inveterate enemies of old, the Egyptians and the Assyrians, now are joined in peace, symbolized by a highway linking their territories.

The final touch is put on this beautiful picture of peace by the lofty and generous spirited author of vv 24-25, as Egypt and Assyria share equally in Israel's prerogatives as God's chosen people. Terms such as *my people* and *the work of my hands* had hitherto been reserved for Israel; here it is acknowledged that if Yahweh is creator of all, he is also Lord of all, not only to judge but also to bless. (Some commentators suggest that *Assyria* in vv 23-24 refers to the Syrians and that these verses speak of a resolution of the hostilities between the Seleucids and the Ptolemies in the Hellenistic period. But if any specific historical background is to be sought, the Persians, who replaced the Babylonians, could be intended. However, even that hypothesis seems unnecessary. Egypt and Assyria were former oppressors of Israel and enemies of each other; as such they stand as types to illustrate the glorious power of Yahweh's reconciling grace.)

ISAIAH THE PROTESTER: 20:1-6

20 In the year that the commander in chief, who was sent by Sargon the king of Assyria, came to Ashdod and fought against it and took it, —²at that time the LORD had spoken by Isaiah the son of Amoz, saying, "Go, and loose the sackcloth from your loins and take off your shoes from your feet," and he had done so, walking naked and barefoot—³the LORD said, "As my servant Isaiah has walked naked and barefoot for three years as a sign and a portent against Egypt and Ethiopia, ⁴so shall the king of Assyria lead away the Egyptians captives and the Ethiopians exiles, both the young and the old, naked and barefoot, with buttocks uncovered, to the shame of Egypt. ⁵Then they shall be dismayed and confounded because of Ethiopia their hope and of Egypt their boast. ⁶And the inhabitants of this coastland will say in that day, 'Behold, this is what has happened to those in whom we hoped and to whom we fled for help to be delivered from the king of Assyria! And we, how shall we escape?'"

This chapter relates to an event that is known to us also from Assyrian documents, namely, the revolt of the Philistine city Ashdod against the Assyrians in 714 and the conquest and punishment of the city in 711; it also tells us of the message Isaiah delivered in these circumstances. The message was delivered in the form of the symbolic, prophetic action of going about *naked* (which perhaps here means only semi-clothed) *and barefoot*, in the manner in which a prisoner of war would be led off. A prophetic act was intended to give special impact to a message, to give it higher visibility, and, in a sense, to actualize it. (For other examples of prophetic actions, see 8:1-4; Jer 19:1-13; 27:1-12; Ezek 4:1-8; 5:1-12; 37:15-22.) Ostensibly the sign was directed to Egypt (vv 3-4 —on the virtual identification here of Egypt and Ethiopia, see above on chap. 18), but Isaiah would no doubt have been more concerned about its impact on Judah and King Hezekiah, for Judah, too, had been invited to join in the revolt against Assyria.

From Assyrian records in the days of Sargon II we learn that not only Ashdod but also Gath and other territories were involved (see Map 1). The Assyrians replaced Ashdod's king with his brother only to have the populace replace him with a usurper. Assyria moved very quickly to crush the rebellion and, having overwhelmed Ashdod, carried off a massive booty. So far were the Egyptians from rendering help that when the usurper fled there for sanctuary, they handed him over to the Assyrians. If the embassy from the Egyptians to Judah described in chap. 18 relates to this period, it is clear that much of the initiative came from the Egyptians. But Isaiah's warning is that they are unreliable allies. They may have instigated the rebellion, but it was others who suffered the consequences. On this occasion Isaiah's advice was apparently heeded; Judah did not suffer from the Assyrians, so presumably they were not deeply involved in the conspiracy (*HI*, 281-82). Isaiah's explanation of his prophetic action (vv 3-4), which undoubtedly goes back to the beginning of the revolt in 714, speaks of the Egyptians being led away, but that is not what, in fact, happened. The piece has been formulated some time after the events (v 1 can announce the fate of Ashdod), in order to present its message anew — probably when Judah was solicited to join the revolt against Sennacherib after the death of Sargon II in 705.

ANNOUNCEMENT ON THE FALL OF BABYLON: 21:1-10

21 The oracle concerning the wilderness of the sea.
  As whirlwinds in the Negeb sweep on,
    it comes from the desert,
    from a terrible land.
  2 A stern vision is told to me;
    the plunderer plunders,
    and the destroyer destroys.
  Go up, O Elam,
    lay siege, O Media;
  all the sighing she has caused
    I bring to an end.
  3 Therefore my loins are filled with anguish;
    pangs have seized me,
    like the pangs of a woman in travail;
  I am bowed down so that I cannot hear,
    I am dismayed so that I cannot see.
  4 My mind reels, horror has appalled me;
    the twilight I longed for
    has been turned for me into trembling.

5 They prepare the table,
      they spread the rugs,
      they eat, they drink.
   Arise, O princes,
      oil the shield!
6 For thus the Lord said to me:
   "Go, set a watchman,
      let him announce what he sees.
7 When he sees riders, horsemen in pairs,
      riders on asses, riders on camels,
   let him listen diligently,
      very diligently."
8 Then he who saw cried:
   "Upon a watchtower I stand, O Lord,
      continually by day,
   and at my post I am stationed
      whole nights.
9 And behold, here come riders,
      horsemen in pairs!"
   And he answered,
      "Fallen, fallen is Babylon;
   and all the images of her gods
      he has shattered to the ground."
10 O my threshed and winnowed one,
      what I have heard from the LORD of hosts,
      the God of Israel, I announce to you.

Since this oracle looks to the immediate fall of Babylon, it is probably to be dated shortly before 539, when the city fell to Cyrus II of Persia. If this is correct, the mention of Elam and Media (see Map 2) in v 2 is somewhat surprising, for Elam had not been a power to be reckoned with for about a century and the Medes had been the first to fall to Cyrus as he set about establishing the empire which would finally topple Babylon. The probable explanation is that these peoples, now subject to Cyrus, might be expected by the poet to provide contingents of troops for the assault upon Babylon; less probable is the suggestion that a deliberately archaic, poetic manner is adopted so that the peoples sweeping in from the east can be referred to by these ancient names. In spite of the expressions of grief over the violence to come (vv 3-4), there is recognition of the suffering Babylon has caused and some exulting in her fall (vv 2, 9-10), so it is unlikely that this oracle could come from an earlier period of Assyrian attacks on Babylon (e.g., under Sargon II); Judah was then Babylon's ally and her fall would have brought no rejoicing.

The designation *wilderness of the sea* (v 1) has occasioned some puzzlement, but it probably is thought to be an apt designation for lower Mesopotamia. The resurgent Neo-Babylonians are called Chaldeans after Kaldu, the portion of Mesopotamia which borders on the Persian Gulf; but an alternative designation for their place of origin, rendered Sealand in English, suggests a relation to the sea or water.

The poem is powerfully and imaginatively written and has great emotional impact. Verse 5 may reflect a tradition that the Babylonians were preparing to feast when the Persian army swept down on them; it depicts a sudden switch from revelry to preparation for battle. The prophet is constituted a watchman (v 6 — cf. Ezek 33:1-9, where a different form of the same Hebrew verb is used) and keeps diligent vigils, giving indications of the outcome of the battle (vv 7-8). The answer, when it comes, carries some anti-pagan polemic, for the reference to the idols which have been shattered in the fall of Babylon indicates both that these worthless gods could not save her and that her false worship was among the crimes for which she was punished (v 9). The poem closes with a consoling address to Judah as *threshed and winnowed one* that assures that Babylon's days of oppressing are over.

ORACLE CONCERNING DUMAH: 21:11-12

11 The oracle concerning Dumah.
   One is calling to me from Seir,
      "Watchman, what of the night?
      Watchman, what of the night?"
12 The watchman says:

> "Morning comes, and also the night.
> If you will inquire, inquire;
> come back again."

These two verses have a certain poignant, haunting beauty to them, but they are also among the most obscure in the Bible. The message conveyed by the brief dialogue they contain is perhaps not too difficult. If the exchange between questioner and watchman were simply what the words express, it would hardly have been included here. If the *watchman* is, rather, a prophet (see above on v 6, though a different Hebrew word is employed there), the *night* would also be a veiled reference to something else, probably a period of trial and oppression. The response might then indicate that relief is in sight, that the relief would be only temporary, but that this is no final response; thus the door is left open to hope.

The difficulty comes with relating this message to any particular historical situation. The only geographical reference in the oracle itself is to *Seir*, i.e., the mountainous region east of the Arabah (the continuation of the Jordan rift south of the Dead Sea — see Map 1), which largely coincided with Edomite territory; Seir is often used as a metonym for Edom. The inscription relates the oracle to *Dumah*, and probably an oasis in Arabia is intended (see Gen 25:14, where Dumah is listed among the sons of Ishmael, and Map 2). The import would be that the request for a preview of the future comes from Arabia, that the call is directed from the edge of the desert (Seir) to the prophet, who is presumably Judean and in Jerusalem. The language of the piece suggests that it is considerably later than Isaiah, but this helps little in determining the historical situation. If it is intended to be related to the previous oracle, we might think of an occasion late in the period of Babylonian domination; some have thought specifically of the moment when Nabonidus, the last Babylonian king, terminated a long stay in Arabia to return to Babylon (545). But it is also possible that the inscription is only the editor's attempt to relate the oracle to what follows.

ORACLE CONCERNING ARABIA: 21:13-15

13 The oracle concerning Arabia.
   In the thickets in Arabia you will lodge,
      O caravans of Dedanites.
14 To the thirsty bring water,
      meet the fugitive with bread,
      O inhabitants of the land of Tema.
15 For they have fled from the swords,
      from the drawn sword,
   from the bent bow,
      and from the press of battle.

The introductory words are a problem in this oracle, too, in that they are missing in the Septuagint and the Hebrew does not have the normal spelling for Arabia. However, in this case the references in the oracle itself, to Dedan and Tema, both oases in Arabia (see Map 2), remove the doubt. The verses indicate that an attack has been made upon caravans of the Dedanites and that continued danger counsels spending the night in the desert in spite of the hardships of the journey; the people of Tema are urged, in sympathetic terms, to go out to them to provide them with supplies. There is no way of knowing with any security who the attackers were or when the action is to be dated. Arabs were among those subjected by the Assyrians (and later by the Babylonians) and at times they were in revolt against the overlords. Along with Judah and others they revolted at Sennacherib's death, and some think Sargon II's retaliation gives the background for this piece. The context (i.e., chap. 21, with its reference to the fall of Babylon) might better favor the attack made by the last Babylonian king, Nabonidus, in 555.

THE END OF KEDAR'S GLORY: 21:16-17

16 For thus the Lord said to me, "Within a year, according to the years of a hireling, all the glory of Kedar will come to an end; 17 and the remainder of the archers of the mighty men of the sons of Kedar will be few, for the LORD, the God of Israel, has spoken."

This short passage is unlike the preceding ones in being in prose and having no *massa'* ("oracle") introduction. Kedar (see Map 2) was famous for its wealth in flocks (see 60:7; Jer 49:28-29; Ezek 27:21) and for its caravan trade. The men of Kedar are seen as a hostile, warlike lot in Ps 120:5-7, and the present piece regards them as worthy of Yahweh's destructive and imminent judgment. These verses are probably inserted here because of the previous ones, which also deal with Arab groups (and cf. Gen 25:13-14, which links Kedar with Dumah and Tema). On *hireling* used with a measure of time, see above on 16:14.

ORACLE AGAINST AN UNREPENTANT JERUSALEM: 22:1-14

22 The oracle concerning the valley of vision.
　　What do you mean that you have gone up,
　　　　all of you, to the housetops,
　2　you who are full of shoutings,
　　　　tumultuous city, exultant town?
　　Your slain are not slain with the sword
　　　　or dead in battle.
　3　All your rulers have fled together,
　　　　without the bow they were captured.
　　All of you who were found were captured,
　　　　though they had fled far away.
　4　Therefore I said:
　　"Look away from me,
　　　　let me weep bitter tears;
　　do not labor to comfort me
　　　　for the destruction of the daughter
　　　　　　of my people."

　5　For the Lord GOD of hosts has a day
　　　　of tumult and trampling and confusion
　　　　in the valley of vision,
　　a battering down of walls
　　　　and a shouting to the mountains.
　6　And Elam bore the quiver
　　　　with chariots and horsemen,

and Kir uncovered the shield.

⁷ Your choicest valleys were full of chariots,
    and the horsemen took their stand at the gates.

⁸ He has taken away the covering of Judah.

In that day you looked to the weapons of the House of
the Forest, ⁹and you saw that the breaches of the city of
David were many, and you collected the waters of the
lower pool, ¹⁰and you counted the houses of Jerusalem,
and you broke down the houses to fortify the wall. ¹¹You
made a reservoir between the two walls for the water of
the old pool. But you did not look to him who did it, or
have regard for him who planned it long ago.

¹² In that day the Lord GOD of hosts
        called to weeping and mourning,
        to baldness and girding with sackcloth;

¹³ and behold, joy and gladness,
        slaying oxen and killing sheep,
        eating flesh and drinking wine.
    "Let us eat and drink,
        for tomorrow we die."

¹⁴ The LORD of hosts has revealed himself in my ears:
    "Surely this iniquity will not be forgiven you
        till you die," says the Lord God of hosts.

This section may be classified form critically as an
announcement of doom (though by some as invective-
threat) in which the first thirteen verses form a reproach and
the last pronounces the judgment. The title, "oracle concerning the valley of vision," is taken from v 5; like the other
massa' titles in chaps. 13-23 it has been supplied by an
editor, though why the piece, which relates strictly to Jerusalem, is placed in the collection of oracles against the
nations is unclear. The passage is a very important one,
though it abounds with unsolved difficulties. There is general agreement that in substance it comes from Isaiah and
most agree that it relates to the events of 701, the lifting of
Sennacherib's siege of Jerusalem. The details of the preparation for the siege given in vv 8b-11 are claimed by some to

be a later addition (precisely a description from the time of
the final assault on Jerusalem by Nebuchadnezzar in 588),
but there is no solid basis for this. The same is to be said of
the position of those who hold that vv 5-8a are a later
addition.

The death of Sargon II in 705 tempted Hezekiah, in
concert with a number of other Assyrian vassals, to revolt
against his successor Sennacherib. Just as Isaiah had
opposed submission to Assyria in the first place (see above
on chaps. 7-8) and just as he had opposed rebellion in 714
(see above on chap. 20), so on this occasion did he most
bitterly oppose Hezekiah's decision to revolt in 705 (for
further details, see below on chaps. 28-31). Sennacherib's
invasion, intended to punish the rebels and bring them to
heel, devastated the lands, destroyed forty-six fortified cities, and left many dead; Hezekiah had to pay a heavy
indemnity from the Temple treasury (2 Kgs 18:13-16) and
was stripped of much of his territory. (On the report of a
miraculous delivery of Jerusalem on this occasion, see
below on chaps. 36-37.)

The inhabitants of Jerusalem apparently took the lifting
of the siege as an occasion for great rejoicing, and this is
what is described in vv 1-2a, 13. Isaiah condemns this
revelry, in part because the people treat the departure of the
Assyrian army as though it were a victory, whereas in fact
they should have been lamenting the numbers who had died
and should have been grieving for the terrible devastation
inflicted on the land. It would have been bad enough had
they acquitted themselves with bravery, but this seems not
to have been the case (vv 2b-3; Assyrian records speak of
desertions among Hezekiah's soldiers). A further reason for
Isaiah's bitter complaint is that the disaster should have led
them to reflect on the blindness of the policy which led them
to such unhappy consequences, but the wild rejoicing shows
this did not happen. How far they are from true repentance
is betrayed by the words attributed to them in v 13. The
saying does not mean that they expect to die on the morrow;
rather, it says that they may as well live for the day since they
don't know what the morrow will bring and the inevitability

of death counsels enjoyment now (cf. the sentiments expressed by the wicked in Wis 2:1-8 and the words of Siduri addressed to Gilgamesh, *ANET* 90). But to repent and reflect over the evils of today is a preparation for a better tomorrow, and since they will not do this, Isaiah picks up the reference to death to say their sin will not be forgiven until death.

Verses 5-8a contain problems and no little obscurity. "Valley of vision" is not a place name; if Isaiah is referring to a specific place, it would probably be the Hinnom Valley, which flanked Jerusalem on the west, as being the place described in this prophetic vision. The prefixing of the reference to Yahweh's "day" to the description of the violence which had come upon them (v 5, picked up again in v 12) amounts to a quasi-identification of the assault with the "day of the Lord" (2:12-21; Amos 5:18-20).

The reference to Elam and Kir in v 6, the only identification given of the invaders, is a rather strange way of describing an Assyrian attack, and this is one of the arguments given for denying vv 5-7 to Isaiah. The problem is particularly acute in that Elam was an ally of the Babylonians in their struggle to throw off the Assyrian yoke in the late eighth century. However, neither of these problems is helped much by taking these verses, as some do, to refer to the final Babylonian assault on Jerusalem in 588. Assuming that Isaiah was speaking shortly after an event that was on everyone's lips, there would have been no need to name Assyria; and Elamites could well have been included in their auxiliary troops, for it was not unusual for combat units to be formed from prisoners of war or mercenaries of conquered peoples (as David did from the Philistines). Little is known of Kir, whose precise location in Mesopotamia is unknown, for it is referred to elsewhere in the Old Testament only as the place to which the Syrians were exiled (2 Kgs 16:9; Amos 1:5) and as their legendary homeland (Amos 9:7).

The reproach contained in vv 8b-11, namely, that the inhabitants of Jerusalem, while taking all possible pains to strengthen the city's defenses, did not look to Yahweh, in

whose hand lay Jerusalem's origins, and from whose hand
would come her present and future, accords very well with
Isaiah's teaching. His conviction was that Judah's deliverance lay in seeking to discern Yahweh's purpose and conforming their plans to it; any other course was folly and led
inevitably to disaster. Now they had reaped the bitter fruit
of their folly but, celebrating their escape from total destruction as victory rather than defeat, they failed to draw any
lesson for the future or to heed Yahweh's call for repentance
for the past (v 12). Therefore Isaiah saw no hope of forgiveness for the future (v 14).

CONCERNING SHEBNA AND ELIAKIM: 22:15-25

15   Thus says the Lord GOD of hosts, "Come, go to this
steward, to Shebna, who is over the household, and say to
him: 16What have you to do here and whom have you
here, that you have hewn here a tomb for yourself, you
who hew a tomb on the height, and carve a habitation for
yourself in the rock? 17Behold, the Lord will hurl you
away violently, O you strong man. He will seize firm hold
on you, 18and whirl you round and round, and throw you
like a ball into a wide land; there you shall die, and there
shall be your splendid chariots, you shame of your master's house. 19I will thrust you from your office, and you
will be cast down from your station. 20In that day I will
call my servant Eliakim the son of Hilkiah, 21and I will
clothe him with your robe, and will bind your girdle on
him, and will commit your authority to his hand; and he
shall be a father to the inhabitants of Jerusalem and to the
house of Judah. 22And I will place on his shoulder the key
of the house of David; he shall open, and none shall shut;
and he shall shut, and none shall open. 23And I will fasten
him like a peg in a sure place, and he will become a throne
of honor to his father's house. 24And they will hang on
him the whole weight of his father's house, the offspring
and issue, every small vessel, from the cups to all the
flagons. 25In that day, says the LORD of hosts, the peg
that was fastened in a sure place will give way; and it will

be cut down and fall, and the burden that was upon it will
be cut off, for the LORD has spoken."

At first glance this seems a relatively simple passage in
which Isaiah tells of the deposition of one official, Shebna
(vv 15-19), his replacement by another man, Hilkiah (vv
20-23), and the later deposition of Hilkiah (vv 24-25). The
two men in question are known to us from other passages (2
Kgs 18:18, 26, 37; Isa 36:3, 22; 37:2), in which Hilkiah does
indeed hold the office of *over the household* (or, less literally
but more correctly, "master of the palace"), that from which
Shebna is said to be deposed in our present passage.

However, there are complications. The first verse of this
passage (v 15) originally began with the words of introduction "Against Shebna, the master of the palace" *(RSV:* "he
who is over the household"); then followed the command of
the Lord, *Come, go to this steward and say to him.* Thus the
identification of the *steward* against whom this oracle was
directed with Shebna rests solely on introductory words
supplied by a later hand, though they may well be correct.
The term "steward" (Heb.: *soken*) is not elsewhere used of
an official in the Old Testament (though its cognate is found
in other Semitic languages); conceivably it is used here
loosely as an equivalent for "master of the palace" (Heb.:
'al-habbayit), the "major-domo," who was the highest of the
king's officials. In the passages listed above, Shebna is
named as "secretary" *(sopher)*, another very high office,
equivalent to our Secretary of State; thus although in these
texts Eliakim does appear as "master of the palace" and
although Shebna holds the second place, subordinate to
Eliakim, Shebna is far from having fallen from grace.

The reason for the very strong words against Shebna (or
the unnamed official later identified as Shebna) is not clear.
Ostentation and pretentiousness, seen in the carving out of a
fine tomb for himself and in his ceremonial chariots (vv 16,
18), are part of it, but Isaiah also reproaches him as *shame of
your master's house,* which would point to something more
serious. It has therefore been suggested (especially in view of
the context, following the "valley of vision" piece of vv 1-14)
that he, as a royal official, was foremost among those urging

on Hezekiah the disastrous policy of revolt against Assyria. This is possible and would make the threat of exile (v 18) appropriate, but no certainty is possible.

It is often asserted that vv 20-23, which speak of Eliakim's elevation, are from another, later, hand, and that v 19 was provided as a transition piece. One does not expect the threat of deposition after the threat of exile, it is true. On the other hand, the arguments for this view are not wholly convincing; for example, there is no evidence that Shebna was in fact either exiled or disgraced, so one questions the invention of a prophecy foretelling an event that had not taken place (*HI*, 300). Moreover, the words of vv 20-23 are not addressed to Eliakim but to someone whose place he is taking. The things said of Eliakim's office are instructive and are intended to associate him closely with the royal house and with royal functions. The term *father* (v 21) refers to the kindly care he will exercise (cf. Gen 45:8; Job 29:16; in Judg 5:7 Deborah is "a mother in Israel"; and in Isa 9:6 the messianic king will be "Everlasting Father"). The handing over of *the key of the house of David* (which may represent the actual ceremony of investiture of office) is a way of giving, both symbolically and in practice, full control over the royal family and the palace. (This passage helps to explain "the power of the keys" given to Peter in Matt 16:18-19.) *RSV*'s *throne* (v 23) is a legitimate translation of the Hebrew *kisse'*, but the word can mean "seat," in a more general sense, and that would be preferable here (cf. *NAB*'s "place of honor"). Verses 24-25 are undoubtedly from a later time, when Eliakim's line had fallen into disfavor and had been removed from this post.

ORACLE CONCERNING TYRE: 23:1-18

23 The oracle concerning Tyre.
> Wail, O ships of Tarshish,
>> for Tyre is laid waste, without house or haven!
> From the land of Cyprus
>> it is revealed to them.
> 2 Be still, O inhabitants of the coast,

O merchants of Sidon;
   your messengers passed over the sea,
3   and were on many waters;
   your revenue was the grain of Shihor,
     the harvest of the Nile;
     you were the merchant of the nations.

4 Be ashamed, O Sidon, for the sea has spoken,
     the stronghold of the sea, saying:
   "I have neither travailed nor given birth,
     I have neither reared young men
     nor brought up virgins."

5 When the report comes to Egypt,
     they will be in anguish over the report about Tyre.

6 Pass over to Tarshish,
     wail, O inhabitants of the coast!

7 Is this your exultant city
     whose origin is from days of old,
   whose feet carried her
     to settle afar?

8 Who has purposed this
     against Tyre, the bestower of crowns,
   whose merchants were princes,
     whose traders were the honored of the earth?

9 The LORD of hosts has purposed it,
     to defile the pride of all glory,
     to dishonor all the honored of the earth.

10 Overflow your land like the Nile,
     O daughter of Tarshish;
     there is no restraint any more.

11 He has stretched out his hand over the sea,
     he has shaken the kingdoms;
   the LORD has given command concerning Canaan
     to destroy its strongholds.

12 And he said:
   "You will no more exult,
     O oppressed virgin daughter of Sidon;
   arise, pass over to Cyprus,
     even there you will have no rest."

¹³   Behold the land of the Chaldeans! This is the people; it
was not Assyria. They destined Tyre for wild beasts. They
erected their siege towers, they razed her palaces, they
made her a ruin.

¹⁴ Wail, O ships of Tarshish,
      for your stronghold is laid waste.

¹⁵ In that day Tyre will be forgotten for seventy years, like
the days of one king. At the end of seventy years, it will
happen to Tyre as in the song of the harlot:

¹⁶ "Take a harp,
        go about the city,
        O forgotten harlot!
    Make sweet melody,
        sing many songs,
        that you may be remembered."

¹⁷ At the end of seventy years, the LORD will visit Tyre, and
she will return to her hire, and will play the harlot with all
the kingdoms of the world upon the face of the earth.
¹⁸Her merchandise and her hire will be dedicated to the
LORD; it will not be stored or hoarded, but her merchandise will supply abundant food and fine clothing for those
who dwell before the LORD.

This is the last of the oracles against foreign nations and it
presents more than its share of difficulties. A literary *inclusio* is formed by the repetition of the *Wail,. . . laid waste* of v
1 in v 14, which gives evidence that this much of the poem
was originally one piece, whatever later interpolations there
may have been or however much the Hebrew may have
suffered in transmission. In fact, vv 5 and 13 (the latter in
prose) are frequently taken as later glosses. Verses 15-18 are
built up of probably three separate additions to the original
oracle.

The title (v 1a) relates this piece to Tyre, no doubt correctly, but vv 2, 4, and 12 refer to Sidon, and this has led to a
confusing variety of theories. The hypotheses set forward
pretty well cover the range of possibilities: the poem was
originally composed for the destruction of Sidon and later
adapted to apply to Tyre or vice versa; or it was originally

intended to refer to both cities and to Phoenicia in general (see Map 2). Although no certainty is possible, the best position seems to be to accept the editor's designation of Tyre as the concern of the oracle (note also the understanding of the later additions in vv 15-18) and to understand *Sidon* to be a general designation for Phoenicia, a function also to be attributed to *Canaan* in v 11.

The historical background of the piece has been found in various periods, from the Assyrian (Sennacherib's attack on Phoenicia during the revolt of 705-701) to the Persian (Artaxerxes III in 343) down to the Greek (Alexander the Great's attack on Tyre in 332). Most probably the attack in question was that of the Assyrian king Esarhaddon (680-669) on Tyre in 671 in response to Tyre's entering into league with Egypt under Tirhakah in an attempt to shake off Assyria's oppressive rule. This attack followed an earlier one on Sidon (679) and in each case Assyrian records boast of their conquest.

Tyre and Sidon were both prosperous seaports along the Phoenician coast; their favorable locations made it possible for them to acquire great wealth by means of the commerce that flowed through them. They had fleets of ships that sailed to distant points, and they founded settlements that helped maintain their influence far from home. The alphabet they used and disseminated was the ancestor of the Greek alphabet and also of ours. David entered into covenant with Hiram, king of Tyre, and Solomon obtained Lebanon cedars from him for his building projects (2 Sam 5:11-12; 1 Kgs 5:1-11). Omri, king of Israel, married his son Ahaz to Jezebel, a Phoenician princess, whose name became the very epitome of wickedness.

While the poem is not Isaian in authorship, it does have power and beauty. In grand, somewhat emotional style, various entities are addressed, some by way of personification: *ships of Tarshish, inhabitants* and *merchants, Sidon, daughter of Tarshish, daughter of Sidon*. In all cases they are told to weep and mourn for the catastrophe which has overtaken them; this seems to consist less in the destruction of the city than in the loss of trade and prosperity this occasions, though the inhabitants are advised to betake themselves to Tarshish (v 6) or Cyprus (v 12), apparently to avoid the danger of more to come.

The term *Tarshish* (vv 2, 6, 10) is most properly applied to ships (1 Kgs 10:22) to designate them as large sea-going vessels; the term itself probably means "refinery" and the designation "*tarshish* ships" would have been coined by the Phoenicians themselves for ships which carried the products of their overseas mining and refining operations (in Cyprus and Sardinia). But in vv 6 and 10 (perhaps also in v 1), the poet may be simply associating the term "Tarshish" with the place of origin of the ships; in this case the reference would probably be to Tartessos, on the coast of Spain. That there is an address to *daughter of Tarshish* in v 10 is uncertain, for the Hebrew is corrupt; the real sense of the verse seems to be that since the harbor (of Tyre) is no more, the inhabitants are being told to cultivate the land or to flee or to return to their own land. The reference to the Nile is missing in the Septuagint and does not belong.

The poem, difficult as it is, is not without its religious value. The author takes his starting point from an actual historical event (or events), and though neither Israel nor Judah appear to be involved even remotely, Yahweh, the Lord of history and of all the earth, is seen to be at work here (vv 8-9). The only sin referred to is that of pride (v 9), but that is sufficient. The willingness to put trust in human power, riches, and glory is a way of exalting man above God and calls for Yahweh's response (cf. 2:6-21). When man-made works are swept away, even such things as magnificent as the harbors at Tyre and Sidon, those who trusted in them learn how fragile are all human strivings, and that is a message which runs throughout the whole piece.

Verses 15-18 are a later addition that somewhat softens the blow to Tyre by holding out hope that she can flourish again — if "flourish" can apply to a tired old harlot who manages to return to business. It would appear that the starting point for these verses was vv 15b-16 (beginning with *it will happen*), which, by way of a taunt, applied to Tyre a ditty composed for other circumstances. To this is added the more gentle words (vv 15a, 17) that speak of Tyre's restoration after seventy years; after Jeremiah's prophecy (Jer 29:10; cf. Dan 9:2; Zech 1:12) this may have been considered the appropriate period for an expected restoration. Hostility against Tyre continues to be expressed here for her commerce is considered harlotry, but v 18 would seem to come from someone of a broader spirit, who sees Tyre's profit dedicated to Yahweh and to his ministers. Thus, on a fitting, somewhat universalistic note, these oracles against foreign nations come to a close.

THE APOCALYPSE OF ISAIAH: CHAPTERS 24-27

Although it has become traditional to call these chapters "The Apocalypse of Isaiah," the term is rather misleading on two counts: this section is not by Isaiah and only in a somewhat qualified sense can it be considered an apocalypse. The latter point is a matter difficult to discuss because the term "apocalyptic" is a subject of no little debate (see the discussion in the Excursus of *OTM*, Vol. 15). This section does contain some apocalyptic features. One may mention in particular such items as universal destruction (24:1-3, 5-6: 26:21), cosmic upheaval (24:4, 18b-20, 23a), and the end of death (25:8). In more general terms one may point to the pattern of judgment on sinful nations (24:1-13; 25:2; 26:5, 21; 27:7-11), deliverance for God's people (sometimes symbolized by Jerusalem — 25:8-11; 26:1-6; 27:2-5, 12-13), victory for Yahweh (24:23b; 25:1-5; 27:1), and indications of unending bliss (25:8). But many other standard features of apocalyptic are missing. For example, the work is not pseudonymous; its insertion into the Isaiah collection may have misled many into thinking it was by Isaiah, but these chapters contain no assertions concerning authorship or origin. We find no clear succession of world empires, no bizarre visions, no angel interpreter, no speculation concerning the end-time. There are eschatological concerns, but these are not expressed in characteristically apocalyptic fashion.

Virtually all agree that these chapters do not form a unified composition; among other indications is the alternation of lyric sections with what, for lack of a better term, can be called eschatological prophecies. This has led some to postulate an original stratum of such prophecy (consisting, e.g., of 24:1-3, 13, 17-23; 25:6-8; 27:1, 12-13) into which have been inserted lyric compositions (hymns, prayers) from another hand, the whole being later expanded with other additions. H. Wildberger, in his very thorough commentary, has proposed a basic groundwork consisting of 24:1-6 (expanded by vv 7-9, 10-12, and 13); 24:14-20; and 26:7-21, to which has been added eschatological passages (24:21-23; 25:6-8, 9-10a, 10b-11, 12), the songs concerning the city (see below — 25:1-5; 26:1-6), and various eschatological additions (27:1, 2-5, 6-11, 12, 13).

The dating of the section is also problematic, especially since it reached its present form by stages and contains no clearly identifiable historical allusions. There are several references to an unnamed city, apparently a wicked one, which has been destroyed (24:10, 12; 25:2; 26:5), and this has often been the starting point for attempts to date the whole. The reference has been taken to be the capture of Babylon by Cyrus in 539, by Xerxes I in 485, or by Alexander the Great in 332; to the overthrow of Dibon (because of the reference to Moab in 25:10), to the destruction of Samaria by John Hyrcanus near the end of the second century, etc. In all probability such attempts are mistaken, for the references to "the city" seem to be generic rather than specific, in the sense that "the city" does not represent a particular one but stands as the embodiment of all the nations and peoples hostile to God and his work; for this reason it is seen as the object of his judgment.

Since it is likely that the collection of prophetic books already formed a completed part of the canon by the time of the author of Sirach (see the "Foreword" to the translation of his book by his grandson, who states that "the Law, the Prophets, and the rest of the books" were assiduously studied by his grandfather), in the early second century, dates so low as some of those proposed seem to be excluded. Wildberger associates what he calls the "groundwork" with the Persian period (and see *HI*, 431-32) and relates it to the struggles and disappointments of the returned exiles and the Jewish community of the fifth century (see *OTM*, Vol. 13); the additions and reworkings referred to above come sometime later, but it is virtually impossible to assign a date to them.

This collection, in spite of the complicated nature of its growth, gives a unified conception of how God's work in history will finally reach its term, and therefore its position after the collection of oracles against the nations (chaps. 13-23) is neither haphazard nor purposeless. It provides a framework within which to understand those other oracles, which are seen now not simply as God's dealing with individual nations but as steps on the way to the final age. (*OTA*, 3, #215.)

UNIVERSAL JUDGMENT: 24:1-13

24 Behold, the LORD will lay waste the earth and make it
  desolate,
  and he will twist its surface and scatter its inhabitants.
² And it shall be, as with the people,
    so with the priest;
    as with the slave, so with his master;
    as with the maid, so with her mistress;
  as with the buyer, so with the seller;
    as with the lender, so with the borrower;
    as with the creditor, so with the debtor.
³ The earth shall be utterly laid waste and utterly despoiled;
  for the LORD has spoken this word.

⁴ The earth mourns and withers,
  the world languishes and withers;
  the heavens languish together with the earth.
⁵ The earth lies polluted
  under its inhabitants;

for they have transgressed the laws,
　　violated the statutes,
　　broken the everlasting covenant.
6 Therefore a curse devours the earth,
　　and its inhabitants suffer for their guilt;
　therefore the inhabitants of the earth are scorched,
　　and few men are left.
7 The wine mourns,
　　the vine languishes,
　　all the merry-hearted sigh.
8 The mirth of the timbrels is stilled,
　　the noise of the jubilant has ceased,
　　the mirth of the lyre is stilled.
9 No more do they drink wine with singing;
　　strong drink is bitter to those who drink it.
10 The city of chaos is broken down,
　　every house is shut up so that none can enter.
11 There is an outcry in the streets for lack of wine;
　　all joy has reached its eventide;
　　the gladness of the earth is banished.
12 Desolation is left in the city,
　　the gates are battered into ruins.
13 For thus it shall be in the midst of the earth
　　among the nations,
　as when an olive tree is beaten,
　　as at the gleaning when the vintage is done.

Although vv 1-6 are often taken as an original unity, there
is a division of sorts after v 3, seen not only in the pharase *for
the Lord has spoken his word*, but also in the *inclusio*
contained in the repetition of *lay waste* (vv 1 and 3). However, the destruction described in vv 1-3 requires an explanation, and this is provided in vv 4-6. The manner of the
destruction to come is not made clear; the description may
perhaps suggest an earthquake, but it is rather vague. It is
the Lord who acts, and he is not restricted to the categories
known from past experience of nature. In great detail the
author lists the classes of society which will be struck. Many

categories are in fact listed, but the completeness comes not in naming all (it would be possible to produce a much longer list) but in the listing of pairs of opposites (*slave-master, buyer-seller*, etc.), by which is intended all that lies between the two extremes (much as heaven and Sheol in 7:11 or sitting and rising in Ps 139:2). Thus no one will stand outside the Lord's new act.

Destruction is spoken of in vv 1-3; in vv 4-6 it becomes explicit that this is a judgment, and the sins that have merited this punishment are rehearsed. Basically this is a forsaking of *the everlasting covenant*, by which may be meant the covenant with Noah (see Gen 9:16), both because of the terminology and because it (like the present judgment) was understood to extend to all mankind. But the reference to *laws* and *statutes*, if they are original and not a gloss, would point to the Mosaic covenant. Biblical authors easily think of the earth itself being afflicted by the sins of those who dwell on it (cf. Hos 4:3).

The picture already painted is now completed with two vignettes and a summary. In vv 7-9 is depicted the loss of mirth and joy; special reference is made to wine, and we are reminded of what is said of Moab in 16:8-10 (and see Sir 32:4-5 on the joys of wine with music). In vv 10-12 occurs the first of several references to *the city*, here (only) designated as *city of chaos*. As has already been suggested (see above, p. 6.133), we are probably not to understand a particular city but to see here the embodiment of the world inimical to God and subject to his judgment. Although Jeremiah depicted judgment as a return to the primal chaos (Jer 4:23; cf. Gen 1:2), the Hebrew *tohu* basically means "barren, deserted," and no more than that may be intended here. Again there is a reference to distress for *lack of wine* and joy, which suggests a shallow, empty, worldly spirit on the part of those who have more serious things to be concerned about. The city whose *gates are battered into ruins* (v 12) is left a prey of every enemy. Verse 13 utilizes the imagery of 17:6 (there applied to Israel, the northern kingdom); given that background, it may allude to a remnant (see also v 6).

SONG OF PRAISE FOR YAHWEH'S JUDGMENT: 24:14-20

¹⁴ They lift up their voices, they sing for joy;
over the majesty of the LORD they shout from the west.
¹⁵ Therefore in the east give glory to the LORD;
in the coastlands of the sea, to the name of the LORD,
the God of Israel.
¹⁶ From the ends of the earth we hear songs of praise,
of glory to the Righteous One.
But I say, "I pine away,
I pine away. Woe is me!
For the treacherous deal treacherously,
the treacherous deal very treacherously."

¹⁷ Terror, and the pit, and the snare
are upon you, O inhabitant of the earth!
¹⁸ He who flees at the sound of the terror
shall fall into the pit;
and he who climbs out of the pit
shall be caught in the snare.
For the windows of heaven are opened,
and the foundations of the earth tremble.
¹⁹ The earth is utterly broken,
the earth is rent asunder,
the earth is violently shaken.
²⁰ The earth staggers like a drunken man,
it sways like a hut;
its transgression lies heavy upon it,
and it falls, and will not rise again.

Here we encounter the first of the lyric sections referred to above (p. 191). Whatever its origin, its present meaning relates to the context in which it has been placed, though it relates more closely to vv 1-6 than to vv 7-13. Thus the praise rendered to Yahweh is for the judgment which he is to enact upon the earth and for the righteousness he manifests in so doing. Who it is that renders this praise is not stated; *they* clearly are not the inhabitants of "the city." No doubt they are those who come safely through the judgment (and therefore could be called "the saved"), but there is nothing to indicate they are a miserable few (as in vv 6, 13). It is not unreasonable to suppose that these "saved" are Israel or the faithful remnant thereof, but the text itself does not indicate this and the author may have had a far more universalistic vision. The geographical ambit far exceeds that of Israel, for although vv 14-15 are much more obscure than *RSV*'s *west ...east* would indicate, v 16 does speak of *the ends of the earth*, and there is no clear reason for restricting this to Israel's Diaspora. The Old Testament not infrequently speaks of the nations praising the God of Israel (e.g., Ps 117:1), and Psalm 98 does this in the context of a description of his judgment on all the earth.

After the hymn of praise there is an abrupt return to the judgment scene, emphasis being placed upon the impossibility of escape from it (for the guilty) and its fearfulness. The first-person speaker of v 16b (*and I said...*) is identified in v 17 as *inhabitant of the earth*, the object of God's judgment, and we are reminded that in the Book of Revelation it is against "those who dwell upon the earth" that God's plagues are directed (3:10; 6:10; 8:13, etc.). The trio of terror, pit, and snare are found also in Jer 48:43-44 in much the same sense, i.e., fleeing from one means capture by the next, except that here it is applied universally, whereas in the Jeremiah text the reference was to Moab. We are reminded also that Amos' description of the "day of the Lord" saw the hapless one fleeing from one danger only to fall into another (Amos 5:18-20). The cataclysm is described in horrendous terms involving elements both of flood and of earthquake. The opening of the windows of heaven alludes not only to P's account of the great flood (see Gen 7:11; 8:2) but also to the cosmology behind it. In Gen 1:6-7 God separated the waters above from the waters below, thus marking off from the primal chaos what he was to organize into earth and sea and sky; to allow the waters above to pour in again is a way of returning all to the original chaos. The author is invoking images to convey something of the cosmic nature of the calamity; so also the earthquake imagery which follows points to something beyond a merely natural disaster (see above on vv 1-3).

YAHWEH OVER THE POWERS OF HEAVEN AND EARTH: 24:21-23

21 On that day the LORD will punish
the host of heaven, in heaven,
and the kings of the earth, on the earth.
22 They will be gathered together
as prisoners in a pit;
they will be shut up in a prison,
and after many days they will be punished.
23 Then the moon will be confounded,
and the sun ashamed;
for the LORD of hosts will reign
on Mount Zion and in Jerusalem
and before his elders he will manifest his glory.

The cosmic and eschatological nature of the coming event is dramatically emphasized in this piece, which, in spite of its brevity, ranges from heaven to earth, from the imprisonment of the wicked to Yahweh's enthronement, from the punishment of his enemies to glorification of his friends. *On that day* refers, in this instance, to "the day of the Lord." The expression *host of heaven* most frequently refers to the stars, usually simply as God's creatures (Neh 9:6; Ps 33:6; Isa 40:26; 45:12), but in this sense they would not be the object of God's judgment. Sometimes the stars are the object of superstitious pagan worship (Deut 4:19; Jer 19:13; Zeph 1:5); conceivably the term was already being applied to angelic beings (cf. Dan 8:10), including those in revolt against God (see above on the mythological background of 14:12-20 and cf. the development of the Gen 6:1-4 story in the Enochic literature). Something like that may lie behind the present text; the parallel between *host of heaven* and *kings of the earth* suggests that they each are rulers in their sphere of activity. No great slaughter is here described, but rather imprisonment until the time of punishment; *after many days* suggests an intermediate period.

The *glory* of Yahweh which will now be manifested (v 23) will be so great that even the light of the sun and moon will seem pale by comparison. This term "glory" (Heb. *kabod*) often describes a visible, overwhelming splendor, as at the theophany on Mt. Sinai (Exod 24:17) or the dedication of the Temple, where its presence made the ministry of the priests impossible (1 Kgs 8:10-11). The enthronement of Yahweh on Mt. Zion may be said to be the final goal of his judgment, which is therefore seen to be ultimately positive. This positive aspect is seen also in the presence of the elders (of Israel, no doubt) before him. The elders were those responsible for order and rule in Israel in the days before the monarchy. But this passage is strongly reminiscent of Exod 24:1-2, 9-11, where seventy elders, along with Moses and others, see God on Mt. Sinai. Many think that 25:6-8, with its reference to a feast, continues the present passage and was separated from it by the insertion of the hymn of 25:1-5.

HYMN ON THE FALL OF THE CITY AND ITS EFFECTS: 25:1-5

25 O LORD, thou art my God;
    I will exalt thee, I will praise thy name;
  for thou hast done wonderful things,
    plans formed of old, faithful and sure.
² For thou hast made the city a heap,
    the fortified city a ruin;
  the palace of aliens is a city no more,
    it will never be rebuilt.
³ Therefore strong peoples will glorify thee;
    cities of ruthless nations will fear thee.
⁴ For thou hast been a stronghold to the poor,
    a stronghold to the needy in his distress,
    a shelter from the storm and a shade from the heat;
  for the blast of the ruthless is like a storm against a wall,
⁵   like heat in a dry place.
  Thou dost subdue the noise of aliens;
    as heat by the shade of a cloud,
    so the song of the ruthless is stilled.

This poem manifests many features of psalms of praise and thanksgiving, but both in form and content it is unique and must have been composed for its present context by an author thoroughly steeped in the language of the psalms. The reference to the *wonderful* aspect of what God has planned also betrays echoes of Isa 9:6; 28:29; and 29:14. What God is about to do regarding *the city* is something he has planned from of old. The completeness and permanence of its destruction are insisted upon (*heap, ruin, a city no more, never be rebuilt*). While the author began by praising God for what he had planned, once it has come to pass it will provide occasion for the conversion to Yahweh of *peoples* (the Hebrew has the singular) and *nations* (v 3). This is because in bringing the city to its well-deserved end Yahweh manifests both his power and his justice; the peoples recognize this and thus glorify and reverence him. In this universalistic sentiment the author echoes the thought, and sometimes the diction, of a number of Old Testament passages (Ps 47:7-9; 67:2-7; 96:7-10, 13; 99:1-3; 102:15, 21-22; Isa 2:2-4; Jer 3:17; Zeph 3:9-10; Zech 2:10-11; 8:20-22). In his judgment on the city God also shows himself the protector of the weak and poor, who suffer from the oppressive power of the city. In spite of the general nature of the terms *poor* and *needy*, the author probably had in mind the oppressed remnant of Israel, who are here said to find protection in Yahweh for every need (see below on 26:6, though the Hebrew terms do not coincide exactly). The piece contains an implicit contrast between *the fortified city*, now become *a ruin* and thereby proving to have offered but deceptive security, and Yahweh, who proves in fact to be *a stronghold to the needy in his distress*.

THE ESCHATOLOGICAL BANQUET: 25:6-8

6 On this mountain the LORD of hosts will make for all peoples a feast of fat things, a feast of wine on the lees, of fat things full of marrow, of wine on the lees well refined. 7And he will destroy on this mountain the covering that is cast over all peoples, the veil that is spread over all

nations. [8]He will swallow up death for ever, and the Lord GOD will wipe away tears from all faces, and the reproach of his people he will take away from all the earth; for the LORD has spoken.

As was suggested above, this passage is a continuation of the development which began in 24:21-23 but which was interrupted by the insertion of the song of 25:1-5. There is no doubt, then, that *this mountain* is Mt. Zion. Yet the introduction of 25:1-5 has also introduced a universalistic note which is here heightened by the description of the great feast that Yahweh will make *for all peoples*. The theme of the pilgrimage of the nations to Mt. Zion is found in a number of the passages cited above on vv 1-5 (especially that of Isa 2:2-4), but the table hospitality described here hardly has a parallel. To appreciate its full impact we should remember that, for the Semite, as for other peoples to a lesser degree, to extend table fellowship is a guarantee of friendship and peace. Thus something is said of the future relations among the nations (including Israel, which is certainly present), but also of their relationship to God. Consonant with this, God removes the ignorance (*covering, veil*) which has in the past kept the nations from knowing and obeying him. The eschatological nature of the scene is revealed in the reference to the end of death: if death comes to an end, there is no more "history as usual." Nothing here is said of the fate of those who have already died; i.e., there is no reference to resurrection. The image of God wiping tears away, much as a mother comforts a weeping child, is one of the most tender and consoling in all of Scripture; it is utilized again in Rev 21:4. If God wipes away the tears, there will be no future occasion for them.

A SONG OF THANKSGIVING: 25:9-12

[9] It will be said on that day, "Lo, this is our God; we have waited for him, that he might save us. This is the LORD; we have waited for him; let us be glad and rejoice in his salvation."

¹⁰ For the hand of the LORD will rest on this mountain, and Moab shall be trodden down in his place, as
straw is trodden down in a dung-pit. ¹¹And he will spread
out his hands in the midst of it as a swimmer spreads his
hands out to swim; but the LORD will lay low his pride
together with the skill of his hands. ¹²And the high fortifications of his walls he will bring down, lay low, and cast
to the ground, even to the dust.

This section was added to the preceding in at least two
stages (vv 9-10a, 10b-12), the first as beautiful as the second
is ugly.

The first part is a joyous proclamation that faith in Yahweh has not been misplaced: those who *have waited* for him
rejoice in the salvation he has brought (i.e., that which is
described in vv 6-8 and which inspired this addition). Faith
expressed as "waiting" is found in Isaiah (see above on 8:17)
and, in particular, in the psalms (see Ps 25:3, 5, 21; 27:14;
37:9, 34; 40:1, etc.), as well as elsewhere. If the object of hope
were always immediately present, there would be no test of
faith; those who "wait," even when all seems dark and the
Lord's power absent, are the ones who exercise faith, and it
is they who rejoice in its fulfillment. So also in the text from
Isaiah referred to (8:17), he and his circle were waiting for
the Lord who had "hidden his face from Israel." Our present
text shows its connection with the preceding verses not only
in the joy expressed, but also by the reference to *this mountain*, i.e., Mt. Zion.

To this beautiful piece, which continued the universalistic
spirit of vv 6-8, another author has added some lines aimed
at excluding Moab from the universal salvation depicted.
Near neighbors and relatives (see below on 34:5) are often
the object of greater antipathy than distant enemies. In Deut
23:3-6 it is said that the Moabites (and Ammonites) are to be
excluded from the Lord's assembly and that one was not to
seek their peace or prosperity; and this text of Deuteronomy
is specifically cited in Neh 13:1 as justification for the postexilic separatist measures. And we have encountered other

passages among the oracles against the nations that manifested particular dislike for Moab (see above on 15:9; 16:6-7, 12-14). Nevertheless, the present author has outdone these in his desire to see Moab trodden down in a dung-pit. The Hebrew text is in part disturbed and in certain particulars the meaning is unclear.

A HYMN OF JUDAH'S REDEEMED CONCERNING TWO CITIES: 26:1-6

26 In that day this song will be sung in the land of Judah:
   "We have a strong city;
      he sets up salvation
      as walls and bulwarks.
 2 Open the gates,
      that the righteous nation which keeps faith
      may enter in.
 3 Thou dost keep him in perfect peace,
      whose mind is stayed on three,
      because he trusts in thee.
 4 Trust in the LORD for ever,
      for the LORD God
      is an everlasting rock.
 5 For he has brought low
      the inhabitants of the height,
      the lofty city.
   He lays it low, lays it low to the ground,
      casts it to the dust.
 6 The foot tramples it,
      the feet of the poor,
      the steps of the needy."

The opening words, *in that day*, as in so many of its other occurrences in these chapters, indicates both the beginning of a new section and also that the action described is still in the future (even though as in v 5, the past tense is used). We have already encountered references to Mt. Zion (=Jerusalem) in these chapters, whether by name or not (24:23; 25:6,

10) and will do so again (27:13). Similarly, we have references to "the city (of chaos)," the embodiment of wicked resistance to God (24:10, 12; 25:2; see also below on 27:10, which may, however, refer to Samaria), but this is the only place in which they are found within the same compositional unit. The two cities are, in fact, brought into deliberate comparison and contrast, and in this respect we are reminded of the contrast between "the fortified city" and Yahweh himself in 25:1-5.

The *lofty city* of v 5 can be assumed to be strong and to have had walls and bulwarks, as is specifically said of the *strong city* in v 2. Yet the one is strong not so much because of fortifications but because it enjoys God's special protection (see the references to trust in God in vv 3-4); the other one, strong as it may be, is marked down for destruction because it stands for the worldly spirit hostile to God. That this city is *lofty* may suggest its strength (for a city to be built on a height—as was the case with Jerusalem itself—was already a certain measure of strength and security against attack), but it also occasions the contrast between its former state and its latter condition (*brought low*). As elsewhere in these chapters we meet reminiscences of the authentic oracles of Isaiah, in this case of the "day" which Yahweh will have against all that is proud, lofty, lifted up, and high (see 2:12, 17).

The contrast between the two cities is set within a context of concern for God's people. The introductory words present this piece as one which will *be sung in the land of Judah* (v 1), and vv 2-4 no doubt have returning Israelites in mind when it speaks of *the righteous nation* which will enter the strong city. There is a particular insistence on faith as each of these three verses speaks of it (and see above on 25:9). No doubt it is also the oppressed of Israel who trample down the lofty city; there is a reminiscence here of 25:4 (*poor* and *needy*, though the Hebrew vocabulary corresponds only in part).

Thus we have a "tale of two cities," of God's city and the city of the proud. Those who trust in God will enter the security of his city, while the proud will fall with the lofty city. (On requirements for entering God's gates, see Ps 15; 24:3-6, the so-called "entrance liturgies," to which this piece is sometimes compared.)

COMMUNAL SUPPLICATION FOR THE FINAL AGE: 26:7-21

7 The way of the righteous is level;
   thou dost make smooth the path of the righteous.
8 In the path of thy judgments,
   O LORD, we wait for thee;
   thy memorial name
   is the desire of our soul.
9 My soul yearns for thee in the night,
   my spirit within me earnestly seeks thee.
   For when thy judgments are in the earth,
   the inhabitants of the world learn righteousness.
10 If favor is shown to the wicked,
   he does not learn righteousness;
   in the land of uprightness he deals perversely
   and does not see the majesty of the LORD.
11 O LORD, thy hand is lifted up,
   but they see it not.
   Let them see thy zeal for thy people, and be ashamed.
   Let the fire for they adversaries consume them.
12 O LORD, thou wilt ordain peace for us,
   thou has wrought for us all our works.
13 O LORD our God,
   other lords besides thee have ruled over us,
   but thy name alone we acknowledge.
14 They are dead, they will not live;
   they are shades, they will not arise;
   to that end thou hast visited them with destruction
   and wiped out all remembrance of them.
15 But thou hast increased the nation, O LORD,
   thou hast increased the nation; thou art glorified;
   thou has enlarged all the borders of the land.

16 O LORD, in distress they sought thee,
    they poured out a prayer
    when thy chastening was upon them.
17 Like a woman with child,
    who writhes and cries out in her pangs,
    when she is near her time,
  so were we because of thee, O LORD;
18   we were with child, we writhed,
    we have as it were brought forth wind.
  We have wrought no deliverance in the earth,
    and the inhabitants of the world have not fallen.
19 Thy dead shall live, their bodies shall rise.
    O dwellers in the dust, awake and sing for joy!
  For thy dew is a dew of light,
    and on the land of the shades thou wilt let it fall.

20 Come, my people, enter your chambers,
    and shut your doors behind you;
    hide yourselves for a little while until the wrath is past.
21 For behold, the LORD is coming forth out of his place
    to punish the inhabitants of the earth for their iniquity,
  and the earth will disclose the blood shed upon her,
    and will no more cover her slain.

The composition that occupies the rest of chap. 26 displays many of the characteristic elements of the psalms of supplication (lament), including confidence of being heard (vv 7-9, 12-15) and complaint (vv 11, 16-18). However, whereas the typical psalm of supplication is a prayer for help and deliverance in a particular danger in which the individual or community finds itself, this composition relates to the particular distress and needs of those who face the last days.

The development of thought is not always easy to follow, but it helps to keep in mind that the author speaks for a community in distress, that God's help is looked for, that this help is not simply an *ad hoc* intervention but an eschatological deliverance that reaches to all creation.

In v 7 the speaker establishes an important premise of Israel's faith: God's ways of dealing with people are right;

the way of the righteous is level and *smooth*. And in accordance with this premise, the supplicants *wait for* the Lord (v 8; see above on 25:9). Although the diction makes one think of the speaker and his community as the faithful of Israel, the range of concern is not so narrow: all *the inhabitants of the world* are able to *learn righteousness* from the justice which is manifested in the Lord's own doings (v 9). This does not hold good for *the wicked*, however, who will not therefore share in the glory that is to dawn upon the righteous (v 10); from them, who now appear as the source of the suffering of the righteous, deliverance is asked through God's fiery judgment (v 11). This help from the Lord for the just is expected most vividly, for he is the source of all good (v 12). Hope is buoyed up by the contrast between the foreign rulers who have at times held sway over God's people but who are now dead, reduced to the weak state of the shades in Sheol (see above on 14:10-11, 15-17), and Yahweh, whom alone Israel has acknowledged as its ruler; and there is an additional contrast between these dead rulers and the living Israel, in whose expansion (here by anticipation) God will be glorified (vv 13-15).

After so vivid an expression of faith the speaker returns to the *distress* of the actual situation and to the supplication which it calls forth; of their own power they have been able to accomplish nothing (vv 16-18).

Verse 19 represents a great turning point after the lament which precedes it. This verse is often taken to refer to resurrection from the dead (and, by most who take it that way, as a much later interpolation), but it is more likely that the reference to the dead coming to life is a metaphor for the restoration of Israel; in terms of imagery it does not go beyond (if it even equals) that of Ezekiel's valley of dry bones (Ezek 37:1-14), which speaks in national rather than individual terms. We would have here a contrast between the adversaries who are consumed by Yahweh's death-dealing *fire* (v 11) and God's people who are vivified by his life-giving *dew* (v 19). The closing verses (vv 20-21) invite God's people to seek safe refuge until the time of judgment is past. The phrase *inhabitants of the earth* here coincides with the wicked who fall before God's judgment (see above on 24:16), very different than the usage of v 9, but very similar to that of v 18 (in both of which the Hebrew term for *earth* is different than that in v 21). That *the earth will disclose the blood shed upon her* is indicative of the general nature of the judgment to come: crimes previously concealed will now be revealed (cf. Gen 4:10) and dealt with. This reference to bloodshed perhaps gives some support to the suggestion that the covenant referred to in 24:5 is that with Noah, for within the context of that covenant God speaks of requiring a reckoning for bloodshed (Gen 9:5-6). To view the present text in the light of 24:5 would accord with the position of those who see 24:1-6 and 26:7-21 as parts of the basic text of the Isaiah Apocalypse (see above, p. 191).

THE SLAYING OF THE CHAOS MONSTER: 27:1

27 In that day the LORD with his hard and great and strong sword will punish Leviathan the fleeing serpent, Leviathan the twisting serpent, and he will slay the dragon that is in the sea.

This verse probably comes as an addition to the "hymn of the redeemed" of the previous chapter; it brings the action of 26:19-21, especially, to a fitting climax. This is the first of a series of four additions (which together make up chap. 27) which come after the main development of the Isaiah Apocalypse in chaps. 24-26. The present verse takes up a theme well-known in ancient Semitic mythology. According to the *Enuma Elish*, the ancient Akkadian cosmogonic myth, Marduk, the creating god, had to first overcome Tiamat, a monster goddess identified with the primordial chaos. This chaos monster shows up in various guises, Leviathan being one of them; the Lothan of Ugarit, whose name is simply a variant of Leviathan, is described in terms very similar to the present text as "the slippery serpent, the tortuous serpent." The theological dualism of the pagan myths was not acceptable to Israel's official faith, which saw Yahweh as the sole divine power, and in the biblical cosmogony (Gen

1:1—2:4a) there is no struggle. However, the theme was not infrequent in poetic passages, where the monster appears under the names of Leviathan and Rahab or simply as "the dragon" (see Job 3:8; 9:13; 26:12; Ps 74:13-14; 89:10; 104:26; Isa 30:7; 51:9). Obviously the figure is to an extent an embodiment of cosmic evil, and its appearance in the present verse is intended to say that *in that day* Yahweh will bring to an end even the most powerful sort of evil that can be conceived of as existing. What is radically different about this procedure is that in this text Yahweh's victory over the dragon is put at the end rather than at the beginning. It is possible that Leviathan is here a symbol for a worldly power whose demise would then be indicated by Yahweh's victory; see Isa 30:7, where Egypt is given the title "Rahab quelled."

THE SONG OF THE VINEYARD REVISITED: 27:2-6

2 In that day:
"A pleasant vineyard, sing of it!
3 I, the LORD, am its keeper;
every moment I water it.
Lest any one harm it,
I guard it night and day;
4 I have no wrath.
Would that I had thorns and briars to battle!
I would set out against them,
I would burn them up together.
5 Or let them lay hold of my protection,
let them make peace with me,
let them make peace with me."

6 In days to come Jacob shall take root,
Israel shall blossom and put forth shoots,
and fill the whole world with fruit.

This new addition is provided by a poet who felt that for the picture of the blessed future to be complete there was needed an annulment of the threatening "song of the vineyard" of 5:1-7 (on which see above). Accordingly, this piece is an undisguised allusion to that song and an explicit reversal of many of its details. Thus, whereas in the earlier composition Yahweh had broken down the walls of the vineyard and given it over to trampling, now he is *its keeper*; previously he had commanded the clouds not to rain upon it, now he waters it *every moment*; the *thorns and briars* that once were allowed to grow up he now wishes to do battle against!

Although the general sense of the piece is thus very clear, there are a number of difficulties, some of which are apparent in the translation and others which are not. One may ask, for example, whether the import of the *thorns and briars* is exhausted in its reference back to the earlier piece or whether Yahweh's wish to "do battle" against them indicates external enemies—an indication that may be heightened by the invitation to *make peace* (v 5). Some have suggested the tensions between Jews and Samaritans in the period of the restoration as the background. The Hebrew is unclear and faulty at points and therefore amenable to various emendations, so that it is possible to find quite diverse interpretations for vv 4-5. Verse 6 is probably a new addition to vv 2-5; its imagery is somewhat reminiscent of Hos 14:5-8.

A PEOPLE WITHOUT DISCERNMENT: 27:7-11

7 Has he smitten them as he smote those who smote them?
   Or have they been slain as their slayers were slain?

8 Measure by measure, by exile thou didst contend with them;
   he removed them with his fierce blast in the day of
      the east wind.

9 Therefore by this the guilt of Jacob will be expiated,
   and this will be the full fruit of the removal of his sin:
 when he makes all the stones of the altars
      like chalkstones crushed to pieces,
      no Asherim or incense altars will remain standing.

10 For the fortified city is solitary,
   a habitation deserted and forsaken, like the wilderness;

> there the calf grazes,
> > there he lies down, and strips its branches.
> 11 When its boughs are dry, they are broken;
> > women come and make a fire of them.
> For this is a people without discernment;
> > therefore he who made them will not have compassion
> > > on them,
> he that formed them will show them no favor.

This new addition, unlike the previous two in this chapter, appears to have little to do with the developments in chaps. 24-26. Again we are faced with a passage whose Hebrew text is doubtful in places and whose translation and interpretation are unclear; whether these verses form a unity is also disputed, for some commentators separate vv 7-9 from vv 10-11. One of the difficulties in attempting to interpret the piece is that there are almost no clear identifications: subject and objects in vv 7-8 are nameless, as are the *fortified city* of v 10 and the *people without discernment* of v 11. There is, however, the reference to Jacob (=Israel) in v 9, while the fact that God (still unnamed) made and formed the people of v 11 again points to his people. However, this is not an Israel restored to God's favor, but, in all probability, the Samaritans (cf. Sir 50:26, which refers to them in similar, slighting terms). These were the people inhabiting Samaria and the central territory between Judah and Galilee. According to 2 Kgs 17:24-34 they were a mixed population of various displaced peoples, though in fact the bulk was made up of Israelites who remained after the fall of Samaria and the deportation by the Assyrians of the more influential classes. When the Jews returned from Babylon and began to rebuild the Jerusalem Temple, the Samaritans asked to join with them in the work, asserting that they, too, were Yahweh-worshippers, but were rudely rebuffed (Ezra 4:1-3). Undoubtedly the pagan and syncretistic elements that had crept into Israel's worship before the fall of Samaria (see especially Hosea) continued to be present, and in greater degree, in the following centuries. In any case, the Jews who returned from Babylon did not consider them co-religionists. The present text, if this understanding is correct, both recognizes them as enjoying a special status before Yahweh and as still subject to his wrath for failure to amend.

Thus vv 7-8 would be saying that God has dealt far more severely with those who afflicted Israel (the Assyrians) than he had with his own people; these he *contended with* (a legal term is used) and had driven them away (the language here is very strong and seems to mean more than simply exile). The only way to expiation is the radical removal and destruction of the cult objects that go with false worship (v 9). The *Asherim* were wooden poles set up in conjunction with altars (see Deut 12:3; Judg 6:28; Isa 17:8) and named for the goddess Asherah. The *fortified city* of v 10 is often identified as Samaria; if this is correct, the text may refer to a future rather than a past destruction, for the destruction by the Assyrians would seem to be too early and that by John Hyrcanus in 108 too late to explain this text. The attentive reader is almost certain to read this verse in the light of previous references to "the city" in these chapters, and it is unlikely the one who added it intended otherwise. Those who have forsaken Yahweh, though he himself had formed them (v 11), will not enjoy his graciousness but will share the fate of others who fall under his judgment.

THE RETURN OF GOD'S PEOPLE: 27:12-13

12 In that day from the river Euphrates to the Brook of Egypt the LORD will thresh out the grain, and you will be gathered one by one, O people of Israel. 13And in that day a great trumpet will be blown, and those who were lost in the land of Assyria and those who were driven out to the land of Egypt will come and worship the LORD on the holy mountain at Jerusalem.

These verses form a final addition intended to bring the collection of chaps. 24-27 to a fitting conclusion. As attractive as they are, these verses do not manifest the broad universalism of some of the passages we have encountered.

The geographical references in v 12 mark the southernmost limit of the Promised Land (on *the Brook of Egypt*, see 1 Kgs 8:65) and, idealistically conceived, the easternmost. Jews who lived beyond these borders were in the Diaspora and the idyllic time to come would have them all return. The threshing or beating out of grain suggests a separation, no doubt from the gentiles, who are not therefore a concern in this text. Egypt and Assyria are named as the lands of exile; the latter stands for Mesopotamia in general, whence many have been exiled by Assyria and Babylonia, but the Jews in Egypt had gone there of their own accord. No matter; in the days to come all would return. We meet in this text the *great trumpet* which will become an important instrument in apocalyptic texts as the means of signifying the great day has come. The closing words name God's holy mountain and Jerusalem, so richly overlaid with redemptive themes, not simply as a place of refuge and security (the primary reference in 26:1-4), but as a place of worship.

ISAIAH'S FINAL PERIOD: CHAPTERS 28-33

After the oracles against the nations (chaps. 13-23), which contain a mixture of words of Isaiah and later compositions, and the Apocalypse of Isaiah (chaps. 24-27), which are wholly from a later period, we come to another collection, chaps. 28-33, which consists, in the main, of authentic words of Isaiah. (More accurately we might speak of chaps. 28-32, since chap. 33 is a later addition to the collection.) Most of the material contained here comes from the crisis of 705-701, during which Isaiah attempted, unsuccessfully, to dissuade Hezekiah from revolting against Assyria, now Judah's overlord, after the death of Sargon II (705). This period is again the subject of chaps. 36-39, but that section is a largely narrative appendix taken, with some variations, from 2 Kgs 18:13-20:19; it may preserve some words of Isaiah, but it cannot rank as a collection of his oracles.

WOE TO THE DRUNKARDS OF SAMARIA: 28:1-6

28 Woe to the proud crown of the drunkards of Ephraim,
    and to the fading flower of its glorious beauty,
        which is on the head of the rich valley of those over-
        come with wine!
  2 Behold, the Lord has one who is mighty and strong;

like a storm of hail, a destroying tempest,
like a storm of mighty, overflowing waters,
he will cast down to the earth with violence.
³ The proud crown of the drunkards of Ephraim
will be trodden under foot;
⁴ and the fading flower of its glorious beauty,
which is on the head of the rich valley,
will be like a first-ripe fig before the summer:
when a man sees it, he eats it up
as soon as it is in his hand.

⁵ In that day the LORD of hosts will be a crown of glory,
and a diadem of beauty, to the remnant of his people;
⁶ and a spirit of justice to him who sits in judgment,
and strength to those who turn back the battle at the
gate.

This threat, delivered against the ruling class of the northern kingdom in the form of a "woe," almost certainly stems from the period between the overthrow of Israel by Assyria in 732, with the reduction of its territory that that entailed, and its destruction, again by the Assyrians, in 722. It has been plausibly suggested that the rebellion in 724 of Hoshea, the last king of Israel (which now consisted only of Samaria and the surrounding territories) provided the occasion for this oracle. This would date the oracle considerably earlier than the rest of the Isaianic material in chaps. 28-31, but its inclusion here can probably be explained in that it provides a useful backdrop for vv 7-22, which is really the main focus of attention. This latter section is directed against the ruling class in Judah, primarily to condemn their short-sighted policy toward Assyria, and begins with an indictment of their drunkenness, just as vv 1-4 tell of the disastrous consequences of Samaria's revolt and begins with an allusion to its leaders' drunkenness. It is possible Isaiah revived this earlier oracle for the crisis of 705; since there was a parallel between Samaria's earlier situation and Judah's present situation, the lesson contained in Samaria's fate would have been powerfully brought home. Verses 5-6 are a later addi-

tion; without them vv 7-22 would follow immediately upon
vv 1-4.

Samaria was built upon a hill (1 Kgs 16:24) and, with its
walls surrounding the summit, could remind one of a crown
or garland on a human head; here Isaiah likens it to a ring of
flowers which quickly fall to the ground to fade and be
trampled upon (vv 1, 3-4a). In v 4b the image of early fruit
quickly devoured replaces that of the wilting flowers. The
onslaught of the Assyrians is described as a storm, irresistible, terrifying, and destructive (v 2).

A later, probably postexilic, hand has introduced the
happier picture of salvation in vv 5-6; now the crown imagery is used to designate Yahweh and his saving power for the
remnant (see above on 4:2). The elements of *spirit*, *judgment*, and *strength* in this piece are reminiscent of the
description of the ideal Davidic king of the future in 11:1-5.

JUDAH'S DRUNKEN PRIESTS AND PROPHETS: 28:7-13

7 These also reel with wine
    and stagger with strong drink;
the priest and the prophet reel with strong drink,
    they are confused with wine,
    they stagger with strong drink;
they err in vision,
    they stumble in giving judgment.
8 For all tables are full of vomit,
    no place is without filthiness.

9 "Whom will he teach knowledge,
    and to whom will he explain the message?
Those who are weaned from the milk,
    those taken from the breast?
10 For it is precept upon precept, precept upon precept,
    line upon line, line upon line,
    here a little, there a little."

11 Nay, but by men of strange lips
    and with an alien tongue

the LORD will speak to this people,
12   to whom he has said,
"This is rest;
     give rest to the weary;
and this is repose";
     yet they would not hear.
13 Therefore the word of the LORD will be to them
     precept upon precept, precept upon precept,
          line upon line, line upon line,
          here a little, there a little;
     that they may go, and fall backward,
          and be broken, and snared, and taken.

Although occasion for Isaiah's condemnation of the priests and prophets is taken from the public display of their drunkenness, the real reason goes far deeper. This oracle is closely related to the following one (vv 14-22), and both have to do with Judah's foreign policy and those who shape it. As a number of indications in chaps. 28-31 make clear, in the period following 705 Egypt solicited Judah's cooperation in a plan of widespread revolt against Assyria (30:1-5; 31:1-3); this plan Isaiah vehemently opposes, but Hezekiah, urged on by the leading classes, falls in with it. In the present passage Isaiah speaks out against two of these groups which, on this point at least, were closely allied. Certain prophets had cultic functions and were numbered among the Temple personnel. On this occasion priests and prophets were celebrating together, perhaps a religious feast or perhaps even the conclusion of the covenant with Egypt (see below on v 15). Prophets who received their livelihood from Temple and court could be depended upon to back royal policy and to produce victory oracles as needed (see 1 Kgs 22:1-13; Mic 3:5) and to refrain from hard sayings (30:10). The impact of Isaiah's prophetic word could be counteracted if others who ranked as prophets contradicted him, and it is clear that this is what happened.

The words *these also* of v 7 are intended to link the present passage with the condemnation of Samaria's leaders (vv 1-4). Isaiah suggests that drunkenness is responsible for the inability of *the priest and the prophet* to declare what they ought (*vision* and *judgment* in v 7). Their response is to reject his admonition with a taunt: they are not children that they should have to receive instruction from him! (v 9). *RSV*'s *precept upon precept*, etc., in v 10 is a doubtful solution to a very difficult verse; the text of the first part of the verse simply does not add up to normal Hebrew words, and it is not clear that it is supposed to. The mocking words read like repetitious sing-song (*sau lasau sau lasau qau laqau qau laqau*) and it has been suggested that they represent a learning exercise or a very young pupil's recitation, something like our ABC's. In any case, Isaiah turns this taunt back upon them. They don't like the way Yahweh instructs them through his prophet? Very well! he will instruct them through much harsher masters. The reference (*strange lips, alien tongue*) is to the Assyrians, whose advent the present policy assures.

Yet this is not what Yahweh had willed for his people (referred to as *this people* in v 11 to indicate displeasure; see 6:9; 8:6, 11); in v 12 Isaiah speaks of the rejection of an oracle previously given that urged *rest* and *repose* as the proper way of dealing with the current situation; in these same circumstances he urged "returning and rest" and "quietness and trust" (30:15), just as earlier he had urged Ahaz to remain tranquil (7:4) and had compared Yahweh's strength to the gentle waters of Shiloah (8:6). He believed that the way to peace was not through frenetic preparations for war or pacts with Egypt but through submission to the saving will of God as revealed in his word. But this word, he says, they rejected. (*OTA*, 4, #507.)

Verse 13 appears to be an editorial addition taken from v 10 and 8:15.

THE ARROGANT RULERS OF JERUSALEM: 28:14-22

> [14] Therefore hear the word of the LORD, you scoffers,
> who rule this people in Jerusalem!

15 Because you have said, "We have made a covenant with death,
     and with Sheol we have an agreement;
   when the overwhelming scourge passes through
     it will not come to us;
   for we have made lies our refuge,
     and in falsehood we have taken shelter";
16 therefore thus says the Lord GOD,
   "Behold, I am laying in Zion for a foundation
     a stone, a tested stone,
   a precious cornerstone, of a sure foundation:
     'He who believes will not be in haste.'
17 And I will make justice the line,
     and righteousness the plummet;
   and hail will sweep away the refuge of lies,
     and waters will overwhelm the shelter."
18 Then your covenant with death will be annulled,
     and your agreement with Sheol will not stand;
   when the overwhelming scourge passes through
     you will be beaten down by it.
19 As often as it passes through it will take you;
     for morning by morning it will pass through,
     by day and by night;
   and it will be sheer terror to understand the message.
20 For the bed is too short to stretch oneself on it,
     and the covering too narrow to wrap oneself in it.
21 For the LORD will rise up as on Mount Perazim,
     he will be wroth as in the valley of Gibeon;
   to do his deed — strange is his deed!
   and to work his work — alien is his work!
22 Now therefore do not scoff,
     lest your bonds be made strong;
   for I have heard a decree of destruction
     from the Lord GOD of hosts upon the whole land.

Although the opening *therefore* of v 14 closely relates this piece to the previous passage and although the basic content of the two is very similar, the address to *you . . . who rule this people* marks it as a separate composition. The prophets and the priests were very influential groups, but the ones here concerned would be the bearers of civil authority, members of the upper class and of the royal court, those who advised the king, helped make policy, and put it into effect.

It is not infrequently asserted that *covenant with death* (v 15) is the leaders' own description of the pact they had made (in which case the reference could be to the pagan god Mot, whose name means "death"), but in fact this is an instance of Isaiah putting into the mouths of others not what they said but words that describe what he perceives to be the reality; they no more spoke of a covenant with death then they did of making *lies our refuge* (v 15) or of telling the prophets to "prophesy illusions" (30:10). The covenant in question was no doubt one with Egypt and provided for Egyptian military help for Judah in their attempt to throw off the Assyrian yoke. But because Judah will now expose itself to the deadly peril of Assyrian retribution, trusting in Egyptian help that will not materialize (31:3), they are indeed making *lies* their *refuge* and *death* shall be a proper characterization of their covenant. It will not preserve them from the *overwhelming scourge* that will come, namely, Assyrian might, here depicted as a storm that carries all before it (vv 15, 17-18; see 8:7-8, where Assyria is likened to a river overflowing its banks).

With the saying about the *cornerstone*, Isaiah contrasts the path the Lord wills with what the people had chosen. The stone is laid *in Zion* and ultimately represents the saving strength of Yahweh himself (and may relate to forms in which that strength has been promised, e.g., the Zion tradition). But it is of no use unless trust is reposed in it and this trust becomes the basis of action, and so the stone bears the legend, which is probably thought of as chiseled into it, *he who believes will not be in haste* (v 16). Probably we should read "stone of testing" (rather than *tested*), faith being the condition for approval and survival. Plummet and measuring line continue the testing theme, as well as the architectural imagery, aptly standing for *justice* (*mishpat*) and *righteousness* (*sedaqah*) (v 11), which are norms against which action is measured and judged. These form the true criteria for all that shall come to pass, and the deceptive facade will collapse, leaving Judah open to the destruction that the neglect of its true source of strength and its attempts at power-brokering have earned it (v 18).

The closing lines of this oracle (vv 19-22) do not present a very intelligible development and may be composed in part of glosses (especially v 19 and v 22). Verse 20 is clearly a proverb, such as Isaiah could easily have used; it would indicate a situation in which no solace or comfort was possible. Isaiah could also have used the allusions to two instances in which Yahweh gave victory to Israel; *Mount Parazim* refers to David's defeat of the Philstines (2 Sam 5:17-25) and *the valley of Gibeon* to Joshua's defeat of the five Canaanite kings of the south during the conquest of the Promised Land (Jos 10:9-14). Yahweh's *work* is *strange* and *alien* because now his hand is turned against a people who look to foreign covenants instead of to the help of him who first gave the land to them. In his early period, too, Isaiah spoke of the action planned by Yahweh as his "work" (5:12, 19).

In spite of the basically threatening tone of this passage, the positive aspects of it should not be overlooked. There is nothing conditional about the laying of the *cornerstone* nor of its salvific import. It may bring no help to those who were formulating Judah's policy at the time, the scoffers who would not heed the prophet's words, but as Yahweh's work it would not be without effect. To those with faith (and again we note Isaiah's demand, as in the days of Ahaz—see especially 7:9) it would be their firm assurance for the future. Since it is laid *in Zion*, we have a clear hint of the positive role the Zion tradition played in Isaiah's teaching.

THE PARABLE OF THE FARMER: 28:23-29

23 Give ear, and hear my voice;
   hearken, and hear my speech.
24 Does he who plows for sowing plow continually?
   does he continually open and harrow his ground?
25 When he has leveled its surface,

> does he not scatter dill, sow cummin,
> and put in wheat in rows
> and barley in its proper place,
> and spelt as the border?

26 For he is instructed aright;
> his God teaches him.

27 Dill is not threshed with a threshing sledge,
> nor is a cart wheel rolled over cummin;
> but dill is beaten out with a stick,
> and cummin with a rod.

28 Does one crush bread grain?
> No, he does not thresh it for ever;
> when he drives his cart wheel over it
> with his horses, he does not crush it.

29 This also comes from the LORD of hosts;
> he is wonderful in counsel,
> and excellent in wisdom.

Although there are many passages in Isaiah that manifest contact with the wisdom tradition, this one contains the greatest concentration of wisdom traits. It begins with the sort of call to attention that is characteristic of the wisdom instruction (see above on 1:10 and cf. Prov 1:8; 4:1; 5:1; 22:17), employs rhetorical questions, draws a lesson from the observable order, traces wisdom to instruction received from God (see Ps 25:8-12), praises Yahweh's counsel, and employs characteristic wisdom terminology (especially the somewhat rare word for wisdom in v 29, *tushiyah*). Yet it deals with a theme that is, for the most part, at least, foreign to the wisdom tradition, namely, the action of God in history. For this reason, although Isaiah here speaks very much like a wisdom teacher, the message conveyed is fundamentally prophetic and totally consistent with what we find elsewhere in his oracles.

Isaiah's reason for utilizing this manner of speech is not difficult to find. There have already been ample indications of Isaiah's conflict with circles of "the wise" in the days of

Ahaz (see above on 1:10; 5:12, 19; 6:9-10; 11:2) and we will soon meet the same sort of thing in the present collection, which pertains to the time of Hezekiah (see below on 29:13-14, 15-16). We have seen that this relates, in part, to the failure of "the wise" to live up to the ethic they had imbibed from their tradition concerning the treatment of the oppressed, but also in large part to their role as advisers to the king and to their pernicious influence in directing him to policies condemned by Isaiah's prophetic word. Here Isaiah adopts the manner of a wisdom teacher in order better to address them and to counter their teaching.

The basic thrust of the parable has been interpreted in many ways. There are those who say, for example, that it indicates the time has come for an end to the punishment Yahweh has been inflicting on Judah through the Assyrians, but this is far from clear. What we find in the parable are a series of actions that could seem to the uninitiated to be unconnected and other actions which could seem inconsistent (i.e., different ways of preparing different crops for use). A parable is most often used for polemical purposes (see the "song of the vineyard" in 5:1-7); the hearer is called upon to answer questions, and in answering them his own objections are answered. So here it would appear that objections have been raised against apparent inconsistencies in Isaiah's message concerning Yahweh's action in history. This could well be because Isaiah had opposed submission to Assyria as vassal in the days of Ahaz and now opposed revolting against them in the days of Hezekiah. Isaiah is saying here that seemingly diverse and unrelated actions can fit into a purposeful pattern of behavior. This is not to say that the passage becomes immediately intelligible; in 29:14 he speaks of overturning the wisdom of the wise, and here he says that Yahweh's *plan*/policy (*'esah*—see above on 5:12, 19; 8:9-10; 14:24-27) is *wonderful*, i.e., marvelous, astounding, and incomprehensible. This would hardly be said if it were merely a question of bringing his punishment against Judah to an end. However the interpretation which sees reference to punishment has at least this justification, that behind the *stick* and *rod* mentioned in v 27 are the same

Hebrew words translated as "rod" and "staff" in 10:5; if the reference to punishment is present, it is not that it is ended but that it has the nature of chastisement rather than destruction (vv 27-28).

There is in the reference to the *wonderful* aspect of Yahweh's counsel an echo of the name "wonder counselor" given to the ideal future king in 9:6.

SIEGE AND DELIVERANCE OF ARIEL: 29:1-8

29 Ho Ariel, Ariel,
    the city where David encamped!
  Add year to year;
    let the feasts run their round.
2 Yet I will distress Ariel,
    and there shall be moaning and lamentation,
    and she shall be to me like an Ariel.
3 And I will encamp against you round about,
    and will besiege you with towers
    and I will raise siegeworks against you.
4 Then deep from the earth you shall speak,
    from low in the dust your words shall come;
  your voice shall come from the ground
      like the voice of a ghost,
    and your speech shall whisper out of the dust.

5 But the multitude of your foes shall
      be like small dust,
    and the multitude of the ruthless like passing chaff.
  And in an instant, suddenly,
6   you will be visited by the LORD of hosts
  with thunder and with earthquake and great noise,
    with whirlwind and tempest, and the flame of a
      devouring fire.
7 And the multitude of all the nations that fight
    against Ariel,
    all that fight against her and her stronghold
    and distress her,
  shall be like a dream, a vision of the night.

⁸ As when a hungry man dreams he is eating
    and awakes with his hunger not satisfied,
  or as when a thirsty man dreams he is drinking
    and awakes faint, with his thirst not quenched,
  so shall the multitude of all the nations be
    that fight against Mount Zion.

There is much that is mysterious and disputed about this oracle. What is not subject to question is that it relates to Jerusalem, begins with a siege (by Yahweh) against it, and ends with a wonderful deliverance. But this already excites wonder and suspicion: if Yahweh himself lays siege to the city, whence comes the wonderful deliverance? Some commentators have explained the text as reflecting the marvelous deliverance of Jerusalem from Sennacherib's siege in 705; but there are historical problems connected with that whole account, and it does not seem likely that Isaiah wavered from his vehement condemnation of Judah's revolt or from his promise that it would lead to disaster (see below on chaps. 36-37). Others would see a repentance on the part of the inhabitants of Jerusalem (in their speaking *from low in the dust* in v 4), but there is no clear reference to repentance there, and the natural understanding of v 6 (the "visitation" of the Lord in *thunder, earthquake,* and *devouring fire*) continues the theme of the Lord's assault on Jerusalem.

It should also be noted that the passage begins with a woe (*hoy*) pronounced on Ariel (rather than *RSV's Ho*). The most probable explanation, therefore, is that we are dealing with a threat against the city composed by Isaiah, but softened by a promise of deliverance from a later hand. There are no allusions to specific events to help date the piece, nor is any sin of Jerusalem named to explain Yahweh's assault on her, but its inclusion in this part of the book suggests that it belongs to the period shortly after 705; the policy of revolt against the Assyrians from this period would also explain Isaiah's threat against the city.

Although Jerusalem is not named, and although the term by which she is addressed, *Ariel,* cannot be explained with any certainty, there is no doubt that it is Jerusalem which is spoken of here. The Hebrew *'ari'el* is used to mean "altar hearth" in Ezek 43:15-16, and that is probably what it means here, though as a metonym for the city. The reference to David's encampment (probably intended in a hostile sense) helps to identify it and reminds that it had fallen before (to a hero, to be sure, but now it is the Lord himself who attacks). The round of cultic celebrations may continue, but they will not appease the Lord or turn him back. It is the distress of the siege that occasions the *speaking from the dust* of v 4. If v 5a, b are skipped over as a later addition, the full threat of 5c-6 becomes apparent: *you* refers to Ariel, which has been addressed in the second person throughout, and the accompaniments of the Lord's visitation make clear its hostile intent. Verse 7 would be part of the later adaptation, with v 8 a later, more prosy, expansion. The additions reflect an interpretation of the Zion theme that would see Jerusalem the object of divine deliverance in all circumstances, but this is incompatible with the opening verses, which see the Lord himself as the attacker. The Zion tradition played a significant role in Isaiah's thought, but only in the nuanced sense we saw in 28:16, which involves the kind of trust in Yahweh which determines policy.

THE BLINDNESS OF THE LEADERS: 29:9-12

9 Stupefy yourselves and be in a stupor,
    blind yourselves and be blind!
  Be drunk, but not with wine;
    stagger, but not with strong drink!
10 For the LORD has poured out upon you
    a spirit of deep sleep,
  and has closed your eyes, the prophets,
    and covered your heads, the seers.
11 And the vision of all this has become to you like the words of a book that is sealed. When men give it to one who can read, saying, "Read this," he says, "I cannot, for it is sealed." 12And when they give the book to one who cannot read, saying, "Read this," he says, "I cannot read."

Verses 9-11a form a short, detached saying from the 705-701 period, while vv 11b-12 are a much later addition which comments on and interprets it. The background for vv 9-11a is undoubtedly the negotiations and political decisions that preceded the revolt of 701. Whereas in his vocation narrative Isaiah had spoken of the Lord commissioning him to bring the deafness, blindness, and hardness of heart that was the condition for Judah's leaders' mad rush to destruction (6:9-10), here he speaks of them blinding and stupifying themselves. Something of the prophet's incredulity as he sees them preparing disaster for themselves shows through in his words. Such blindness hardly seemed possible without the Lord's act, and so he speaks of him pouring sleep upon them, as though by means of a powerful narcotic, to close their eyes and cover their heads. The identification of eyes and head with prophets and seers is the work of a glossator who understood the lines as an allegory rather than a simple metaphor. The special word for sleep used here (*tardemah*) regularly refers to a condition that comes from the Lord (see Gen 2:21; 15:12; 1 Sam 26:12; Job 4:13; 33:15).

Although vv 11-12 as a whole are usually taken as a later addition, it is perhaps better to take the first part of it with v 10b, read without the glosses (thus giving *he has closed your eyes/and covered your heads,/so that the vision of all this /has become to you like the words of a sealed book*), as part of the original text. The description of their incomprehension of the prophetic revelation suits the context and is intelligible. But a later hand provided a prose addition to spell it out and perhaps apply it to a new situation.

THE WISDOM OF THE WISE SHALL PERISH: 29:13-14

13 And the Lord said:
"Because this people draw near with their mouth
  and honor me with their lips,
    while their hearts are far from me,
  and their fear of me is a commandment of men learned
    by rote;

14 therefore, behold, I will again
    do marvelous things with this people,
    wonderful and marvelous;
and the wisdom of their wise men shall perish,
    and the discernment of their discerning men
       shall be hid."

Because certain phrases of v 13 have often been taken out of context as a polemic against the cult, or at least against external observance as opposed to inner obedience, we are conditioned to understand this passage in those terms. However, remembering that it almost certainly belongs to the same historical background as the other materials in these chapters, we should observe that v 14, which is closely joined to v 13 (*therefore*), is spoken against the wise men. Thus the hypocrisy of which the people are accused in v 13 relates not to the cult nor to provisions of the Law (concerning which we find virtually no reference in Isaiah) but to their high claims to want to do God's will, while at the same time rejecting the word of God given through the prophet, following, instead, the ways mapped out by their human teachers. *RSV's commandment* (*miswah*) in v 13 might better be "precept," a term used in any circumstances in which the speaker enjoys some sort of authority, including that of teacher (Prov 2:1; 3:1; 4:4; 6:20, etc.); *by rote* is not expressed in the Hebrew.

The *wise men* whom the people follow are the royal advisers who abet Hezekiah in the plan to covenant with Egypt for military aid in their revolt against Assyria. The text puts much emphasis on the *marvelous things* the Lord is about to do, in Hebrew the same root (*pl'*) being used three times. The same terminology is sometimes used of God's mighty deeds on behalf of Israel (Exod 15:11; Ps 77:11, 14), but now, it is clear, the words are being used in a threatening sense. God's counsel is wonderful (28:29, where the same root is used), not the least because it often is not what human calculation expects. Isaiah apparently has found no way to counter the influence of the royal advisers (even offering a sign to Ahaz, at a previous time, did not help—7:11), but he indicates that when Yahweh has completed his work the total bankruptcy of their *wisdom* will be apparent to all.

THE PARABLE OF THE POTTER: 29:15-16

> 15 Woe to those who hide deep from the LORD their counsel,
>   whose deeds are in the dark,
>   and who say, "Who sees us? Who knows us?"
> 16 You turn things upside down!
>   Shall the potter be regarded as the clay;
>   that the thing made should say of its maker,
>   "He did not make me";
>   or the thing formed say of him who formed it,
>   "He has no understanding"?

At an earlier time Isaiah had reproached the Assyrians for failing to recognize their place in God's scheme; he had pronounced a "woe" against God's "rod" and "staff" (10:5) and had asked (rhetorically) whether the axe could vaunt itself against the one who wields it (10:15). In a similar way he now pronounces a *woe* against Judah's rulers and asks whether the *clay* can change places with the potter. In each case it was a matter of lack of comprehension of one's place in God's scheme of things, yet the different imagery, clay rather than axe, may not be without significance. To represent Assyria as an instrument, a tool, suggests that its import lies in the use God wishes to make of it and does not go beyond that. But to represent Israel as clay suggests God's creative activity (see 45:9; Jer 18:4, 6; Job 10:9; 33:6), with all the concern that involves, as well as the condition of total dependence of the creature before its Creator and the obedience that implies. And since Israel's election is frequently thought of as the result of God's creative activity (Deut 32:6; Isa 43:1, 7, 15), this imagery does not rule out but rather emphasizes that it is God's *chosen* people who are rebelling.

The occasion for these words would be the machinations of Judah's leaders during the events preceding 705; again it is a matter of human *counsel*, which, by implication, is opposed to the Lord's counsel. Whether the reference to their hiding their plans from the Lord means they attempted to keep Isaiah in the dark or simply alludes to the secrecy which so often surrounds political negotiations cannot be known. Clearly the words attributed to the clay (*he did not make me, he has no understanding*) are not statements of Judah's leaders; rather, as on other occasions, Isaiah places in their mouths words that express the attitudes conveyed by their actions (cf. 30:10-11). Actions speak louder than words.

TRANSFORMATION IN THE NEW AGE: 29:17-24

17 Is it not yet a very little while
  until Lebanon shall be turned into a fruitful field,
  and the fruitful field shall be regarded as a forest?
18 In that day the deaf shall hear
  the words of a book,
 and out of their gloom and darkness
  the eyes of the blind shall see.
19 The meek shall obtain fresh joy in the LORD,
  and the poor among men shall exult in the Holy one of
    Israel.
20 For the ruthless shall come to nought and the scoffer cease,
  and all who watch to do evil shall be cut off,
21 who by a word make a man out to be an offender,
  and lay a snare for him who reproves in the gate,
  and with an empty plea turn aside him who is in the right.

22 Therefore thus says the LORD, who redeemed Abraham,
  concerning the house of Jacob:
   "Jacob shall no more be ashamed,
    no more shall his face grow pale.
23 For when he sees his children,
  the work of my hands, in his midst,
  they will sanctify my name;
 they will sanctify the Holy One of Jacob,
  and will stand in awe of the God of Israel.
24 And those who err in spirit will come to understanding,
  and those who murmur will accept instruction."

These beautiful verses come from a time long after Isaiah,
from the exilic or postexilic period, for they speak of a new
age in eschatological terms that have much in common with
Deutero-Isaiah (chaps. 40-55) but are different than anything we find in the words of Isaiah himself. They do resem-
ble, however, the Apocalypse of Isaiah (chaps. 24-27). They
fit rather strangely into the present context, for chaps. 30-31
will continue in much the same vein as the materials in
chaps. 28-29, but the editor who placed them here no doubt
wished to provide a hopeful note for the future to relieve the
otherwise rather harsh succession of oracles. And the verses
relate to the previous context in that some elements of them
reverse unfavorable aspects of the preceding verses; cf., e.g.,
vv 9-12 with v 18 and vv 15-16 with v 24.

"Transformation" is perhaps the keynote of the passage.
It begins by describing a marvelous transformation to take
place in the world of nature and in so doing points to the
wonderful character of the age to come — which is expected
to burst in very soon (*Is it not yet a very little while . . .?*).
Lebanon, already famous for its cedars, is to be *turned into
a fruitful field.* The transformation of *the fruitful field* into *a
forest* is somewhat difficult to comprehend as a move in the
same direction. It helps little to note that the word translated *fruitful field* ("orchard grove" would perhaps be better) in both halves of the verse is *karmel*, which could
equally well be rendered "(Mt.) Carmel," proverbial for its
luxuriant fruitfulness. Whether we take it to mean "orchard
grove" or "Mt. Carmel," the meaning has to be that its fruit
trees will be so abundant that it can be likened to a forest.

In any case, this transformation in nature is symbolic of
and points to more important transformations: the deaf and
the blind hear and see, the meek and the poor rejoice, the
ruthless and the scoffer are silenced, and those who have
been straying turn back to God.

It is not certain whether the *deaf* and *blind* (v 18) are to be
understood literally or whether these terms stand as metaphorical language for a spiritual condition; that the deaf
hear the words of a book can suggest a new receptiveness to
revelation in written prophecy (which is perhaps also

intended above in vv 11-12). The *meek* and the poor come to
stand, eventually, for those who place their trust exclusively
in the Lord, his justice, and his might. Originally the terminology of poverty referred simply to a socio-economic condition, but already in Amos 2:6 "needy" stands in parallel to
"righteous" if for no other reason than that they were more
righteous than the rich who oppressed and cheated them.
There is also the fact that the poor, by the mere fact that they
had no resources of their own in which to trust, turned to the
Lord alone in their needs (thus the reference to them in v 19
forms a good counterpoint to the condemnation in the
preceding and following chapters of those who refuse to
trust in the Lord). And so the terminology comes often to
designate those who trust and are faithful, without emphasis
on their economic condition (note the "blessed are the poor
in spirit" of Matt 5:3), often identified with the righteous
remnant who can be contrasted with the faithless, with the
rich and powerful who oppress them, and with the repro-
bate (see above on 25:4; 26:6).

In vv 19-21 the *meek* and *poor* appear in a context which
brings out their religious qualities and also shows them to be
the victims of the *ruthless* and the *scoffer*, with whom they
are contrasted. Although the occasion of the *fresh joy* that
shall obtain for the poor is deliverance from those who
wrong them, the fact that it takes the form of exultation in
the Holy One of Israel demonstrates something of their
religious dispositions. Israel's conception of the new age
involves elimination of the evils which afflict the present age
and make it less than ideal, and so the unjust judgments that
the faithful can suffer from because of the unscrupulous will
cease. In Israel's religious faith there is no possibility of a
glorious new age which is not founded upon and characterized by justice. (On *him who reproves in the gate*, v 21, see
OTM, Vol. 7, p. 56, on Amos 5:10.)

Verses 22-24 give the appearance of having been built
upon the preceding, so they probably come from a still later
hand. They concern themselves with a group in between the
"poor" and the "ruthless," namely, the erring in Israel. Verse
23 should begin "when his children see the work of my hands

...," or, more probably, "when he sees the work of my hands ..." ("he" being Jacob embodied in his descendants). The meaning is that the great things God is about to do will bring about the conversion of those in Israel who are in need of it, and *they will sanctify* his *name*. The name and the person who bears it are identical and so to sanctify God's name is to sanctify God himself. To "sanctify" means basically to make holy, and no mortal can add anything to God's holiness. But the range of meaning includes both the praise of God, by which we declare or acknowledge his holiness in private and public prayer, and that kind of behavior which effectively shows that one's whole life belongs to God through consecration and obedience.

PHARAOH AND YAHWEH'S REBELLIOUS CHILDREN: 30:1-5

30 "Woe to the rebellious children,"
    says the LORD,
    "who carry out a plan, but not mine;
  and who make a league, but not of my spirit,
    that they may add sin to sin;
2 who set out to go down to Egypt,
    without asking for my counsel,
  to take refuge in the protection of Pharaoh,
    and to seek shelter in the shadow of Egypt!
3 Therefore shall the protection of Pharaoh turn
    to your shame,
  and the shelter in the shadow of Egypt to your
    humiliation.
4 For though his officials are at Zoan
    and his envoys reach Hanes,
5 every one comes to shame
    through a people that cannot profit them,
  that brings neither help nor profit,
    but shame and disgrace."

In this *woe* Isaiah again speaks of the uselessness, and worse, of Judah's turning to Egypt for help; the trust they place in Pharaoh, by encouraging them to a revolt they might not otherwise have been emboldened to, becomes an occasion of their own downfall. While some commentators relate the verses to the events of 714-711, the period of 705-701 seems more probable. Here Judah is actively seeking Egyptian help (in 714-711 it was Egypt which took the initiative; see on 18:1-6), and this may have been at a time when Assyrian forces were already beginning to threaten.

Verse 1 contains the gist of the whole piece; Egypt is not named there, it is true, but the identity of the third party is, for Isaiah, irrelevant. Judah's making of a plan that is not from Yahweh is already condemned as rebellion, and we are reminded of earlier texts in which it was made clear that since Yahweh has a plan/policy (*'esah*), any attempt to establish human plans was both futile and foolish (5:19; 7:5; 8:10; 14:24, 26-27; 28:29; 29:15-16). The people of Judah are addressed as *children*, and we are reminded that in the wisdom tradition it was the role of the sage to form and impart counsel (Prov 1:25, 30; 8:14; 19:20) to learners who were addressed as "children." The diction is not unlike that found in 1:2-3, where Yahweh's "children" are seen to be without understanding. But in a matter in which Judah's survival hangs in the balance and in which they are determined to seek help from purely human resources instead of from Yahweh's might, it is not simply a question of foolishness but of piling sin on top of sin.

Verse 2 does not really speak of asking Yahweh's *counsel*; literally it speaks of inquiring of his mouth, i.e., of asking for an oracle. This was common practice in Israel/Judah (1 Kgs 22:5; 2 Kgs 3:11; 22:13; Jer 37:17; 38:14) and in the ancient world in general. That Hezekiah, who is presented as having frequent contact with Isaiah, should not have done so, suggests a suspicion of what the response would be and an unwillingness to hear it. Possibly the sin Isaiah here condemns is simply the refusal to hear his message. In either case it is a matter of the king being willing to be persuaded by court officials, the strategists, the "wise," but of being unwilling to listen to the word of Yahweh through his prophet.

There is deliberate and heavy irony in Isaiah's depicting of Judah making Pharaoh their *refuge* and *shadow*, for this is terminology regularly used of the Lord in the protection he grants to those who look to him (see, e.g., Ps 27:1; 28:8; 31:3; 37:39; 43:2; 52:7; 90:1; 91:1; 121:5; sometimes the expression is "shadow of his wings": Ps 17:8; 57:1; 63:7). This is to say that they are putting Pharaoh and Egypt in the place of God (and 31:3 will say that "the Egyptians are men, not God"). The Pharaoh at this time was Shabako (710-696), a very vigorous ruler who may have inspired confidence in his ability to deal with the Assyrians, but Isaiah insists that it is a false confidence that will lead only to defeat and shame. It was in the mouth of an Assyrian official that the characterization of Egypt as "that broken reed of a staff, which will pierce the hand of any man who leans upon it" was put (2 Kgs 19:21; Isa 36:6), but the sentiment would have suited Isaiah admirably. In the event, Isaiah turned out to have been quite correct in his assessment even of the military realities: after Assyrian forces had appeared in Palestine to quell the revolt, the Egyptian army marched out to do battle with them at Eltekah and was defeated.

A FUTILE TREK THROUGH THE NEGEB: 30:6-7

> 6 An oracle on the beasts of the Negeb.
> Through a land of trouble and anguish,
>   from where come the lioness and the lion,
>   the viper and the flying serpent,
> they carry their riches on the backs of asses,
>   and their treasures on the humps of camels,
>   to a people that cannot profit them.
> 7 For Egypt's help is worthless and empty,
>   therefore I have called her
>   "Rahab who sits still."

The title given this short piece, *an oracle on the beasts of the Negeb*, is the work of a later editor; it is drawn from the creatures mentioned in v 6 but does not express the contents very well. Although one cannot be certain, both context and content encourage the idea that the reference is to the embassy from Judah to Egypt that 30:2 supposes. If the seaward road were not available (as it might not have been if Assyrian forces were already threatening), the trip would have to be made with great hardship through the arid steppe south of Judah that is named the Negeb. This was the home of dangerous creatures and also of weird ones that encouraged even weirder legends (such as the *flying serpent* of v 6). The caravan of asses and camels carrying riches *to a people that cannot profit them* would be bringing presents to Pharaoh to obtain his intervention. Isaiah rightly foresees that whatever help Egypt may attempt to provide will be useless. Again Isaiah bestows a name which summarizes his teaching (see 7:3, 14; 8:2-3; 9:6). *Rahab* is one of the names of the ferocious chaos monster (see above on 27:1), though what the Hebrew text intends to say of her is somewhat obscure (cf. *NAB's* "Rahab quelled," which is based on an emendation). The general sense of the name is clear from the end of v 6: the mighty beast (Egypt) is no longer fearsome.

ISAIAH'S ETERNAL WITNESS: 30:8-17

⁸ And now, go, write it before them on a tablet,
   and inscribe it in a book,
that it may be for the time to come
   as a witness for ever.
⁹ For they are a rebellious people,
   lying sons,
sons who will not hear
   the instruction of the LORD;
¹⁰ who say to the seers, "See not";
   and to the prophets, "Prophesy not to us what is right;
speak to us smooth things,
   prophesy illusions,
¹¹ leave the way, turn aside from the path,
   let us hear no more of the Holy One of Israel."
"Because you despise this word,
   and trust in oppression and perverseness,
   and rely on them;

13 therefore this iniquity shall be to you
  like a break in a high wall, bulging out, and
    about to collapse,
  whose crash comes suddenly, in an instant;
14 and its breaking is like that of a potter's vessel
  which is smashed so ruthlessly
  that among its fragments not a sherd is found
    with which to take fire from the hearth,
    or to dip up water out of the cistern."

15 For thus said the Lord GOD, the Holy One of Israel,
  "In returning and rest you shall be saved;
    in quietness and in trust shall be your strength."
  And you would not, 16 but you said,
  "No! We will speed upon horses,"
    therefore you shall speed away;
  and, "We will ride upon swift steeds,"
    therefore your pursuers shall be swift.
17 A thousand shall flee at the threat of one,
    at the threat of five you shall flee,
  till you are left
    like a flagstaff on the top of a mountain,
    like a signal on a hill.

This passage seems almost like a concluding summary of what Isaiah has had to say during the crisis of 705-701. This impression is heightened by the reference to writing it down, an action whose intention would be to preserve the prophetic word so that later its fulfillment could be verified. Again we meet reference to rebellious children, to their rejection of Yahweh's word, to his (earlier) call for quiet trust, and to the final ruin that is to come upon them.

The section begins quite abruptly with the command to *write it*, and no antecedent is provided fot the "it." This leaves room for much speculation as to what precisely was to be written down. Possibly it was an account of the things which Isaiah had to say during this period of his ministry, and the document could then have provided the basic content of chaps. 28-31 of the book. This explanation would allow us to see a parallel with the written testimony of 8:16, which is generally understood to have been the basic text of Isaiah's Memoirs (see above, p. 82). In any case, the present text reminds us again of the predictive element in prophecy: Isaiah was so certain that the word of Yahweh spoken through him would come to pass that he wanted it preserved so that its truth could be ascertained by events. This was not intended in any "I told you so" spirit. Isaiah had preached concerning Yahweh's "purpose" so that the people, by planning their own affairs in conformity with it, could find peace and security. Thus were they called upon to manifest their living faith that Yahweh was in control of things and to exercise obedience to what his "purpose" in history required of them at this moment. Because they were unwilling to do this the disaster Isaiah foretold would come. But with it would come also a realization of their disobedience and want of faith, and therefore also the opportunity for repentance and the impetus for a totally different kind of behavior in later times. It was for this that Isaiah wanted *a witness for ever*.

Verse 9 again reminds us of Isaiah's conflict with "the wise." The people are *children* who will not listen to Yahweh's *instruction* (*torah*; see above on 1:10; 2:3; 5:24; and 8:16). Because "the wise," in promoting a foolish and disastrous policy, have forfeited all rights to the term (cf. 29:14), Isaiah attributes all wisdom to Yahweh and makes him the source of all that the wisdom tradition attributed to human teachers. Only the messianic king would possess such attributes as wisdom, knowledge, counsel, and that only because he was the recipient of Yahweh's spirit (11:2). But this terminology also calls attention to the intensely personal nature of the relationship that Isaiah understands to exist between Yahweh and his people; it is not a matter of transgressing law or even covenant but of rejecting the wise counsel of a loving father (cf. 1:2-3, where Judah's problem is described as that of children who do not understand).

On the device of placing words in the mouths of his adversaries, see above on 28:15; 29:15-16. Though they almost certainly did not speak the words attributed to them

(vv 10-11), their actions have revealed their inmost sentiments, which had nothing to do with the piety and obedience they should have manifested. Therefore disaster
would come, a disaster which could be conceived in part as
punishment for their sin but perhaps even more as the
inevitable consequence of foolish and imprudent policy.
Judah had no obligation to revolt against their Assyrian
overlords; on the contrary, Isaiah's message assured them
that in Yahweh's good time the Assyrian might would come
to an end. Israel's tradition of the holy war claimed all
victory for Yahweh, and one of the conditions for this was
the recognition that Israel's power of arms was not responsible for bringing it (Judg 7:2-7; Ps 20:7-8). If Judah, disre-
garding all this, chose to become embroiled in military
action and enter into covenant with foreign powers, the
consequence would be military defeat, with all the devastation that entailed.

The defeat and devastation is described through two
images, the collapsing wall and the broken pot. The collapsing wall is the more dynamic of the two and presents Judah's
iniquity as that fatal flaw which causes that which appeared
so strong to crumble and come crashing down. But the
second image continues the message of the first. A broken
pot is irreparable, but sometimes something can be salvaged
(e.g., many of the written records which come from Palestine are written on potsherds), but in the crash here described not a single fragment large enough to be of any sort of
use will remain. (See further on this passage above, Introduction, p. 34.)

In vv 15-17 we have again something very similar to 28:
16-17, namely, a reference back to Yahweh's invitation to
faith and trustful waiting, along with a note on Judah's
rejection of the invitation and on the consequences this
brings. We should probably translate "in waiting and rest"
rather than *RSV's in returning and rest*. What is required is
not mere passivity, but that strength that consists in recog-
nizing how temporary, how inconsequential, how inconclu-
sive are all human machinations: *in quietness and in trust*

shall be your strength (cf. the holy war formula in Exod 14:14: "the Lord will fight for you, and you have only to be still"). The consequences of Judah's refusal are now depicted in more realistic terms, without imagery, as military defeat. But here it is the reversal of the holy war paradigm: traditionally Yahweh's fear fell upon the enemy and they would flee before a handful of Israelites, but now the reverse is true. The final image is that of hopeless isolation; 1:8 contains a rather similar image of isolation and suggests that perhaps here, too, there is a reference to the survival of Jerusalem in the general devastation.

A PROMISE OF RESTORATION: 30:18-26

18   Therefore the LORD waits to be gracious to you;
    therefore he exalts himself to show mercy to you.
For the LORD is a God of justice;
    blessed are all those who wait for him.
19 Yea, O people in Zion who dwell at Jerusalem; you shall weep no more. He will surely be gracious to you at the sound of your cry; when he hears it, he will answer you. 20And though the Lord give you the bread of adversity and the water of affliction, yet your Teacher will not hide himself any more, but your eyes shall see your Teacher. 21And your ears shall hear a word behind you, saying "This is the way, walk in it," when you turn to the right or when you turn to the left. 22Then you will defile your silver-covered graven images and your gold-plated molten images. You will scatter them as unclean things; you will say to them, "Begone!"
23 And he will give rain for the seed with which you sow the ground, and grain, the produce of the ground, which will be rich and plenteous. In that day your cattle will graze in large pastures; 24and the oxen and the asses that till the ground will eat salted provender, which has been winnowed with shovel and fork. 25And upon every lofty mountain and every high hill there will be brooks running with water, in the day of the great slaughter, when the

towers fall. [26]Moreover the light of the moon will be as the light of the sun, and the light of the sun will be sevenfold, as the light of seven days, in the day when the LORD binds up the hurt of his people, and heals the wounds inflicted by his blow.

The assurance with which this piece begins, that Yahweh is waiting to be gracious, relates to the previous context only in the sense that the threatened judgment has already taken place. It therefore supposes the destruction of Jerusalem and v 18 must date from sometime after 587; vv 19-26 are a further development on the theme, sometimes in rather extraordinary terms that approach apocalyptic, and are undoubtedly considerably later; this later section supposes that the return to the land has already taken place.

Verse 18, with its *blessed are all those who wait for him*, picks up a good Isaian theme (see 8:17, where the same vocabulary of waiting occurs). Isaiah had already spoken of the need to wait for the Lord to act in his own good time, and the present author now extends that to those who are impatient for the promised restoration. The same Hebrew verb is used of the Lord at the beginning of the verse, who therefore is also "waiting" for the proper moment. The *justice* referred to here (*mishpat*) is to be understood as "right order" rather than reward or punishment.

Verse 19 speaks no longer of the Lord waiting, but of his being willing to answer as soon as he is called upon; at the same time it reveals that those who have returned to Zion still have occasion to weep and to cry out to him (cf. 61:3; 62:6-7). Verse 20 strikes an odd note in the present context if it is really to be understood to refer to *bread of adversity* and *water of affliction*. The expressions can better be rendered as "the bread you need" and "water for which you thirst" (see *NAB*); or, with an emendation, it could be translated "bread instead of adversity," etc. Although some commentators would delete the reference to *your Teacher*, there seems no need for this. The Hebrew has the plural, but this is regularly taken as a plural of majesty to refer to the Lord.

This concept builds very nicely on Isaiah's polemic against the human imparters of wisdom that he had encountered and upon his presentation of Yahweh as the source of true wisdom and *torah*. Faithful people have always longed to know with certainty what is required of them (which is why there has always been such a strong tendency to take refuge in exact sets of rules), and in this passage is the promise that the desired guidance would one day be given in an unmistakable manner. Here the immediate result of this divine instruction is the forsaking of pagan and idolatrous ways, which therefore must have been one of the failings the author saw in the people he was addressing; again there is an echo here of other passages in Isaiah (2:8, 20) but also of the abuses of the postexilic period (57:4-13; 65:11-12; 66:3-4).

The remaining verses describe the future joy in most extraordinary terms of fertility and prosperity. The somber allusion to *the day of great slaughter* points to a development in which the "day of the Lord" is thought of as one of bloody destruction of Yahweh's (and Israel's) foes, such as we find in 66:15-16 and Joel 3:11-15, though the reference to the downfall of the towers was probably suggested by Isaiah's own description of the "day of the Lord" (2:15). The same is true of the mention of *every lofty mountain and every high hill* (v 25), which approximates the language of 2:14 except that here the note of destruction has been replaced with the positive one of abundant water. The transformation which will increase the brilliance of sun sevenfold approaches the sort of thing found in later apocalyptic, though it exceeds only in the matter of degree some of the imagery found in Trito-Isaiah (cf. 58:10; 60:2-3, 19-20).

YAHWEH'S JUDGMENT ON ASSYRIA: 30:27-33

27 Behold, the name of the Lord comes from far,
   burning with his anger, and in thick rising smoke;
   his lips are full of indignation,
   and his tongue is like a devouring fire;
28 his breath is like an overflowing stream

that reaches up to the neck;
to sift the nations with the sieve of destruction,
    and to place on the jaws of the peoples a bridle that leads
    astray.

29 You shall have a song as in the night when a holy feast is kept; and gladness of heart, as when one sets out to the sound of the flute to go to the mountain of the Lord, to the Rock of Israel. 30 And the Lord will cause his majestic voice to be heard and the descending blow of his arm to be seen, in furious anger and a flame of devouring fire, with a cloudburst and tempest and hailstones. 31 The Assyrians will be terror-stricken at the voice of the Lord, when he smites with his rod. 32 And every stroke of the staff of punishment which the Lord lays upon them will be to the sound of timbrels and lyres; battling with brandished arm he will fight with them. 33 For a burning place has long been prepared; yea, for the king it is made ready, its pyre made deep and wide, with fire and wood in abundance; the breath of the Lord, like a stream of brimstone, kindles it.

Commentators disagree on the Isaian authenticity of this piece, and those who favor it sometimes judge vv 29 and 32 as later additions. Although Isaiah speaks elsewhere about the destructive punishment Yahweh will visit upon Assyria, this text speaks of it being accomplished by *rod* and *staff* (vv 31-32); since these are not apt instruments of destruction (and destruction is certainly what is intended), they seem to have been picked up from 10:5. There Assyria was Yahweh's rod and staff for chastising Judah; here, in what can be termed an adaptation and a reversal of that reference, they become the means of Yahweh's destruction of Assyria. The order of the text appears to be disturbed; see *NAB*, which transfers v 29 after v 32 (and cf. *OAB*, which proposes a somewhat more complicated rearrangement).

The early verses of the piece contain traditional elements of a theophany — *smoke, fire*, etc. — and all this suits very well the "coming" of the Lord which is proclaimed in v 27. There are many vehicles of God's self-revelation in the Old

Testament; for example, his saving work on behalf of Israel (40:5) or even a thunderstorm (Psalm 29). In the present case it would be his righteous judgment on the nations, specifically on the Assyrians. The description of Yahweh breathing out fire (vv 27, 33), strange as it may seem, is not unique in the Old Testament (see Ps 18:8, 15). The astounding shift of imagery between v 27 (*smoke, fire*) and v 28 (*overflowing stream*) is not uncharacteristic of the piece, which combines quite a range of images. The *overflowing stream* bit rests on 8:7-8, only there it was Assyria flooding Judah; thus we have another instance of reversing the import of a text that spoke of Assyria's devastating Judah into Yahweh's destruction of Assyria. The meaning of the Hebrew term translated *sift* and *sieve* is quite uncertain.

Since Assyria is named (v 31) and the use of earlier Isaiah texts (see above on v 28 and vv 31-32) also points to the Assyrians, the piece is to be dated before the fall of Nineveh in 612; however, the depth of animosity expressed suggests a time well before the end, while Assyria was still vigorous and actively oppressing Judah. The author sees this destruction of Assyria as an occasion of joy and glee for Judah, such that he readily presents it as accompanied with the sort of song and musical instruments with which a religious feast is celebrated; Yahweh's destruction of Assyria is a liturgical act, so to speak, carried out to the accompaniment of Judah's songs of praise and joy.

There is much that is obscure and doubtful about the final verse (v 33), but the general import is not in doubt: the climax of Yahweh's offensive against the Assyrians will be consumption by fire in a funeral pyre. Again something of the unbridled animosity comes through in the gusto of the description and the kindling by the breath of the Lord. The Hebrew word that *RSV* translates *burning place* is not otherwise found in the Old Testament, but a small emendation gives "Topheth," a name given to a place outside Jerusalem, in the Hinnom Valley, where the pagan sacrifice of infants by burning was carried out (2 Kgs 23:10), and it may be that the author intended that the destruction of the Assyrians would have place there. Partly under the influence of this understanding, many would read "Molech" in place of *king* (*melek*), since the Old Testament understands that such infant sacrifices were made to a pagan god of that name (see Lev 18:21; 20:2-5; 2 Kgs 23:10), but the sense then becomes very tortured.

WOE TO THOSE WHO TRUST IN EGYPT: 31:1-3

31 Woe to those who go down to Egypt for help
    and rely on horses,
  who trust in chariots because they are many
    and in horsemen because they are very strong,
  but do not look to the Holy One of Israel
    or consult the LORD!
2 And yet he is wise and brings disaster,
    he does not call back his words,
  but will arise against the house of the evildoers,
    and against the helpers of those who work iniquity.
3 The Egyptians are men, and not God;
    and their horses are flesh, and not spirit.
  When the LORD stretches out his hand,
    the helper will stumble, and he who is helped will fall,
    and they will all perish together.

Again we return to the theme which has occupied so much of chaps. 28-31, namely, the foolishness of revolt against the Assyrians and the pointlessness of looking to Egypt for help. The present piece is closely connected with the similar "woe" of 30:1-5 and may come from about the same time. Again it is a question of Judah taking the initiative (so we are in a different situation from that of 18:1-6), perhaps suggesting they are already hard-pressed. Verse 2 is not part of the original woe-oracle, but a later interpolation which interrupts the otherwise clear connection between v 1 and v 3; the reference to *wicked* and *evildoers* suits the language of the psalms very well, but is rather generalized for the present context, which speaks of Judah and Egypt.

As in 30:1-5, it is again a matter of placing trust in the wrong thing, in a multitude of chariots rather than in that strength which comes from the Lord; again it is a matter of failing to seek to learn what is his word for this situation (v 1, as in 30:2). Verse 3 gives a precious insight into the biblical contrast between "flesh" and "spirit," which relate, respectively, to weakness and power (rather than to that which is material and that which is immaterial). The contrast between *flesh* and *spirit* is made clear in the preceding contrast between *men* and *God*: if the Egyptians were God, they could be of help (but they are only men); and (surprising to our ears!) if their horses were spirit they could help, but they are only flesh. Because Judah has chosen to put trust in that which is of its nature weak and helpless, they prepare their own destruction. The Egyptians will fail in their attempt to bring help and those who relied on them will meet disaster.

SALVATION FROM THE LORD FOR A REPENTANT JERUSALEM: 31:4-9

4 For thus the LORD said to me,
  As a lion or a young lion growls over his prey,
    and when a band of shepherds is called forth against him
  is not terrified by their shouting
    or daunted at their noise,
  so the Lord of hosts will come down
    to fight upon Mount Zion and upon its hill.
5 Like birds hovering, so the Lord of hosts
    will protect Jerusalem;
  he will protect and deliver it,
    he will spare and rescue it.
6 Turn to him from whom you have deeply revolted, O people of Israel. 7For in that day every one shall cast away his idols of silver and his idols of gold, which your hands have sinfully made for you.
8 "And the Assyrian shall fall by a sword, not of man;
    and a sword, not of man, shall devour him;
  and he shall flee from the sword,
    and his young men shall be put to forced labor.
9 His rock shall pass away in terror,

> and his officers desert the standard in panic,"
> says the LORD, whose fire is in Zion,
> and whose furnace is in Jerusalem.

The authorship, unity, and import of this passage are so disputed that it is difficult to find two commentators who hold to the same interpretation. There is general agreement that v 7 is a later interpolation, taken over from 2:20 and/or 30:22. Some authors will concede v 4 to Isaiah but understand it as threat rather than promise: Yahweh will come down to fight *against* (not upon) Mt. Zion, which (in the lion imagery) is the prey which none can take from him. This supposes that all the other expressions in the passage which suggest promise of deliverance — and which make up the bulk of it — are a series of later developments.

Although no certainty can be claimed, the passage can be taken in a more unified way, as an expression of the tradition of Yahweh's special protection of Zion (Jerusalem). It would thus stand as a reminder from Isaiah, presented in a conditional way, of the protection Yahweh is willing and able to supply, *provided* they will look to him for the help that is needed. On this understanding, the passage would be the other side of the coin to the "woe" immediately preceding (31:1-3): Judah can expect either disaster or safety, depending on whether they look to Egypt or to Yahweh for help. The words which describe a rescue by Yahweh are accompanied by a call for "return" to the one from whom they have rebelled (v 6; cf. 30:1, 9), and although this verse, just as v 7, is probably a later addition, it would not be out of harmony with Isaiah's thought.

In this sense the simile of the lion becomes more intelligible: the emphasis is not on the prey having just now been seized or being in danger from the lion, but rather on the fact that the lion regards it as his own and allows no one to deprive him of it. In terms of the Zion tradition, Jerusalem stands in that relation to Yahweh, the one who has founded and chosen it (see above on 1:26; 14:32; 17:12-14). But, as has already been made clear, this protection is available only through faith, and no unconditional promise is made.

In this sense the passage aligns itself with texts such as 28:16 and 30:15. The imagery of the hovering birds (v 5) is not easily intelligible either in itself or as a development on v 4, something which is true in any interpretation, but it does help to reinforce rather emphatically the message of rescue and safety.

As in some other texts, there is a close connection between the Zion tradition and the holy war tradition. In the circumstances of the holy war it would not be Judah's valor or strength in battle, but the Lord's own action which would bring about the defeat of his adversaries (v 8), an end which is often accomplished through a numinous terror which falls upon the enemy to send them flying in confusion. In the case at hand, the Assyrians are doomed to sword, flight, or captivity, as even the officers, the backbone (*rock*) of their force, melt in terror.

THE KINGDOM OF RIGHTEOUSNESS AND INTEGRITY: 32:1-8

32 Behold, a king will reign in righteousness,
    and princes will rule in justice.
2 Each will be like a hiding place from the wind,
    a covert from the tempest,
  like streams of water in a dry place,
    like the shade of a great rock in a weary land.
3 Then the eyes of those who see will not be closed,
    and the ears of those who hear will hearken.
4 The mind of the rash will have good judgment,
    and the tongue of the stammerers will speak readily and
  distinctly.
5 The fool will no more be called noble,
    nor the knave said to be honorable.

6 For the fool speaks folly,
    and his mind plots iniquity:
  to practice ungodliness,
    to utter error concerning the LORD,
  to leave the craving of the hungry unsatisfied,

and to deprive the thirsty of drink.
7 The knaveries of the knave are evil;
     he devises wicked devices
   to ruin the poor with lying words,
     even when the plea of the needy is right.
8 But he who is noble devises noble things,
     and by noble things he stands.

These verses are a peculiar blend of wisdom and prophecy. It may be said that although they are the composition of
a sage, they could never have been written without the
prophetic tradition, most specifically that of Isaiah. The
opening words *Behold, a king will reign* ... are often taken
to designate the messianic ruler of the prophets' expectation, but it is more probably a generalized picture of what an
ideal king would be like, what conditions would be like
under him, viewed from the perspective of the wisdom
tradition. This generalized picture is often brought out by
translating the opening words "when (or if) a king rules in
righteousness. ..." Yet it was only the prophetic tradition
that taught the wise men to look forward with expectation
to a messianic future in which the ideal would be realized,
either by depicting it directly or by promising that the evils
of the present would pass away. Not a few phrases of the
present piece seem to be reversals of Isaiah's comments on
his own time — reversals intended not to deny the truth of
his observations, but to depict a new situation in which his
strictures have had their effect, especially as they relate to
the rulers and to the wise. The piece falls into two parts, vv
1-5 and vv 6-8, the second of which acts as an expansion on
certain points raised in the first.

The parallelism between what is said of the *king* and what
is said of the *princes* (*sarim*) in v 1 is one of the indications
that it is not a matter of a messianic king to come; king and
princes together make for a well-ordered society. The wisdom tradition concerned itself with the qualities of righteousness and justice (*sedeq, mishpat*) as endowments of
king and princes (see Prov 8:15-16; 16:10, 12-13; 20:8, 26, 28;
25:5; and cf. Job 34:18-19). In v 2 the advantages of a society

blessed by rulers with such qualities are expressed in images suggesting safety and refreshment, while in vv 3-4 is depicted the curing of certain limitations of mind and body. The non-closing of the eyes and ears seems to be a reversal of the unhappy circumstances of Isaiah's ministry (6:9-10; and cf. 29:9-10). When a society is sick, values are reversed: good is called evil, sweet is called bitter, and vice versa (cf. 5:20; and see 3:5), but in the ideal society which is here envisioned, the wicked and the foolish will be seen for what they are.

Three of the terms used in v 5, *fool, knave,* and *noble,* are now singled out for further commentary (vv 6-8), perhaps by a later hand. Here we encounter something of the wisdom tradition's concern for just judgment and for the poor, as the fool, to the utter neglect of God's will, leaves the hungry in their need, and the knave, by perversion of justice, deprives the poor of their right. This equation of the fool with the wicked is also characteristic of the wisdom tradition. But in the new order here envisioned, people of this sort will no longer prevail, and so the passage ends with a glance at the *noble things* that the noble one (a reference back to the ideal rulers of v 1) plans and carries into effect.

FATE OF THE COMPLACENT WOMEN: 32:9-14

9 Rise up, you women who are at ease, hear my voice;
    you complacent daughters, give ear to my speech.
10 In little more than a year
    you will shudder, you complacent women;
for the vintage will fail,
    the fruit harvest will not come.
11 Tremble, you women who are at ease,
    shudder, you complacent ones;
strip, and make yourselves bare,
    and gird sackcloth upon your loins.
12 Beat upon your breasts for the pleasant fields,
    for the fruitful vine,
13 for the soil of my people
    growing up in thorns and briers;
yea, for all the joyous houses

in the joyful city.
14 For the palace will be forsaken,
   the populous city deserted;
the hill and the watchtower
   will become dens for ever,
a joy of wild asses,
   a pasture of flocks;

   A number of commentators attribute this oracle to
Isaiah, some specifically relating it to the time immediately
after the Assyrian withdrawal in 701. Indeed, it does manifest some points of contact with genuine Isaian words. For
example, the reference to the place as *the joyful city* (v 13)
agrees with Isaiah's strictures on Jerusalem in 22:2. Isaiah
does use the sort of "call to attention" formula with which
this piece opens (see 1:10 and 28:23), and he did have some
harsh things to say about the haughty daughters of Zion in
3:16-26. Nevertheless, the very contrast of that piece with
this one argues against common authorship; there is also the
fact that, as much as he threatened Jerusalem, Isaiah never
spoke of its destruction in the fashion of the present oracle;
there is also some linguistic usage that would date this one to
a period later than Isaiah. Although *the joyful city* (v 13),
the populous city (v 14) is not named, the chances are very
good that these words were spoken of Jerusalem. The most
likely time would have been shortly before that city's fall to
Nebuchadnezzar in 587.
   The piece begins, as we have mentioned, with a call to
attention. The message delivered after this is that within a
fairly brief time (the exact import of the Hebrew expression
is not certain) everything in which they now place confidence and take pleasure will be gone; therefore they already
have reason to tremble and go into mourning (of which
stripping, dressing in sackcloth, and beating the breast
would be expressions). There are to be no new crops from
vine or field, for the arable land would be given back to
briars and to the trampling of livestock (cf. 7:24-25). A
further sign of the desolation spread by an invading army is

seen in the abandonment of houses, the palace, and of the city in general. The term translated *hill* in v 14 (*'ophel*) designates the mount captured by David from the Jebusites and the earliest part of Jerusalem. Thus the fate of the city has come full circle, as it is taken from the power of the then reigning son of David and returned to pagan control.

Our knowledge of the editing of Isaiah's oracles is very incomplete, so it is difficult to know when and by whom this oracle was inserted, coming, as it does, so close to the end of the collection consisting of chaps. 28-33. Was it the editor's intention to demonstrate that even worse things than Isaiah had threatened had come to pass? Certainly his warnings about the folly of Judah's behavior were fully vindicated. But Isaiah also held out hope, so the collection will be filled out and completed with the hopeful lines which follow the present ones and by chap. 33.

RESTORATION THROUGH THE SPIRIT: 32:15-20

[15] until the Spirit is poured upon us from on high,
and the wilderness becomes a fruitful field,
and the fruitful field is deemed a forest.
[16] Then justice will dwell in the wilderness,
and righteousness abide in the fruitful field.
[17] And the effect of righteousness will be peace,
and the result of righteousness, quietness and trust for ever.
[18] My people will abide in a peaceful habitation,
in secure dwellings, and in quiet resting places.
[19] And the forest will utterly go down,
and the city will be utterly laid low.
[20] Happy are you who sow beside all waters,
who let the feet of the ox and the ass range free.

The *until* of v 15 obviously intends to bind these verses closely to the preceding and to cover over their immediate threat by holding out future promise, but they come from a different hand and a different age. They breathe forth a peaceful calm with no indication that those addressed are in exile. Because of this and because they show contact with other late passages, these verses are probably to be dated to postexilic times.

The sense of peace, justice, and prosperity that pervades this passage is remarkable, and the author shows at the outset the understanding that these qualities are attainable only through the gift of God. Thus he begins with reference to *spirit poured upon us from on high*. In this he is in accord with 11:1-5, though there it is the messianic king who is the recipient, while here it is presumably the whole people (*my people*—v 18); there it was "the spirit of Yahweh," while here it is *spirit from on high*—in each case the same heavenly gift which enables people to do what they could not otherwise do. (On the import of God's spirit, see above on 11:2.)

Not only does a sense of peace, justice, and prosperity characterize this passage, but there is a strong awareness of the interconnection between the three. After the reference to the transformation in material nature (cf. 29:17 for an almost identical situation), *justice* and *righteousness* (*mishpat* and *sedaqah*) are said to dwell in two of the areas of the nature that have been named (*wilderness* and *fruitful field* — v 16). The concatenation is made explicit as peace, quietness, and trust are designated as *the effect* (literally: work) *of righteousness* (v 17). These effects are said to be *for ever*, and we can see a merciful contrast with the previous passage, where the desolation there described was to be "for ever" (v 14). The blessings of peace, trust, and quiet are ultimately those that relate to human existence rather than the natural world, just as do the qualities of justice and righteousness, and so at length they are bestowed (where some authors might have begun) on *my people* (v 18). In a less positive vein Hosea had seen the land mourning and animals perishing because of human wickedness (Hos 4:1-3). Our present author perceives the same sort of connection between human behavior and the world of nature, and his restoration proceeds in the direction in which it does to emphasize the divine source and the divine gift which makes it possible.

Verse 19 has been the subject of much dispute, for its negative tone fits badly into this oracle of salvation. Even if *the city* were taken to be some enemy capital, *forest* can hardly be something to be destroyed, since it is part of the positive picture in v 15. Thus the verse does not fit here; some consider it an interpolation from a totally different context, while others think it belonged originally after v 14 and was therefore the conclusion of the preceding oracle.

The final editor of this part of the book has closed this collection on the note of promise and hope. He has brought in many themes that were important to Isaiah, themes such as righteousness and justice and has related them to the peace that Isaiah so dearly longed for. He has held these things out as something to come in future times as a gift of God's spirit. In all this he was in accord with the aspirations of Isaiah and even with the promises expressed at more than one point in his oracles.

A LITURGY OF SUPPLICATION AND SALVATION: 33:1-24

33 Woe to you, destroyer,
>who yourself have not been destroyed;
you treacherous one,
>with whom none has dealt treacherously!
When you have ceased to destroy,
>you will be destroyed;
and when you have made an end of dealing treacherously,
>you will be dealt with treacherously.

2 O LORD, be gracious to us; we wait for thee.
>Be our arm every morning,
>our salvation in the time of trouble.
3 At the thunderous noise peoples flee,
>at the lifting up of thyself nations are scattered;
4 and spoil is gathered as the caterpillar gathers;
>as locusts leap, men leap upon it.
5 The LORD is exalted, for he dwells on high;

he will fill Zion with justice and righteousness;
6 and he will be the stability of your times,
abundance of salvation, wisdom, and knowledge;
the fear of the LORD is his treasure.

7 Behold, the valiant ones cry without;
the envoys of peace weep bitterly.
8 The highways lie waste,
the wayfaring man ceases.
Covenants are broken,
witnesses are despised,
there is no regard for man.
9 The land mourns and languishes;
Lebanon is confounded and withers away;
Sharon is like a desert;
and Bashan and Carmel shake off their leaves.

10 "Now I will arise," says the LORD,
"now I will lift myself up;
now I will be exalted.
11 You conceive chaff, you bring forth stubble;
your breath is a fire that will consume you.
12 And the peoples will be as if burned to lime,
like thorns cut down, that are burned in the fire."

13 Hear, you who are far off, what I have done;
and you who are near, acknowledge my might.
14 The sinners in Zion are afraid;
trembling has seized the godless:
"Who among us can dwell with the devouring fire?
Who among us can dwell with everlasting burnings?"
15 He who walks righteously and speaks uprightly,
who despises the gain of oppressions,
who shakes his hands, lest they hold a bribe,
who stops his ears from hearing of bloodshed
and shuts his eyes from looking upon evil,
16 he will dwell on the heights;
his place of defense will be the fortresses of rocks;
his bread will be given him, his water will be sure.

17 Your eyes will see the king in his beauty;
   they will behold a land that stretches afar.
18 Your mind will muse on the terror:
   "Where is he who counted, where is he who weighed
      thete?
   Where is he who counted the towers?"
19 You will see no more the insolent people,
   the people of an obscure speech which you cannot
      comprehend,
   stammering in a tongue which you cannot understand.
20 Look upon Zion, the city of our appointed feasts!
   Your eyes will see Jerusalem,
   a quiet habitation, an immovable tent,
   whose stakes will never be plucked up,
      nor will any of its cords be broken.
21 But there the LORD in majesty will be for us
   a place of broad rivers and streams,
   where no galley with oars can go,
      nor stately ship can pass.
22 For the LORD is our judge, the LORD is our ruler,
   the LORD is our king; he will save us.

23 Your tackle hangs loose;
   it cannot hold the mast firm in its place,
      or keep the sail spread out.
   Then prey and spoil in abundance will be divided;
      even the lame will take the prey.
24 And no inhabitant will say, "I am sick";
   the people who dwell there will be forgiven their iniquity.

This chapter is here taken as a single composition, though
it is to be noted that a number of commentators see vv 1-6 as
an independent unit and vv 7-24 as a second one. The two
are closely related thematically, for both describe deliverance from the Lord in response to his people's need. In
taking the whole chapter as one composition, vv 1-6 are seen
as a summarizing introduction to the whole, containing
both the prayer for deliverance and description (by anticipa-

tion) of the Lord's salvation. In any interpretation vv 7-24 fall into four parts patterned on well-recognized prophetic or liturgical forms: vv 7-9 (lament), vv 10-13 (prophetic oracular response), vv 14-16 (entrance liturgy), and vv 17-24 (prophetic oracle of promise). Although the composition exhibits many contacts with the psalms and even with the wisdom tradition (see especially v 6), it is prophetic in its inspiration and tenor and is to be classified as a "prophetic liturgy" (a term also applied to parts of chaps. 24-27). There is almost universal agreement that the chapter is not earlier than the exile, though a postexilic date, with adherents for both Persian and Greek periods, is more commonly favored; so late a date as Maccabean times seems highly unlikely.

Verses 1-6, referred to above as a "summarizing introduction," begins by identifying a main cause of the distress which prompts the people's lament, namely, a nation (presumably, though the address is individual) characterized as *destroyer* and *treacherous one*. It still exists and poses a danger but is now threatened with being on the receiving end of destruction and treachery. No identification is given; if the poem can be dated in exilic times, Babylon would be the obvious choice. In v 2 appeal is made to Yahweh in language reminiscent of the psalms (cf. Ps 123:3), and almost at once the mood passes to that of confidence of help as the poet speaks of the peoples fleeing as Yahweh arises and of booty being swarmed upon as by locusts (v 4). Yahweh is pictured as enthroned in Zion, which he fills with *justice and righteousness* (the condition for all blessedness — see above on 32:15-20). Verse 6 promises stability to this happy situation and relates it to *wisdom, knowledge,* and *fear of the Lord*, three of the charismatic qualities of the messianic king in 11:1-5. The two passages share not only those three terms, but the *stability* of the present text is the same Hebrew word (*'emunah*) as the "faithfulness" of 11:5. Both passages exhibit wisdom influence and both relate peace and salvation to the same sort of moral qualities.

But now, in vv 7-9, the current distressful situation is described, that from which deliverance is sought. The translation *valiant ones* (v 7) is quite uncertain, but some manuscripts have "men of Ariel" (i.e., the poetic term for Jerusalem in 29:1, 2, 7), and a small emendation would give "envoys of Salem" (another term for Jerusalem — cf. Gen 14:18; Ps 76:2) rather than *envoys of peace*. This would provide good parallelism and a clearer meaning in describing the distress of the inhabitants of Jerusalem. Normal travel and communication have been made impossible (cf. Judg 5:6). The reference to covenants and witnesses (v 8) probably relates to disorders in commercial matters. Although in such circumstances one would indeed expect that farming would be adversely affected, the *languishing* of the fertile places is an imaginative way of driving home the wretchedness of the situation: Lebanon, Sharon (i.e., the fertile coastal plain stretching north from Mt. Carmel), Bashan (the rich pastureland in northern Transjordan), and Carmel are all proverbial for their richness, but Lebanon lay outside Israel's territory at all times, and Bashan and Carmel would not have been in Judah's territory in postexilic times.

The prophetic response of vv 10-13 begins at once with the assurance of Yahweh's intervention by "rising up," language reminiscent of the psalms (cf. Ps 12:5), spoken by the Lord in the first person (v 10). The impotence of his enemies Yahweh describes in terms of what they can *conceive* (*chaff*) and give birth to (*stubble*). Midway through v 11 there is a shift: Yahweh is no longer the speaker but the one being addressed. As in some other texts he is depicted as breathing forth fire to consume his enemies (see above on 30:27, 33), who are depicted as being *burned to lime* (cf. Amos 2:1) and as blazing like dried thorn bushes (v 12). The section ends as Yahweh looks to all, both near and far, to recognize the power he manifests by his acts in history (v 13).

Verses 14-16 are called an "entrance liturgy" because of their resemblance to other passages that have long been so designated; see especially Ps 15:1-5 and 24:3-6. These consist of a dialogue in which the conditions for entering the Lord's sanctuary are asked and a response given in terms of certain required moral dispositions. (Such passages are sometimes inaccurately designated as "entrance torahs" on the incorrect assumption that the question and answer form is sufficient to label something "torah.") In the present case, however, it is not a matter of entering the Lord's sanctuary, but of the danger which faces the sinners among those who already dwell on Zion, his holy mountain. The connection with the preceding section is seen in Yahweh's fiery disposal of his enemies there, the fear experienced by the sinners on Zion here, and the question raised by the proximity of this *devouring fire* and the possibility of existing with it (v 14). The response resembles the "entrance liturgies" referred to above and, like them, lists a series of lofty ethical demands, with emphasis upon the avoidance of oppression, injustice, and violence (v 15). The concluding verse assures that the one who meets these conditions will dwell in security and without need (v 16).

Now that the supplication has been offered for deliverance (v 2) from the present situation (vv 7-9), the promise of the Lord has been heard (vv 10-13), and the moral conditions for living in his presence established (vv 14-16), a beautiful and exuberant description of the future blessedness is given (vv 17-24). The opening promise, that of seeing a king (rather than *RSV's the king*) in his glory, raises at once the question of whether the reference is to a future messianic king (as in 11:1-9), any future ideal king (as is probably the case in 32:1-5), or God himself, and it does not seem possible to provide a certain answer. Given the whole context, especially the preparation for dwelling with God in vv 14-16 and the identification of Yahweh as *our king* in v 22, the third possibility seems most likely; but then it is strange that the article ("*the* king") is missing in Hebrew. In any case, the vision of beauty stretches out to distant vistas (v 17b). The poet even pictures the thoughts of the one now delivered from fear of the overseers and "enforcers" who saw to collecting tribute and imposing the foreign tyrants' will (*your mind will muse* . . .). These strangers with their unintelligible speech will be gone (vv 18-19) — another reversal of previous punishment (cf. 28:11). Attention is now called to the future joy and glory of Jerusalem, described with an eye to its cultic importance (*city of our appointed feasts*) and characterized as permanent like a *tent* that is destined never to be moved; that note may be inspired by a somewhat idealized recollection of Israel's early days and their desert tabernacle.

Whatever the meaning of "a king" in v 17, vv 21-23a make abundantly clear how immediately present the Lord will be and how great the implications of his presence. For one thing, it will be a sure defense, as though he were an impassable river that no sort of ship could negotiate. The reference to the slack *tackle* and *sail* in v 23a continues the same idea, and it is possible that those lines should immediately follow v 21 (see *NAB*). If 32:1-5 spoke of the happy situation in which just rulers ruled, v 22 describes the happier situation in which the Lord himself holds sway and in which he is judge and king and savior.

It would seem difficult to improve on the idyllic conditions depicted in vv 20-23a, but the concluding vv 23b-24 promise, in somewhat prosaic fashion, the taking of spoil from the enemy (which may hark back to v 4) and the absence of illness. A higher note is again reached as the moral aspect of true happiness is touched upon in the acknowledgment that the forgiveness of sin is a part of the happy picture.

JUDGMENT ON THE
NATIONS AND VINDICATION
OF ZION: CHAPTERS 34-35

Chaps. 34-35 are to be taken together as a sort of diptych, the one retailing the fate in store for the nations, considered to be inimical to God's people, with Edom singled out for particular attention, the other describing the glory of the Jerusalem of the restoration. There are obvious similarities between chaps. 34-35 and Deutero-Isaiah, so that some have even postulated a common authorship. A better explanation is that the author of chaps. 34-35 was strongly influenced by Deutero-Isaiah's writings and that his own composition betrays that influence. This would suggest the late sixth century as the earliest time of composition, with a date in the fifth century perhaps more likely. Similarities to the "Apocalypse of Isaiah" (chaps. 24-27) are also noted, so that chaps. 34-35 are sometimes called the "Little Apocalypse." Again it should be noted that we do not find here apocalyptic in the developed sense but rather what may be termed "proto-apocalyptic" (see above on chaps. 24-27).

The pattern of judgment upon the nations followed by Israel's restoration is found elsewhere in the prophetic books, most especially in Ezekiel, whether we think in broader terms of the oracles against the nations (chaps.

25-32) followed by oracles of Judah's restoration (chaps. 33-48), or in narrower terms of the summoning of the nations to fight against Jerusalem and to fall on the mountains of Israel (chaps. 38-39) followed by the detailed account of the new theocracy (chaps. 40-48). This pattern, which is generally attributable to the editors of the prophetic books, is found also on a smaller scale in briefer collections within prophetic books, as in the many examples we have already encountered in Isaiah. In the present case, however, the pattern is attributable to the author, who willed the contrast between the fate of the nations (especially as seen in Edom) and that of God's people. Some scholars have seen these chapters as forming a bridge between the collection of chaps. 1-33 (mainly the oracles of Isaiah of Jerusalem, from the eighth century) and Deutero-Isaiah. If that is the case, it would mean that insertion of the historical appendix of chaps. 36-39, which now separates chaps. 34-35 from Deutero-Isaiah, would have taken place at a later time.

JUDGMENT ON THE NATIONS: 34:1-17

34 Draw near, O nations, to hear,
      and hearken, O peoples!
   Let the earth listen, and all that fills it;
      the world, and all that comes from it.
 2 For the LORD is enraged against all the nations,
      and furious against all their host,
      he has doomed them, has given them over for slaughter.
 3 Their slain shall be cast out,
      and the stench of their corpses shall rise;
      the mountains shall flow with their blood.
 4 All the host of heaven shall rot away,
      and the skies roll up like a scroll.
   All their host shall fall,
      as leaves fall from the vine,
      like leaves falling from the fig tree.

 5 For my sword has drunk its fill in the heavens;

behold, it descends for judgment upon Edom,
   upon the people I have doomed.
6 The LORD has a sword; it is sated with blood,
   it is gorged with fat,
      with the blood of lambs and goats,
      with the fat of the kidneys of rams.
   For the LORD has a sacrifice in Bozrah,
      a great slaughter in the land of Edom.
7 Wild oxen shall fall with them,
      and young steers with the mighty bulls.
   Their land shall be soaked with blood,
      and their soil made rich with fat.

8 For the LORD has a day of vengeance,
      a year of recompense for the cause of Zion.
9 And the streams of Edom shall be turned into pitch,
      and her soil into brimstone;
      her land shall become burning pitch.
10 Night and day it shall not be quenched;
      its smoke shall go up for ever.
   From generation to generation it shall lie waste;
      none shall pass through it for ever and ever.
11 But the hawk and the porcupine shall possess it,
      the owl and the raven shall dwell in it.
   He shall stretch the line of confusion over it,
      and the plummet of chaos over its nobles.
12 They shall name it No Kingdom There,
      and all its princes shall be nothing.

13 Thorns shall grow over its strongholds,
      nettles and thistles in its fortresses.
   It shall be the haunt of jackals,
      an abode for ostriches.
14 And wild beasts shall meet with hyenas,
      the satyr shall cry to his fellow;
   yea, there shall the night hag alight,
      and find for herself a resting place.
15 There shall the owl nest and lay
      and hatch and gather her young in her shadow;
   yea, there shall the kites be gathered,

each one with her mate.
16 Seek and read from the book of the LORD:
  Not one of these shall be missing;
  none shall be without her mate.
For the mouth of the LORD has commanded,
  and his Spirit has gathered them.
17 He has cast the lot for them,
  his hand has portioned it out to them with the line;
they shall possess it for ever,
  from generation to generation they shall dwell in it.

In spite of the violence and carnage here depicted, these verses are distinguished by great poetic power. The piece is not without its inconsistencies, but the development of the theme is quite clear: the nations are summoned to hear a message of judgment and destruction which is pronounced against them (vv 1-4); attention is then directed to Edom and the particular punishment it shall receive; this is first of all depicted in terms of a great sacrificial feast with much slaughter (vv 5-8), then in terms of fearful desolation (vv 9-15); the piece concludes with a reference to written prophecy in which, it is said, all this has been earlier set forth (vv 16-17). There have been attempts to divide the chapter into poetic strophes but little agreement has been reached.

In v 1 we encounter one of the more elaborate examples of the "call to attention" (see above on 1:10; 28:23; 32:9). The terms *nations, peoples, earth,* and *world* stand in parallel to each other, and although any or all of these could include Israel, v 8 and chap. 35 make it clear that God's people are not included in this fearful address. The reason the Lord is *enraged* and *furious* is not immediately apparent in v 2, though v 8 gives an answer of sorts a little later. But v 2 does speak of the Lord having *doomed* these peoples, i.e., of having consecrated them for destruction as a religious act. As objectionable as we would consider the mind-set that believed that God would accept as a religious act the devoting to slaughter of human beings, this is in fact found in the Old Testament, most frequently in connection with the holy war concept (see Deut 20:10-18; Josh 6:17-18; 7:1, 11, 15;

10:1, 28, etc.; 1 Sam 15:3-20; see *OTM*, Vol 4, pp. 23-25, 53, 107-110). The practice was not restricted to Israel, the best known non-biblical instance being described in the text of the so-called Mesha Stone (see *ANET* 320-21). The technical term for that which has been consecrated for destruction is *herem* (used below, v 5), though in this verse the verbal form is used. Usually it is through Israel that an enemy is devoted to destruction; that the Lord here acts without any agent being named is almost without parallel. The gruesome carnage of v 3 contains as much realism as imagination. Wholesale slaughter of the populations of towns and cities would indeed have created mounds of corpses, such as those attested in well-known Assyrian bas-reliefs, quantities of blood, and inevitable stench. We must remember, of course, that the very realism adds to the impact of what is intended as a description of the final divine intervention. Verse 4, on the other hand, speaks in terms that become stereotyped in later apocalyptic of disturbances in the heavenly realms, such as the sky being rolled up or vanishing and the stars falling (see above on 24:18, 21-23; see also 51:6; Rev 6:14). On the term *host of heaven*, see above on 24:21.

Yahweh's word, having done its work in the heavens, now descends to earth, specifically to Edom, *the people I have doomed* (v 5). Why a particular example is made of Edom is not clarified. The patriarchal narratives made Esau (Edom) Jacob's twin brother and predicted their eternal rivalry and Jacob's eventual dominance (Gen 25:21-26), but Deuteronomy made this brotherhood a reason for privileged treatment for Edom (Deut 23:7). While Amos faults the Edomites for hostile action against Israel (Amos 1:11-12), it may have been Edom's behavior after the fall of Jerusalem, apparently encroaching on Judah's territory in the south, that occasions the hostile tone of the present poem. Bitter feelings against Edom are attested in Obadiah (the whole of this short book) and elsewhere (Isa 63:1-6; Jer 49:7-22; Ezek 25:12-14; 35:1-15; Joel 3:19; Mal 1:2-5); a troublesome neighbor is often the object of greater anger than a nation that can stand as the embodiment of all evil (such as Assyria or Babylon), precisely because a brother, a neighbor, should be a support and not opportunistically profit by one's misfortune. The Lord's campaign against Edom is described as a great sacrifice, with its location at Bozrah (v 6), Edom's capital. The picture of sacrificial slaughter fits well with the concept of the *doom* (in the technical sense — *herem*; see above on v 2) under which Edom, along with all the other nations, has been placed (v 5). Only in v 8, where vengeance and Zion's cause are mentioned, is it perhaps suggested why Edom has been singled out; retribution is being exacted for all of Edom's hostile acts. The verse could be a summary explanation for all that has preceded in the chapter (i.e., including God's wrath against the nations), but the fact that references to Edom precede and follow it make that less likely.

The imagery of the manner of Yahweh's vengeance on Edom now changes completely, and from that of sword and sacrifice, we turn to a description that, with its reference to pitch, brimstone, and the smoke that goes up for ever and ever (vv 9-10), calls to mind the overthrow of Sodom and Gomorrah (Gen 19:24-28). This occasions no surprise, for these cities had become proverbial for wickedness (1:9, 10) and their fate a type of Yahweh's direct intervention to bring punishment (as opposed to bringing it throught the instrumentality of another nation) on those deserving of it. The poet's statement that Edom shall be utterly desolate with *none to pass through it* (v 10b) suits the Sodom and Gomorrah imagery very well, but it stands in no little tension with the following verses, which take delight in describing the weird creatures that shall inhabit it (vv 11-15). These include not only animals that were associated with lonely places (owl, raven, hyena) and the more unusual ones (the ostrich), but also legendary or fabled creatures, the *satyr* and the *night hag*. The latter two are both demonic in character. The *satyr*, much like that of classical mythology, was thought of as goat-like in form; it is mentioned elsewhere in the Old Testament, sometimes as the object of Israel's idolatrous worship (Lev 17:7; 2 Chr 11:15; Isa .13:21). Rather than *night hag* we should translate as Lilith, a female demon whose name comes from Akkadian (early Mesopotamian) *lilitu* and has nothing to do with the night (Hebrew *laylah*) in spite of the similarity. This is the only place in the Old Testament that Lilith appears, though extensive legends grew up about her in Jewish folklore and she is even mentioned in the Talmud.

The picture of desolation includes the proliferation of thorns and thistles (v 13a), the sort of description we have found elsewhere, though not always utilizing the same Hebrew terminology (7:24-25; 32:14). The language of destruction includes the *line* and *plummet* (v 11b), presumably because a site was surveyed prior to demolition, imagery which is found elsewhere to convey the same meaning of destruction (2 Kgs 21:13; Amos 7:7-9). Verse 12 seems to be disturbed and there is room for doubt as to what the exact translation should be, but there is no doubt that here, without image or metaphor, is proclaimed an end to Edom's kingdom and ruling class.

One might perhaps have expected that unvarnished statement to come as the conclusion of the series on the desolation and demise of Edom, especially since the take-over by wild creatures had already been introduced in v 11. But the concluding verses of this oracle against Edom see all this foretold in earlier prophecy (v 16) which spoke explicitly only of the portioning out of Edom's territories to the wild creatures (though it certainly intended thereby to signal the end of Edom), so the most detailed accounting of these is given in vv 13-15. The *book of the Lord* undoubtedly refers to earlier written prophecy, which the poet says can be sought out and read. Most of the Old Testament passages against Edom mentioned above (see on v 4) refer to its desolation, but of these only Mal 1:3 speaks of its territory being assigned to wild beasts (jackals). One would expect the author's reference here to be to something in the Isaiah collection, and it may be a matter of an adaptation to Edom of what was said in 13:20-22 concerning Babylon (where also we find, v 19, a comparison to Sodom and Gomorrah). This may be supposing an excess of literalism in the author; it is possible that he is simply fleshing out with poetic license the more general sort of prediction of destruction found in

63:1-6 (where also we find reference, v 4, to the Lord's *day of vengeance*).

ISRAEL'S FUTURE GLORY AND BLESSEDNESS: 35:1-10

35 The wilderness and the dry land shall be glad,
the desert shall rejoice and blossom;
like the crocus ²it shall blossom abundantly,
and rejoice with joy and singing.
The glory of Lebanon shall be given to it,
the majesty of Carmel and Sharon.
They shall see the glory of the LORD,
the majesty of our God.

3 Strengthen the weak hands,
and make firm the feeble knees.
4 Say to those who are of a fearful heart,
"Be strong, fear not!
Behold, your God
will come with vengeance,
with the recompense of God.
He will come and save you."
5 Then the eyes of the blind shall be opened,
and the ears of the deaf unstopped;
6 then shall the lame man leap like a hart,
and the tongue of the dumb sing for joy.
For waters shall break forth in the wilderness,
and streams in the desert;
7 the burning sand shall become a pool,
and the thirsty ground springs of water;
the haunt of jackals shall become a swamp,
the grass shall become reeds and rushes.

8 And a highway shall be there,
and it shall be called the Holy Way;
the unclean shall not pass over it,
and fools shall not err therein.
9 No lion shall be there,
nor shall any ravenous beast come up on it;

> they shall not be found there,
>   but the redeemed shall walk there.
> 10 And the ransomed of the LORD shall return,
>   and come to Zion with singing;
> everlasting joy shall be upon their heads;
>   they shall obtain joy and gladness,
>   and sorrow and sighing shall flee away.

If the vengeful character of the preceding chapter on the fearful fate of Edom is somewhat distressing, it should be remembered that at least part of its purpose is to act as a foil to set off the more positive things that are now said in chap. 35 about the fate in store for God's people. Here, more clearly than in chap. 34, can be seen the influence of Deutero-Isaiah. The resemblance is unmistakable if one compares the reference to the return to *Zion* of the *ransomed* and *redeemed* in vv 9-10 (and *way* in v 8) with 51:10-11. In the latter text, however, in its broader context, it is clear that it is a matter of return to Judah from the Babylonian captivity, whereas in our present chapter the reference is generalized, not related to any particular historical context. This allows one to suppose that the author thinks of a wholesale return of the Jews from the Diaspora (as in 27:12-13, for example), since there is no contextual link to the exile. This is a fairly clear indication that chap. 35 is later than Deutero-Isaiah.

The piece begins with the theme of a wonderful fertility (vv 1-2), and this provides another example of the same sort of adaptation of an earlier text. In Deutero-Isaiah the gushing forth of water in the wilderness and the flourishing of plants therein is in the service of a "new exodus" theme (see 41:18-19): the Jews' return to their own land under the Lord's guidance is seen as a new and more wonderful exodus, the original exodus now functioning as type to antitype. In 35:1-2 similar things are said of the flourishing of the wilderness, but without the background of the return from Babylon to give point to it; now such details are utilized in the service of a generalized description of the fertility Israel would enjoy in the new age. The wilderness (*midbar*), dry land (*siyyah*), and desert (*'arabah*) no longer refer to the Syro-Arabian Desert that the returning Jews would have to cross in order to reach their homeland but rather to the barren places in the Holy Land itself, which therefore is to be blessed with great fertility in the days to come. Except during the rainy season large parts of Palestine are barren of vegetation, especially in the southern part, so these verses point to a real transformation of nature. *Lebanon, Carmel,* and *Sharon* are all areas famous for their flourishing vegetation and abundant fertility and therefore are apt examples for illustrating what the land would be like; the same three are used (along with Bashan) as proverbial for fertility in 33:9, though to a quite different intent (see also 29:17). The *they* who *shall see the glory of the Lord* are not the desert, etc., of vv 1-2, but the phrase looks forward to those referred to in vv 3-4, those of *weak hands* and *fearful heart.* Here we find applied in a more restricted sense what extends universally in 40:5 ("all flesh shall see it [the glory of the Lord] together").

To whom the imperatives of vv 3-4 are directed is not said, but they are probably prophetic messengers; we find something similar in 40:1-2, the opening of Deutero-Isaiah, where unidentified persons are commanded to bring words of comfort and hope to God's people. The reason for the encouraging words which are to be spoken is that *your God will come*; this coming will be manifested in the first instance, apparently, by his *vengeance* (on Edom) and *recompense* (v 4), and in this vocabulary we have one of the few clear references back to the grimmer side of the things to come (34:8).

The coming age, having already been described in terms of a wonderful transformation in nature (vv 1-2), is again characterized by other glorious things to come (vv 5-7) which also have their counterparts in Deutero-Isaiah. It has been pointed out above that in Deutero-Isaiah the gushing forth of water in the wilderness (which consequently flourishes) is a taking up of the exodus theme. At the beginning of this chapter (vv 1-2) there is reference to the wilderness being transformed to flourishing fertility, but no mention of

water; now, in vv 6b-7, the *streams in the desert* motif
appears in terms strongly reminiscent of Deutero-Isaiah (cf.
43:19-21, where there is even mention of jackals). Other
wonderful phenomena mentioned here are the healing of the
blind, deaf, lame, and *dumb*. We have already encountered
one reference to the healing of the deaf and blind (29:18).
Deutero-Isaiah speaks of Israel as deaf and blind (42:18-19),
but he also speaks of God opening the eyes that are blind
(42:7) and of turning their darkness into light before them
(42:16). The present passage may have in mind the healing
of spiritual blindness, such as that in 42:18-19 (and cf.
6:9-10), but the inclusion of the lame and the dumb suggests
it is rather a matter of a wonderful elimination of all such
infirmities (cf. above, 33:24).

Finally, we have, to conclude this chapter, the description
of the *Holy Way* (vv 8-10). As has already been suggested,
this takes up a theme found also in Deutero-Isaiah, though
now cut free from the "new exodus" context which in
Deutero-Isaiah gives it its particular point. The present text
most clearly relates to 51:10-11, where also there is reference
to the *redeemed* and the *ransomed*. The Hebrew term here
translated *highway* (*maslul*) is found nowhere else in the Old
Testament, so it is not that terminology which links the
texts. The word translated *way* (*derek*) is found in this sense
in significant passages in Deutero-Isaiah (sometimes in
parallel with another word for "highway," *mesillah*), such as
40:3; 43:15-21 (where there is a reference to a way both
through the sea and through the wilderness, in a very clear
reference to the exodus from Egypt and to the new exodus);
49:11; and 51:10. Our text clearly has the highway going to
Zion (v 10) but no indication of where it comes from other
than the reference to *wilderness* and *desert* of v 6b (notice
the *there* of v 8). This lack of specification leaves the door
open to understanding a general return from the Diaspora
(and cf. 62:10-12).

If no detail is given as to where the road comes from, great
attention is given to who travels on it. This is done nega-
tively, by excluding the *unclean* and *fools*, and positively, by
specifying the *ransomed* and *redeemed*. The fact that the

highway leads to Zion, the great center of worship, helps to explain the exclusion of the unclean; they are the ones who are unfit (the term most frequently refers to ritual defilement, but it can go deeper than that, as in 6:5) to join in Yahweh's cult. The reference to fools is surprising because the Hebrew term (*'ewil*) is virtually never found outside the wisdom literature (though cf. Isa 19:11); the inclusion is intelligible, however, at least in the sense that in the wisdom tradition the fool and the wicked are virtually identified. Such exclusions are appropriate from what is called the *Holy Way*. Excluded also, for obvious reasons, are dangerous beasts. The final description of the *everlasting joy* of those who enter is the crown of the whole chapter (in fact, of chaps. 34-35), the result of the fertility of the land, the healing of physical ills, and the banishment of the wicked; but it is attached most closely, and most fittingly, with entry into Zion, where the *singing* referred to is in praise of and in thanksgiving to Yahweh, who has brought this all to pass. (*OTA*, 1, #803.)

HISTORICAL APPENDIX: CHAPTERS 36-39

The four remaining chapters are taken almost verbatim from 2 Kgs 18:13-20:19, the principal differences being that 2 Kgs 18:14-16 (Hezekiah's submission to Sennacherib) has no counterpart in the Isaiah text and that Isa 38:9-20 (Hezekiah's canticle of thanksgiving) is not found in the 2 Kings text. The chapters contain three narratives which involve Isaiah and Hezekiah: the story of Sennacherib's assault on Jerusalem and the city's deliverance (36:1-37:38 // 2 Kgs 18:13-19:37); Hezekiah's illness and recovery (38:1-22 // 2 Kgs 20:1-11); and the affair of the Babylonian envoys (39:1-8 // 2 Kgs 20:12-19). This extensive treatment of a canonical prophet in the deuteronomic history is a unique case; some scholars have suggested that the passage was initially composed by Isaiah's disciples, was utilized in 2 Kings, and at some point taken from there and inserted into the Isaiah collection. Yet it is to be noted that, at least in the first two stories, Hezekiah is featured far more than Isaiah, while there is also the peculiar fact that Hezekiah is never mentioned in the Isaiah collection other than in the inscription (1:1) and in these chapters.

Hezekiah is one of the heroes of the deuteronomic historians, and it may be that Isaiah expected great things of him, especially as contrasted with Ahaz (see above on 7:10-17). But in fact Hezekiah, to judge from Isaiah's oracles from the time of 705-701, did not live up to such expectations and was a source of disappointment to the prophet. While the first two of these stories present Hezekiah as a man of deep piety and faith and as enjoying a good rapport with Isaiah, the third presents him in a less favorable light; his dealings with the Babylonian envoys represent the kind of thing Isaiah (as we learn from his oracles) would have condemned, and Hezekiah is said here to have been rebuked by the prophet for an action which is seen to presage the Babylonian captivity, the king appearing as rather cynically unconcerned so long as the blow does not fall in his own day.

Thus the three narratives, in terms of their theological biases, point in different directions and probably did not all originate in the same circles. They fit together into one collection in that they all involve both Hezekiah and Isaiah, though the third one places them in a different relationship than the first two. The first and the last narratives intimately involve the fate of Jerusalem, though again they point in very different directions. In the first Jerusalem is protected by Yahweh by miraculous intervention because Hezekiah placed his trust in him and because of the arrogant blasphemies of the Assyrians. In the third the future destruction of Jerusalem is foretold, a prophecy occasioned by Hezekiah's dealings with the Babylonians. The first narrative raises many difficult historical questions and seems to be at odds with all we have seen of Isaiah's teaching during the period in question. The third, at least, accords very well with Isaiah's insistence that history and Judah's security lie in Yahweh's hands alone and that any attempt to manipulate such matters by reliance on covenants with foreign powers was equivalent to the rejection of Yahweh and would have disastrous consequences. As they stand now, however, the three narratives constitute a unified collection; note especially the reference to the deliverance of Jerusalem in the story of Hezekiah's cure (38:6) and of Hezekiah's cure in the account of the Babylonian envoys (39:1).

Sennacherib's Invasion: Isa 36:1-37:38

As has already been suggested, this account raises some rather severe historical problems, most of them springing directly from the biblical texts themselves. Up to a certain point the events narrated are very clear and find independent confirmation in Assyrian records. The events of 705-701 have already been alluded to a number of times, particularly in the discussions above of Isaiah's oracles in chaps. 28-31. At the death of Sargon II (705) there was a movement among a number of the vassals of Assyria to revolt against the overlord. In the east there were Babylonia and the Elamites, and in the west Tyre and other Phoenician cities, the Philistine cities of Ashkelon and Ekron, certainly Judah, and possibly Moab, Edom, and Ammon. It was in these circumstances that Hezekiah negotiated the treaty with Egypt that Isaiah denounced as a "covenant with death" (see above on 28:15). Vigorous king that he was, Hezekiah took many other measures, including the digging of the famous tunnel through rock in order to assure Jerusalem a supply of water from the spring Gihon. Even his religious reform, by which pagan cult objects were banished and an attempt made to centralize the cult in Jerusalem, was part of the same movement for independence. These activities helped make him the hero of the deuteronomic historians that he was. But all these measures were in vain; as Isaiah had foretold, the revolt brought disaster to Judah. Sargon II was succeeded by Sennacherib (704-681), another very able king. He dealt first of all with the trouble spots nearer to home and so did not turn his attention to the west until 701. His attack fell first of all on Phoenicia, and success there brought the submission of Moab, Edom, Ammon, and others. As Sennacherib brought the battle to the rebellious Philistine cities, the Egyptians, who marched to their relief, were met and defeated at Eltekah (near Ekron). He then turned his attention to Judah. The biblical account reports that he "came up against all the fortified cities of Judah and took them" (1 Kgs 18:13 // Isa 36:1), and Assyrian records specify forty-six fortified cities (plus many other towns), adding that much of the population was deported and that Judah was stripped of much of its territory; Sennacherib could then boast that, with Jerusalem thus isolated, he had "shut up Hezekiah as a bird in a cage." Hezekiah had little choice but to submit; according to 2 Kgs 18:14, he sent word to Sennacherib, who was then besieging Lachish, the message "I have done wrong: withdraw from me; whatever you impose on me I will bear." Biblical and Assyrian records agree that the tribute imposed included thirty talents of gold, though Assyrian records claim a much larger tribute in silver (eight hundred talents) than the thirty talents the Bible admits to (*ANET*, 288).

Up to this point there is very little problem. However, the biblical account speaks of Sennacherib now sending three officials (2 Kgs 18:17), or one official (Isa 36:2), with a great army, to expostulate concerning Jerusalem's resistance (2 Kgs 18:18-37 // Isa 36:3-22). Hezekiah then sends to Isaiah, who assures him that the Assyrian king will return to his own land and there fall by the sword (2 Kgs 19:1-7 // Isa 37:1-7). The Assyrian official (the Rabshakeh) reports to Sennacherib, whom he now finds besieging Libnah, and another message is sent back to Hezekiah. Having received it, Hezekiah enters the Temple to pray. In response, Isaiah speaks a long oracle in which he gives assurance that Sennacherib will not enter the city or shoot an arrow against it but will return home the way he came (2 Kgs 19:8-34 // Isa 37:8-35). The angel of the Lord slays 185,000 in the Assyrian camp, Sennacherib returns to Nineveh, and there he is killed by two of his sons (2 Kgs 19:35-37 // Isa 37:36-38).

The problem does not consist in the miraculous deliverance of the city, if such there was. Biblical faith would allow God this and far more, whether acting directly or through natural causes (e.g., understanding the "angel of the Lord" to be a plague; cf. 2 Sam 24:14-16). Very simply put, the problem may be seen especially in the apparently total turn-around of the three principal characters involved, Sennacherib, Hezekiah, and Isaiah. Sennacherib, according to the story, having imposed terms on Hezekiah and having received his submission, sends to ask why he continues to hold out; neither the biblical text nor Assyrian records give reason to expect that anything more would be expected of Hezekiah. It is true that Sennacherib's failure to take Jerusalem can be considered lenient treatment of Hezekiah, but sufficient explanation for that are Hezekiah's submission and the time and expense a siege of Jerusalem would involve. Assyrian records accord with the Bible as far as 2 Kgs 18:13-16, and the picture is one of total triumph for Assyrian arms. The Rabshakeh's speech does not make any explicit new demands (though Isa 36:16-17 // 2 Kgs 18:31-32a, directed to the people, suggests that total surrender is the issue), but is directed against false confidence, including confidence in Egypt—whom the Assyrians have already defeated!

So also Hezekiah, after having abjectly submitted, is presented in his prayer before Yahweh (Isa 37:16-20 // 2 Kgs 19:15-19) as a model of faith — this same Hezekiah who has persisted in rejecting Isaiah's insistent demands by aligning himself with Egypt and rebelling against the Assyrians. The message he sends to Isaiah and the prayer he directs to Yahweh suggest no change of heart on his part nor any new-found faith; he is simply a model king behaving as a model king ought.

But the hardest of all to understand would be the change on the part of Isaiah. The one who has steadfastly condemned the revolt against Assyria and proclaimed the destruction it would entail now (again without any indication of change of mind) becomes one who promises unconditional deliverance. Many try to explain this change by pointing to the arrogant boasting of the Assyrian officials, but Isaiah was no stranger to Assyria's arrogance (see 10:5-15) that his message to Hezekiah relevant to the revolt should suddenly turn about by 180 degrees. In fact, oracles spoken *after* the Assyrian departure, 1:4-9 and 22:1-14, make it certain that he did not; both oracles suppose a massive destruction has taken place upon a people who still have not learned to repent and need to be urged to do so. The second of the two condemns the rejoicing of the people of Jerusalem at the departure of the Assyrians, but had this been brought about by a wonderful deliverance effected by Yahweh in response to faith, Isaiah would hardly have condemned it.

Even a casual reading raises questions about the unity of the text. For example, the sudden appearance of the Assyrian official(s) and a great army at Jerusalem (36:2 // 2 Kgs 18:17), coming without explanation, as it does, immediately after the account of Hezekiah's submission and payment of tribute, is puzzling. We note that Assyrian spokesmen make two somewhat overlapping addresses on two different trips to Jerusalem (Isa 36:4-20; 37:9-13 // 2 Kgs 18:17-35; 19:9-13). In one case Hezekiah sends word to Isaiah and in the second he goes to the Temple to pray, without further word to Isaiah (37:1-4, 14-20 // 2 Kgs 19:1-4, 14-19), even though the prophet has already given him an unconditional assurance of deliverance (37:6-7 // 2 Kgs 19:6-7); this reassurance is repeated in a poetic oracle of some length (37:21-35 // 2 Kgs 19:20-34). The texts have been subjected to intensive analysis and there is general agreement in finding here two different accounts placed one after the other (Source A and Source B), the second of which is made up of two parallel stories, largely distinct but partly mingled (Source B[1] and Source B[2]). These can be designated schematically as follows:

Source A: 2 Kgs 18:13-16//Isa 36:1 (incomplete)

Source B: $\begin{cases} \text{B}^1\text{: 2 Kgs 18:17-19:9a, 36-37//} \\ \quad \text{Isa 36:2-37:9a, 37-38} \\ \text{B}^2\text{: 2 Kgs 19:9b-35//Isa 37:9b-36} \end{cases}$

Source A tells the story of Hezekiah's revolt, the Assyrian invasion, and Hezekiah's submission and tribute; it agrees substantially with Assyrian reports. Source B tells of the wonderful deliverance but consists of two fairly parallel accounts. The differences between B[1] and B[2] are more in the way of detail than of substance. B[1] contains a much longer and more detailed account of Sennacherib's demands in the Rabshakeh's speech, in which the Rabshakeh skillfully employs a whole range of arguments; it includes some elements that reflect an older historical tradition and others based on more recent theological developments. Isaiah's response to Hezekiah's request for intercession says that Yahweh "will put a spirit in" Sennacherib "so that he shall hear a rumor, and return to his own land"; the "rumor" is perhaps supplied in 37:9a (2 Kgs 19:9a), where Sennacherib is told of the advance of the Egyptian army, and the completion in vv 37-38 (2 Kgs 19:36-37), as Sennacherib returns to Nineveh to die at the hands of his sons. (The biblical account somewhat telescopes events here, for his death in fact occurred only twenty years later, in 681.) In B^2 the address, by unspecified Assyrian messengers, touches only on the powerlessness of Yahweh to deliver Jerusalem from the might of Assyria. Hezekiah goes to the Temple to pray without consulting Isaiah, but receives a response from him that promises safety for the city from siege and arrow; deliverance comes as Yahweh's angel strikes down 185,000 in the Assyrian camp. Later theological motifs are more in evidence in this source. The differences between B^1 and B^2 will be touched on in greater detail below.

Of the historicity of Source A there can be little doubt; the historical problem relates to Source B. Generally speaking there are three interpretations of Source B. One interpretation would see it a continuation of the action described in Source A, as a sort of sequel: the Assyrians return with new demands which Hezekiah refuses to accede to; in this he is supported by Isaiah, who considers that Assyrian arrogance and blasphemy now call for defense of the city by Yahweh. But it would be difficult to explain why new demands were made; by the Bible's own account, Hezekiah's submission was total ("whatever you impose on me I will bear" — 2 Kgs 18:14). Nor does the Rabshakeh's long speech indicate that new demands are being made, nor do the words of those of Judah who speak with him. The address of the Rabshakeh to the people on the wall (Isa 36:13-20 // 2 Kgs 18:28-35) suggests a demand for the surrender of Jerusalem, but there is no reason this would not have been made in the first instance, as soon as Hezekiah acknowledged his hopeless situation; he had no other option; since all his allies had already been vanquished. Sennacherib's imposition of tribute and reduction of Hezekiah's territories indicates the intention of leaving him on the throne, so a demand for the surrender of Jerusalem and deportation of the people does not seem to square with the historical situation.

A second explanation argues that account B must depict an historical event, but recognizes that the events of 701 leave no room for a wonderful deliverance; thus it is postulated that this deliverance took place at a later time, on the occasion of a second revolt by Hezekiah and a second invasion by Sennacherib, perhaps in 688. Much is made of the reference to "Tirhakah, king of Ethiopia," i.e., the Egyptian Pharaoh (37:9 // 2 Kgs 19:9); Tirhakah was not yet Pharaoh in 701 and it is claimed that he would have been too young at that time to have led a military expedition. (For a detailed discussion, see *HI*, 298-309. Those who reject this position would see the reference to Tirhakah as the sort of anachronism that occurs not infrequently in the Bible.) While this "two campaigns" theory cannot be ruled out of court, neither the Bible nor Assyrian sources nor Egyptian sources (and the Egyptians would have been involved — Isa 37:9 // 2 Kgs 19:9) provide any record of the later campaign. It is exceedingly strange that Source B, as detailed as it is in many ways, simply attaches itself to the account of the events of 701 without any hint that more than a decade had passed and that a completely different situation was being introduced. Or is one to assume that the editor who added Source B to Source A was unaware that it dealt with completely different historical events? 2 Kgs 18:13-16 tells of Sennacherib's invasion and states that Hezekiah sent to him at Lachish asking for terms of peace and that he met them; when v 17 continues "and the king of Assyria sent ... from Lachish to King Hezekiah at Jerusalem," one must assume continuity of action.

Thus a third possible explanation can be set forth, the one adopted here, albeit with some hesitation. It supposes that Source B relates to the same event as Source A but that the passage of time and the intervention of theological tradition has brought about a substantial recasting of it. What is

remembered from history is that Hezekiah's revolt brought
Sennacherib to the gates of Jerusalem (the Assyrian records
speak of setting up earthworks there) and the fact that he left
without having taken the city. Under the influence of the
Zion tradition, by which Yahweh himself is the protector of
the city, the deliverance is seen and recounted in a totally
different light. The recasting is not done crudely but with
considerable theological nuance. Yahweh does not uncon-
ditionally protect the city, come hell or high water, but
demands faith; Hezekiah already had the reputation of
being an ideal king, and this made the recasting all the
easier.

If the new account's presentation of Isaiah's intervention
flies in the face of all that prophet had to say concerning the
events of 705-701, it can nevertheless be said that many of
Isaiah's own positions provided some justification for this
and that these positions have been worked into the text.
Thus Isaiah did promise Yahweh's help and deliverance to
those who put their trust in him, he condemned Assyria's
arrogance, and promised their ultimate destruction; he did
make positive use of the Zion tradition, as well as speaking
of the remnant and even Yahweh's zeal (9:7; cf. 37:32).

The story would thus be applying to a concrete historical
occasion what was celebrated in the cult, namely, God's
protection of Zion from all enemies (see especially Psalm
46). It is difficult to know how widely circulated the story
was before the deuteronomic historians elaborated on it and
incorporated it into their history, but something like this
could help explain Jeremiah's warning about misplaced
trust that Yahweh's presence meant automatic safety (Jer
7:4); it would also help explain the suicidal policies which
finally brought the kingdom to an end in 587. Source B[1] and
Source B[2] must have circulated and developed independently, though B[2] appears to have been incorporated later,
after greater theological elaboration; both have been
adapted as vehicles of deuteronomic teaching. The deuteronomic editors have not replaced history with theologized
tradition but have juxtaposed the latter to the former, thus
preserving a fairly bare-faced account of what happened

and presenting us with the anomaly we have in Account A + Account B. It was left to the Chronicler to provide a more consistent account in which there is now no longer any word of submission, but rather a Hezekiah who is steadfast in courage and faith from the outset and who encourages his men not to fear because "there is one greater with us than with him" (2 Chr 32:1-23). The tension is not present in the Isaiah text since 2 Kgs 18:14-16 are omitted.

ADDRESS OF THE RABSHAKEH TO HEZEKIAH'S OFFICIALS: 36:1-10

36   In the fourteenth year of King Hezekiah, Sennacherib king of Assyria came up against all the fortified cities of Judah and took them. ²And the king of Assyria sent the Rabshakeh from Lachish to King Hezekiah at Jerusalem, with a great army. And he stood by the conduit of the upper pool on the highway to the Fuller's Field. ³And there came out to him Eliakim the son of Hilkiah, who was over the household, and Shebna the secretary, and Joah the son of Asaph, the recorder.

⁴And the Rabshakeh said to them, "Say to Hezekiah, 'Thus says the great king, the king of Assyria: On what do you rest this confidence of yours? ⁵Do you think that mere words are strategy and power for war? On whom do you now rely, that you have rebelled against me? ⁶Behold, you are relying on Egypt, that broken reed of a staff, which will pierce the hand of any man who leans on it. Such is Pharaoh king of Egypt to all who rely on him. ⁷But if you say to me, "We rely on the LORD our God," is it not he whose high places and altars Hezekiah has removed, saying to Judah and to Jerusalem, "You shall worship before this altar"?⁸ Come now, make a wager with my master the king of Assyria: I will give you two thousand horses, if you are able on your part to set riders upon them. ⁹How then can you repulse a single captain among the least of my master's servants, when you rely on Egypt for chariots and for horsemen? ¹⁰Moreover, is it without

> the LORD that I have come up against this land to
> destroy it? The LORD said to me, Go up against this
> land, and destroy it.'"

One of the discrepancies between the 2 Kings text and
that of Isaiah is that the latter has no parallel to 2 Kgs
18:14-16; or, to put it another way, Source A is represented
in Isaiah only by 36:1, which tells nothing of Hezekiah's
response to Sennacherib's invasion (before that which is set
forth in Source B), i.e., nothing of his admission of wrong,
of his suing for terms of peace, of his paying of tribute (even
to stripping the Temple of gold). Although other explana-
tions are possible, it seems likely that those verses were
deliberately suppressed in the Isaiah text. Clearly, to go
immediately from the news of Sennacherib's invasion to the
advent of his emissary, without any account of Hezekiah's
surrender, creates a different impression (not to mention the
problems it avoids!) than the reading of the fuller text. One
effect is an enhancement of the consistency and faith of
Hezekiah.

Another difference of the Isaiah text is that for the first
embassy it mentions only one Assyrian official, the Rabshakeh, whereas 2 Kings mentions three officials. The title
means "cupbearer," though in English it is sometimes rendered "chief steward" or "chamberlain"; since the 2 Kings
text names the commander-in-chief first, the Rabshakeh
was probably not primarily a military officer. This is con-
firmed by the account, which presents him as a skilled
diplomat and able to speak in the name of the king. The
location of this encounter is not without interest, for it is
said to be exactly where Isaiah met Ahaz in 7:3; by this
device the lack of faith demonstrated by Ahaz on that
occasion provides a neat foil for the perfect faith Hezekiah
will manifest. Two of the three Jerusalem officials named
have already been encountered (Eliakim and Shebna; see
above on 22:15-25). The title of the third (*mazkir*) is better
rendered "herald" than "recorder"; his function was normally to act as liaison between the king and people, report-

ing on matters that concerned the people to the king and conveying to the people the commands of the king and acting as his official spokesman.

The Rabshakeh begins with the classical messenger formula, "thus says . . . " (v 4) followed by words spoken in the first person in the name of the sender (a procedure used also by the prophets — see above on 7:7; see also 30:12, 15; 37:6, 21, 33; 38:1, 5). The words of the official are a masterpiece, at least in the sense that he skillfully attempts to undermine any source of confidence that Hezekiah might have. *Strategy and power* (v 5) must go together, but he is out to demonstrate that Judah has no source of power. (The words used here are the same as those rendered "counsel and might" in 11:2, gifts of the ideal future king.) Egypt is worse than useless because leaning on it occasions only injury (Isaiah would heartily concur). The Rabshakeh's caution against relying on the Yahweh whose shrines have been removed is often pointed to as a credible pagan misunderstanding: Hezekiah's reform was inspired by the desire to enhance, not diminish the worship of Yahweh, but the Assyrian official would hardly understand this; at the same time his knowledge of Hezekiah's reform is not surprising, for it was part and parcel of Hezekiah's plans to rebel and thus of great interest to the Assyrians. Judah's inability to meet Assyria on military terms is emphasized by the assertion that Judah could not even muster enough men to place on the horses Assyria could provide; it is probable that Judah, which employed horses to draw chariots, did not have a cavalry, a lack the words also allude to. *Captains* probably does not belong in the text (v 9), but the sense is unaffected; the Rabshakeh is saying that Hezekiah would be unable to repulse a single one of the many contingents under Sennacherib (*servants* meaning subordinate military commanders rather than individual soldiers). The speech would cut off Hezekiah's last ground of hope by the assertion that Yahweh had sent the Assyrian against him. This would be an astounding assertion for an Assyrian to make (they marched in the name of their god Ashur); that Yahweh sent the Assyrians accords with Isaiah's teaching (see 10:5-11), though he speaks of punishment, not, as here, of destruction.

THE RABSHAKEH'S ADDRESS TO THE PEOPLE: 36:11-22

[11]Then Eliakim, Shebna, and Joah said to the Rabshakeh, "Pray, speak to your servants in Aramaic, for we understand it; do not speak to us in the language of Judah within the hearing of the people who are on the wall." [12]But the Rabshakeh said, "Has my master sent me to speak these words to your master and to you, and not to the men sitting on the wall, who are doomed with you to eat their own dung and drink their own urine?"
[13]Then the Rabshakeh stood and called out in a loud voice in the language of Judah: "Hear the words of the great king, the king of Assyria! [14]Thus says the king: 'Do not let Hezekiah deceive you, for he will not be able to deliver you. [15]Do not let Hezekiah make you rely on the LORD by saying, "The LORD will surely deliver us; this city will not be given into the hand of the king of Assyria." [16]Do not listen to Hezekiah; for thus says the king of Assyria: Make your peace with me and come out to me; then every one of you will eat of his own vine, and every one of his own fig tree, and every one of you will drink the water of his own cistern; [17]until I come and take you away to a land like your own land, a land of grain and wine, a land of bread and vineyards. [18]Beware lest Hezekiah mislead you by saying, "The LORD will deliver us." Has any of the gods of the nations delivered his land out of the hand of the king of Assyria? [19]Where are the gods of Hamath and Arpad? Where are the gods of Sepharvaim? Have they delivered Samaria out of my hand? [20]Who among all the gods of these countries have delivered their countries out of my hand, that the LORD should deliver Jerusalem out of my hand?'"
[21]But they were silent and answered him not a word, for the king's command was, "Do not answer him." [22]Then Eliakim the son of Hilkiah, who was over the household,

and Shebna the secretary, and Joah the son of Asaph, the
recorder came to Hezekiah with their clothes rent, and
told him the words of the Rabshakeh.

It is to be noted that no new demands, no terms of
surrender have been presented; the Rabshakeh's words have
simply underlined the pointlessness of resistance. Diplo-
mats like to conduct their talks in private, and the Judean
officials are presented as not wanting the people of the city
to hear such plain-spoken (and, in large part, irrefutable)
words. Aramaic was not the language of either Assyria or
Judah, but it was a Semitic language closely related to both;
it was widely spread and commonly used for international
communication, so the request that it be used is reasonable
(v 11). But the Rabshakeh's intention is to undermine the
will to resist in any way he can, so he openly takes his case to
the people, whom, he says, are soon to be driven to repulsive
measures by the rigors of the siege (v 12). Addressing them
in Hebrew (or the dialect of Hebrew spoken in Judah) in the
name of Sennacherib (again the messenger formula — see v
4), he invites them to disregard their king and surrender to
him; in return he promises two things: that for the time
being they will be left in peace to enjoy their own possessions
and that when they are deported it will be to a fertile and
prosperous land (vv 13-17). (It is only in this latter suggestion, directed not to the officials but to the people, that there
is any hint of some demand beyond the tribute Hezekiah has
already agreed to, according to 2 Kgs 18:14-16, namely, the
surrender of the city.)

But now a new theme is introduced, that of boasting
against the Lord. Up to this point the Rabshakeh had said
that help was not to be expected from Yahweh because (a)
Hezekiah had removed his shrines (v 7) and because (b)
Yahweh himself had sent the Assyrians against Jerusalem (v
10). Now it is said that Yahweh is powerless to deliver
Jerusalem, just as the deities of other cities have been powerless against the Assyrians. This theme of arrogant boasting
reflects the Isaian oracle of 10:5-11 (especially vv 8-11) and
in this sense already points to Assyria's fall. The cities

named are some of those which, on earlier campaigns, had been punished for rebellion against Assyria. It is probable that some words have fallen out of the text of v 19 ("Where are the gods of Samaria?" — cf. 10:10-11), since the gods of those other cities could not be expected to deliver Samaria.

The scene thus reaches its climax in the manner it was intended to, namely, by focusing on the question of Yahweh's power to deliver and of the wisdom of putting trust in him. Note that Hezekiah is presented as the active agent in calling for such faith (vv 15, 18); it remains only to see whether or not he has misled the people (v 18). The scene ends with the three Judean officials returning to report to Hezekiah, the distress they feel evident in their rent garments.

EXCHANGE BETWEEN HEZEKIAH AND ISAIAH: 37:1-7

37 When King Hezekiah heard it, he rent his clothes, and covered himself with sackcloth, and went into the house of the LORD. ²And he sent Eliakim, who was over the household, and Shebna the secretary, and the senior priests, clothed with sackcloth, to the prophet Isaiah the son of Amoz. ³They said to him, "Thus says Hezekiah, 'This day is a day of distress, of rebuke, and of disgrace; children have come to the birth, and there is no strength to bring them forth. ⁴It may be that the LORD your God heard the words of the Rabshakeh, whom his master the king of Assyria has sent to mock the living god, and will rebuke the words which the LORD your God has heard; therefore lift up your prayer for the remnant that is left.'"

⁵When the servants of King Hezekiah came to Isaiah, ⁶Isaiah said to them, "Say to your master, 'Thus says the LORD: Do not be afraid because of the words that you have heard, with which the servants of the king of Assyria have reviled me. ⁷Behold, I will put a spirit in him, so that he shall hear a rumor, and return to his own land; and I will make him fall by the sword in his own land.'"

Hezekiah's response to his officials' report of the words of the Rabshakeh is to rend his garments, put on sackcloth, and enter the Temple. These acts may indicate that a state of public penance and supplication was proclaimed. Rent garments and the wearing of sackcloth were external signs of distress, which might be manifested in conjunction with mourning, penance, or supplication, or even all three together; the Old Testament does not make a sharp distinction among these. Hezekiah sends the same three officials, along with the senior priests, to Isaiah to request his intercession, this being one of the important functions of the prophet (see Amos 7:1-6). The reference to prayers *for the remnant which is left* (v 4) is, in the circumstances, surprising. It could reflect the decimation of Judah's forces and the reduction of its territory (see 1:4-9), but more likely, the expression is evidence that the account was composed after Jerusalem's fall in 587. Hezekiah utilizes what was probably a popular proverb (*children have come to the birth* ...) to express their inability to successfully complete the project begun, i.e., the revolt against Assyria. The key theme of the insult offered to Yahweh in the Rabshakeh's words is brought in as a reason Yahweh may hear and act (v 4).

The text does not speak of Isaiah praying but rather presents him as having an answer ready to hand. Again we have the messenger formula, only now the sender is Yahweh rather than the king of Assyria, and again there is reference to the insult offered to the Lord. The *spirit* which Yahweh is to put into Sennacherib is not that spirit of the Lord that had come upon Israel's Judges (Judg 3:10; 6:34; 11:29; 13:25; 14:6, 19; 15:14) and was to come upon the messianic king (Isa 11:2) to enable them to do extraordinary things. Rather this one might be said to be akin to the "evil spirit from the Lord" which so disrupted Saul's life and occasioned his inappropriate behavior (1 Sam 16:14-16, 23; 18:10; 19:9-10). The fact that Sennacherib is to return to his own land because of a *rumor* he was to hear indicates that this account of the deliverance did not see it as effected by miraculous means. It is unfortunate for us that the nature of the rumor is not specified. Commentators speculate that it had to do with trouble at home, but, although that did come at a later time (see below on v 38), there is no historical evidence to point to this in 701. The analysis of Source B[1] followed here suggests that the *rumor* had to do with the advance of Egyptian forces (see below on v 9); in view of Assyria's contemptuous attitude toward Egypt (not to mention Isaiah's!), to retreat at their approach would indeed be inappropriate behavior which could be explained only by the king being possessed by the wrong kind of spirit. (On the telescoping of Sennacherib's return and his death, see below on v 38.)

THE SECOND ASSYRIAN EMBASSY: 37:8-13

[8]The Rabshakeh returned, and found the king of Assyria fighting against Libnah; for he had heard that the king had left Lachish. [9]Now the king heard concerning Tirhakah king of Ethiopia, "He has set out to fight against you." And when he heard it, he sent messengers to Hezekiah, saying, [10]"Thus shall you speak to Hezekiah king of Judah: 'Do not let your God on whom you rely deceive you by promising that Jerusalem will not be given into the hand of the king of Assyria. [11]Behold, you have heard what the kings of Assyria have done to all lands, destroying them utterly. And shall you be delivered? [12]Have the gods of the nations delivered them, the nations which my fathers destroyed, Gozan, Haran, Rezeph, and the people of Eden who were in Telassar? [13]Where is the king of Hamath, the king of Arpad, the king of the city of Sepharvaim, the king of Hena, or the king of Ivvah?'"

Verses 8 and 9b, which explain that the Rabshakeh had to go to Libnah in order to find Sennacherib, because in the meantime he had moved there from Lachish, and that from there a new embassy was sent to Jerusalem, appear to function as bridges between Source B[1] and Source B[2]. B[2] apparently had Sennacherib at Libnah rather than at Lachish. Since Libnah is not far from Eltekah, where Assyrian records say Sennacherib met and defeated the Egyptians (*before* attacking Judah), this makes good sense.

The exact meaning of v 9a is important for knowing how Source B[1] understood the reason for Sennacherib's return, but unfortunately there is a significant difference between the Isaiah text and the parallel 2 Kgs 19:9a. The Isaiah text has *the king heard . . . and (when) he heard (it), he sent . . .*, the *he sent* being the beginning of Source B[2] (or possibly an editorial bridge to B[2]). The 2 Kings text has "and he heard . . . and he returned and he sent . . ." Some scholars see in this "and he returned" an original reference to Sennacherib's return to Nineveh (which notice is then completed in vv 37-38, giving the conclusion of B[1]), though the verb can also be understood adverbially ("and he again sent"). The Septuagint has this same reading for Isaiah, while the Qumran Isaiah A scroll also attests to an original "and he returned" (though it says "he heard and he returned"). On the mention of Tirhakah, see above.

The account makes it clear that a written message was delivered to Hezekiah (v 14), but it was also given orally, though in whose presence we are not told. The previous account depicted Assyria's arrogant boasting against Yahweh's ability to deliver, and the people were told not to let Hezekiah deceive them. The second account goes beyond this in that Hezekiah is urged not to let Yahweh deceive him. One effect of this is that the concern of the piece becomes more directly the truth of the claim that Yahweh is the one true God. The cities that are named in v 12 as proof that no god can deliver from the Assyrians were Aramean cities conquered by the Assyrians (*Eden* elsewhere in the Old Testament being sometimes referred to as Beth-eden — see Amos 1:5); they form a list quite distinct from that in 36:19. The *Hamath, Arpad,* and *Sepharvaim* of v 13 were named in 36:19, but now the rhetorical questions ask *where is the king of . . .?* rather than "where are the gods of . . .?" (There is no certain knowledge concerning the cities of Hena and Ivvah; the presence of their names may rest on a misreading of the text.) The point about the gods has already been made with the first list; the second perhaps is now intended to suggest that, the gods being of no help to save, Hezekiah should provide for his own safety. Sennacherib does not speak of the gods of Assyria but only of what the kings of Assyria have done against the cities of these other gods (and what he will soon do to the city of Yahweh!), so the charge of blasphemy is well-founded.

HEZEKIAH'S PRAYER: 37:14-20

> [14]Hezekiah received the letter from the hand of the messengers, and read it; and Hezekiah went up to the house of the LORD, and spread it before the LORD. [15]And Hezekiah prayed to the LORD: [16]"O LORD of hosts, God of Israel, who art enthroned above the cherubim, thou art the God, thou alone, of all the kingdoms of the earth; thou hast made heaven and earth. [17]Incline thy ear, O LORD, and hear; open thy eyes, O LORD, and see; and hear all the words of Sennacherib, which he has sent to mock the living God. [18]Of a truth, O LORD, the kings of Assyria have laid waste all the nations and their lands, [19]and have cast their gods into the fire; for they were no gods, but the work of men's hands, wood and stone; therefore they were destroyed. [20]So now, O LORD our God, save us from his hand, that all the kingdoms of the earth may know that thou alone art the LORD."

Again Hezekiah goes to the Temple (as in Account B[1] — v 1), but now it is explicitly to pray. His spreading out of the letter of Sennacherib before the Lord is not to be attributed to naivete but rather to that very natural and human desire to show concrete and material proof of that whereof he prayed — almost a sacrament in reverse. The king's prayer is a model of piety and in some ways is the very antithesis of the boasting words of Sennacherib. His words acknowledge Yahweh as the only God, as *God of Israel* and of *all the kingdoms of the earth*, and as creator of all that exists. But he makes a distinction between the previous victories of the kings of Assyria and what Sennacherib now attempts: the *gods* they conquered and destroyed were no gods, mere idols, not that majestic *Lord of hosts, enthroned above the cherubim* over all the earth. Hezekiah's prayer ends with a plea for deliverance, indeed, but the motive alleged is that Yahweh's Lordship may be manifested to all the kingdoms of the earth over whom he rules as God.

Hezekiah's prayer resembles those offered by David and Solomon (see especially 2 Sam 7:18-24 and 1 Kgs 8:22-23), which are attributable to the deuteronomic historians; in its explicit monotheism (not only the confession of Yahweh as God alone, but also the rejection of pagan gods as no gods, *but the work of men's hands, wood and stone*) it is like the development we find in exilic and postexilic texts (see *OTM*, Vol. 12; see 40:18-20; 41:21-24, 28-29; 44:6-8, 9-20). For the latter reason, especially, Source B[2] probably can be judged to have been inserted as part of the exilic redaction of 2 Kings, whence it was taken into the Isaiah collection. The idealization of Hezekiah, partly through the resemblance here seen to David and Solomon, but mostly because of the faith he manifests, is not so much for his glorification as it is for the exaltation of Yahweh for what he is about to do.

ISAIAH'S ORACLE OF DELIVERANCE: 37:21-35

[21]Then Isaiah the son of Amoz sent to Hezekiah, saying, "Thus says the LORD, the God of Israel: Because you have prayed to me concerning Sennacherib king of Assyria, [22]this is the word that the Lord has spoken concerning him:

> 'She despises you, she scorns you —
>   the virgin daughter of Zion;
> she wags her head behind you —
>   the daughter of Jerusalem.

[23] 'Whom have you mocked and reviled?
>   Against whom have you raised your voice
> and haughtily lifted your eyes?
>   Against the Holy One of Israel!

²⁴ By your servants you have mocked the Lord,
      and you have said, With my many chariots
  I have gone up the heights of the mountains,
      to the far recesses of Lebanon;
  I felled its tallest cedars,
      its choicest cypresses;
  I came to its remotest height,
      its densest forest.
²⁵ I dug wells
      and drank waters,
  and I dried up with the sole of my foot
      all the streams of Egypt.

²⁶ 'Have you not heard
      that I determined it long ago?
  I planned from days of old
      what now I bring to pass,
  that you should make fortified cities
      crash into heaps of ruins,
²⁷ while their inhabitants, shorn of strength,
      are dismayed and confounded,
  and have become like plants of the field
      and like tender grass,
  like grass on the housetops,
      blighted before it is grown.

²⁸ 'I know your sitting down
      and your going out and coming in,
      and your raging against me.
²⁹ Because you have raged against me
      and your arrogance has come to my ears,
  I will put my hook in your nose
      and my bit in your mouth,
  and I will turn you back on the way
      by which you came.'

³⁰"And this shall be the sign for you: this year eat what grows of itself, and in the second year what springs of the same; then in the third year sow and reap, and plant vineyards, and eat their fruit. ³¹And the surviving remnant of the house of Judah shall again take root down-

ward, and bear fruit upward; [32]for out of Jerusalem shall go forth a remnant, and out of Mount Zion a band of survivors. The zeal of the LORD of hosts will accomplish this.

[33]"Therefore thus says the LORD concerning the king of Assyria: He shall not come into this city, or shoot an arrow there, or come before it with a shield, or cast up a siege mound against it. [34]By the way that he came, by the same he shall return, and he shall not come into this city, says the LORD. [35]For I will defend this city to save it, for my own sake and for the sake of my servant David."

The Lord gives his reply to Hezekiah's prayer — or rather, indicates what his response and manner of answering it will be — through Isaiah. Thus the king's role here is much greater than the prophet's: it is he who professes faith in Yahweh's power, he who prays, and it is he to whom the favorable response is directed (*because you have prayed to me* — v 21). The long oracle is, in fact, not all one piece. The earliest form of the oracle contained only vv 21-22a, 33-35, the intervening material being composed of two separate interpolations, vv 22b-29 and vv 30-32. This is clear from the fact that the introduction to the oracle, given once in v 21, has to be taken up again in v 33, as well as from the fact that vv 22-29 are addressed to (presumably) Sennacherib, not to Hezekiah. Although these verses manifest some elements of Isaiah's teaching, it is unlikely that they stem originally from him, most especially because vv 22-29, at least, show evidence of influence from Deutero-Isaiah.

The first of the interpolations, vv 22-29, shows no little resemblance to the taunt-song against the king of Babylon in 14:4-23. This is seen in the more general theme of the tyrant who exalts himself, ascends the heights (cf. 14:13-14), fells the cedars and cypresses of Lebanon (cf. 14:8), and possibly the claim of divine prerogatives, if that is what is implied in Sennacherib's boast that he had dried up streams with the soles of his feet (v 25 — *of Egypt* is conjecture; the Hebrew text is unclear); cf. 45:21; 46:10; 51:10. Jerusalem is depicted as a spirited young woman who treats the tyrant with contempt; on the wagging of the head to express scorn, see Job 16:4; Ps 22:7; Jer 18:16. Daughter Zion can be bold because she stands under the protection of the One whom Sennacherib has *mocked and reviled*, the One whose power and control of events is soon to be proved. Sennacherib's boasting related to the victories he had won, the cities he had conquered, but the oracle now reveals that it was Yahweh who planned all this and had brought it to pass (vv 26-27); his victories, therefore, were a proof of Yahweh's power, not of his own. While this reminds us of Isaiah's teaching concerning Assyria as Yahweh's instrument (10:5-11), the diction (*have you not heard*, etc.) and the concept of Yahweh's predetermination of history are very reminiscent of Deutero-Isaiah's description of the victories Yahweh granted to Cyrus, subduing nations before him, all in order to further his own ends (45:1-6). Yahweh knows Sennacherib through and through (cf. Ps 139:1-2 for a similar manner of describing divine knowledge), as only God can know his own creature. Sennacherib's arrogant boasting is therefore inexcusable, and Yahweh will compel him to return to his own country. The image of the bit in the mouth relates to the manner of controlling a horse or mule (see Ps 32:9); the hook in the nose is variously understood to relate to the treatment of a captured animal (cf. Job 40:24; 41:2; Ezek 19:4) or of a prisoner of war (cf. Ezek 38:4), but the former would give better parallelism with the "bit in the mouth" image. This oracle does not suggest the kind of destruction of Sennacherib's army related in v 36, but neither is it incompatible with it.

The second interpolation (vv 30-32), which is no longer directed to Sennacherib but (presumably) to Hezekiah, speaks of a sign, though obviously not in the sense of a marvelous event that assures the future fulfillment of Yahweh's word (as in 7:11). Rather, the *sign* here is a meaningful event (or, more accurately, a series of significant happenings) which will show that what has come to pass is in fulfillment of what Yahweh had previously promised; as in 7:14 (and cf. Exod 3:12), the *sign* is visible only after what it points to comes to pass. Thus this sign could not be a motive for Hezekiah to make a decision (unlike that initially offered to Ahaz in 7:11) but could later confirm the rightness of that faith in which he based his decision. On the historical level the statement is easily intelligible: the Assyrian devastation would make harvesting impossible for the current year as well as plowing and sowing for the coming year, so that only that which grows spontaneously will be available for food; but in the third year normal agriculture can be resumed. Some scholars see in vv 31-32 an allegorical meaning relating to the role to be played by the remnant for the future people, but this is by no means transparent. Again the remnant reference seems to point to a time later than 701 (see above on v 4). The second interpolation is concluded with a good Isaianic phrase taken from 9:7.

Verses 33-36 mark the conclusion of Source B². The oracle introduced by the formula in v 21 and interrupted by vv 22-32 is now reintroduced by the same formula and brought to its conclusion. The promise is that Sennacherib will not be allowed to undertake any hostile actions against the city but would return to his own land without inflicting any harm. Yahweh's defense of the city is *for my own sake and for the sake of my servant David*. The first of the two phrases is reminiscent of Deutero-Isaiah (cf. 43:25; 48:9; 55:5), but the second relates to the Davidic tradition and comes up frequently in the deuteronomic history (see 1 Kgs 11:13, 34; 15:4; 2 Kgs 8:19). Yahweh's honor is involved in the defense of the city he has chosen and of the dynasty he has chosen. Nevertheless, this is far from an eternal commitment to the "inviolability of Zion," as is sometimes said. (A correction for any misunderstanding that this narrative may have occasioned is provided in the last of these three Isaiah-Hezekiah narratives [see below on chap. 39].)

JERUSALEM'S DELIVERANCE AND SENNACHERIB'S DEPARTURE: 37:36-38

36And the angel of the LORD went forth, and slew a hundred and eighty-five thousand in the camp of the Assyrians; and when men arose early in the morning,

> behold, these were all dead bodies. [37]Then Sennacherib
> king of Assyria departed, and went home and dwelt at
> Nineveh. [38]And as he was worshiping in the house of
> Nisroch his god, Adrammelech and Sharezer, his sons,
> slew him with the sword, and escaped into the land of
> Ararat. And Esarhaddon his son reigned in his stead.

As a conclusion to Source B[2], v 36 is both very dramatic
and at the same time incomplete — especially since v 34
leads us to expect some reference to Sennacherib's return
home. It is possible that in the blending together of B[1] and
B[2] part of the narrative has been suppressed in the interests
of a more unified account; in any case, vv 37-38 provide a
satisfactory ending for the combined narrative as it now
stands.

There has been no preparation for the mass destruction of
the Assyrian army described in v 36, so it is sometimes
suggested that this verse did not belong even to B[2] but is a
later addition; yet that would leave B[2] without any explanation for Sennacherib's departure (not even the "spirit" and
the "rumor" of B[1] in v 7), and some explanation would seem
to be required. The Old Testament frequently sees a Yahweh's hand in natural events (cf., e.g., Josh 10:11, where
only incidentally is it revealed that the "great stones" the
Lord hurled down on Israel's enemies from heaven were
hailstones), so there is no rationalization involved in sus-
pecting that the author's *angel of the Lord* is intended to
designate a plague (cf. especially 2 Sam 24:12-16). Nor
ought one to be bothered by the impossibly large figure of
185,000. In any case, however, we are probably not dealing
with an historical event (see above p. 279), and therefore the
attempt that is sometimes made to relate this text to the
story told by Herodotus (II, 141) of an invasion of mice who
gnawed the Assyrian bowstrings is probably mistaken;
while it is true that rodents can be associated with plagues,
that is not the effect Herodotus attributes to them, and there
are other discrepancies of time, place, and detail.

Verses 37-38, in the analysis here followed, would originally have been the conclusion to B[1] (cf. v 7). Although one

would assume from the biblical text that Sennacherib's death came soon upon his return, he did not in fact die until 681. Indications from Mesopotamian documents, while not explicit in all details, suggest that the biblical account of the manner of his death is accurate. Esarhaddon was designated by Sennacherib during his life as his successor, to the chagrin of older brothers (*ANET*, 289-290). Sennacherib did die by assassination, and the Babylonian Chronicle attributes this to one of his sons (*ANET*, 302). No Assyrian deity by the name of Nisroch is known, but we cannot be certain which name originally stood in the text.

HEZEKIAH'S SICKNESS AND HEALING: 38:1-21

38   In those days Hezekiah became sick and was at the point of death. And Isaiah the prophet the son of Amoz came to him, and said to him, "Thus says the LORD: Set your house in order; for you shall die, you shall not recover." 2Then Hezekiah turned his face to the wall, and prayed to the LORD, 3and said, "Remember now, O LORD, I beseech thee, how I have walked before thee in faithfulness and with a whole heart, and have done what is good in thy sight." And Hezekiah wept bitterly. 4Then the word of the LORD came to Isaiah: 5"Go and say to Hezekiah, Thus says the LORD, the God of David your father: I have heard your prayer, I have seen your tears; behold, I will add fifteen years to your life. 6I will deliver you and this city out of the hand of the king of Assyria, and defend this city.

7"This is the sign to you from the LORD, that the LORD will do this thing that he has promised: 8Behold, I will make the shadow cast by the declining sun on the dial of Ahaz turn back ten steps." So the sun turned back on the dial the ten steps by which it had declined.

9A writing of Hezekiah king of Judah, after he had been sick and had recovered from his sickness:
10 I said, In the noontide of my days
        I must depart;

I am consigned to the gates of Sheol
    for the rest of my years.
¹¹ I said, I shall not see the LORD
    in the land of the living;
  I shall look upon man no more
    among the inhabitants of the world.
¹² My dwelling is plucked up and removed from me
    like a shepherd's tent;
  like a weaver I have rolled up my life;
    he cuts me off from the loom;
  from day to night thou dost bring me to an end;
¹³   I cry for help until morning;
  like a lion he breaks all my bones;
    from day to night thou dost bring me to an end.

¹⁴ Like a swallow or a crane I clamor,
    I moan like a dove.
  My eyes are weary with looking upward.
    O Lord, I am oppressed; be thou my security!
¹⁵ But what can I say? For he has spoken to me,
    and he himself has done it.
  All my sleep has fled
    because of the bitterness of my soul.
¹⁶ O Lord, by these things men live,
    and in all these is the life of my spirit.
    Oh, restore me to health and make me live!
¹⁷ Lo, it was for my welfare
    that I had great bitterness;
  but thou hast held back my life
    from the pit of destruction,
  for thou hast cast all my sins
    behind thy back.
¹⁸ For Sheol cannot thank thee,
    death cannot praise thee;
  those who go down to the pit cannot hope
    for thy faithfulness.
¹⁹ The living, the living, he thanks thee,
    as I do this day;
  the father makes known to the children

thy faithfulness.
20 The LORD will save me,
   and we will sing to stringed instruments
all the days of our life,
   at the house of the Lord.

21Now Isaiah had said, "Let them take a cake of figs,
and apply it to the boil, that he may recover." 22Hezekiah
also had said, "What is the sign that I shall go up to the
house of the LORD?"

This narrative has analogies in the wonders worked by
Elijah and Elisha (see 1 Kgs 17:17-24; 2 Kgs 4:1-5:27),
though the emphasis given to Hezekiah and his piety makes
it difficult to classify it simply as a prophetic legend. It is tied
to the previous narrative about Hezekiah by the reference to
deliverance from the king of Assyria (v 6) and probably also
by the chronology indicated; according to 2 Kgs 18:2, Hezekiah ruled for twenty-nine years, and if fifteen years are
added to his life from the point of this narrative (Isa 38:5),
the events related must have been thought to have taken
place in his fourteenth year, which according to 2 Kgs 18:13
// Isa 36:1 was the time of Sennacherib's invasion (i.e., 701).
   Although the presence of Hezekiah's canticle (vv 9-20) is
the largest difference between the form of the story as found
in Isaiah and its source in 2 Kgs 20:1-11, there are a number
of others that are worth noting. In the 2 Kings version the
account falls easily into two parts (which some commentators think were originally two independent stories), Hezekiah's illness and the healing thereof, including the
application of a fig compress by Isaiah (vv 1-7) and Hezekiah's request for a sign and the granting thereof (vv 8-11).
The Isaiah version is somewhat more complicated: there is a
description of Hezekiah's illness and Isaiah's promise of a
cure (vv 1-6); Isaiah volunteers the sign which will assure
Hezekiah he will be healed (vv 7-8); there is appended the
canticle of Hezekiah (vv 9-20); and only after this does
Isaiah call for a fig compress and does Hezekiah ask for a
sign (vv 21-22) — to which request there is no reply, since the

sign has already been given. It seems probable that the
editor who placed this story in the Isaiah collection deliberately omitted Hezekiah's request for a sign (which could
suggest some lack of faith in the prophet's word) and reference to the rather prosaic means (or at least prop) by which
the cure was effected, and that a later harmonizer attempted
to supply the omission, but did so in a rather awkward way.

Isaiah's intervention (v 1) is perhaps somewhat unexpected, though prophetic oracles concerning a gravely ill
king were not unknown (2 Kgs 1:3-6) and were sometimes
sought (2 Kgs 8:7-10); in are frequently found in these
psalms and serve equally well as a motive for being heard.
Hezekiah is presented as having nothing to repent of and
therefore being remarkable in piety. The same favorable
emphasis is given to the king in that he offers his own prayer
rather than asking Isaiah's intercession (as he does in 37:14-
20, but otherwise than in 37:1-4). The reversal of a prophet's
word by a new oracle from the Lord is not without parallel
(cf. 2 Sam 7:1-7), and in this case it is in response to Hezekiah's prayer; it demonstrates both that the prophet's word
(especially when he foretells woe) has a conditional aspect to
it and that Yahweh hears the prayer of the devout supplicant. Yahweh's response goes beyond anything implied in
Hezekiah's prayer in that it promises delivery of the city
from the king of Assyria; the Lord's intention to *defend this
city* (v 6) relates this narrative closely to the preceding (cf.
37:35), from which this motif was no doubt taken precisely
for that purpose; in this piece it occurs almost casually,
whereas there it was a major climax of a dramatic
development.

Isaiah's spontaneous offer of a sign relieves Hezekiah of
the onus of having asked for one (unlike the 2 Kings version
— see above), with the possible implication of doubt concerning the prophetic word. Somewhat astonishingly the
sign is rather more marvelous than the healing it is introduced to confirm; it is on the order of the sun-miracle of
Josh 10:12-14. (In the Isaiah version the sign could be in
confirmation also of Yahweh's defense of the city, but in 2
Kgs 20:8 it relates only to Hezekiah's question about his

restoration to health.) The text probably does not speak of a sundial but of the steps of a staircase leading to a terrace or other structure built by or named for Ahaz.

Whether the psalm of vv 9-20 was actually written by Hezekiah cannot be said with certainty; it is not found in the 2 Kings version of the story, and, being couched in general terms (as in fact most psalms of thanksgiving are), there is nothing to identify it with Hezekiah's particular situation. Hezekiah's brief prayer in v 3 did not specifically ask for healing, so the psalm could conceivably have been inserted to supply that lack (see v 16b). There is, however, a conflict between Hezekiah's protestation of innocence (v 3) and the psalm's admission of sin (v 17b). Although the composition contains many elements of a typical psalm of thanksgiving, it does not conform to the pattern in all respects (e.g., it does not have the sort of *introduction* one normally finds in such psalms). In some respects the piece reads like a psalm of supplication (and by some has been so classified), but this is because the *body* of it contains a detailed account of the trouble from which the psalmist has been delivered and the prayer he offered to God in his distress. This is to be expected, since the opening *I said* is to be understood as introducing the words spoken in the prayer for healing.

As in other cases in which the supplicant describes his dangerous illness, he pictures himself already in the power of the netherworld (Sheol — see above on 14:4-20 and cf. Ps 16:10; 30:3; 86:13; 88:3-7; 116:3). The netherworld is not *the land of the living*, and God's concern and power are hardly thought to extend there (Ps 88:4-5, 10-12). Two images are used to describe the end of life, the striking of a tent and the cutting of a woven cloth from the loom (v 12). Even in suffering the Israelites knew God was in control of events; if on the one hand this meant that God himself was responsible for present suffering (vv 13, 15), on the other it made him the only one to whom one could turn for help (v 14) — a help the faithful one never doubted he would give. The prayer would seem to reach a climax at v 16b, but here the Hebrew is uncertain and obscure: the same is true of the phrase rendered *Lo, it was for my welfare* (and of many others in this text). As is frequently the case in the Old Testament, a connection is seen between present ills and past sins, and so the writer relates his deliverance to God's forgiveness of his sins (v 17b; see Ps 32:1-5; 38:3-5). He returns to the thought of Sheol, but now to contrast the lot of those who go there to that of the living (vv 18-19); the former have no possibility of praising God (cf. Ps 6:5), while the latter find their chief joy in so doing.

The thanksgiving being offered is not merely for the here and now, but it will be prolonged by the proclamation of God's gracious deeds to future generations (v 19b) — a duty Israel recognized both with regard to God's more public benefits to Israel (Exod 13:14-16) and to his individual blessings (Ps 22:30-31). The concluding reference to being *at the house of the Lord* (v 20b) would be more appropriate to the 2 Kings version of the story, for there Isaiah's promise of healing included the assurance that Hezekiah would go to the house of the Lord on the third day, and this detail comes into the king's request for a sign (2 Kgs 20:5, 8). It is perhaps this specific reference to *the house of the Lord* that prompted the editor to add, at the very end, Hezekiah's request for a sign, which now relates only to going to the Temple (v 22), with no specific mention of healing (unlike 2 Kgs 20:8).

While there is some evidence that figs were thought to have healing properties, Isaiah's use of the fig compress is more in the way of sacrament than medicine, as in the many other examples in which something quite inadequate to the task at hand is used as a sign and vehicle of God's healing and restoring power (Exod 15:25; 2 Kgs 4:40-41; 5:10-14; John 9:6-7).

THE BABYLONIAN EMBASSY: 39:1-8

39   At that time Merodachbaladan the son of Baladan, king of Babylon, sent envoys with letters and a present to Hezekiah, for he heard that he had been sick and had recovered. ²And Hezekiah welcomed them; and he showed them his treasure house, the silver, the gold, the spices, the precious oil, his whole armory, all that was found in his storehouses. There was nothing in his house

or in all his realm that Hezekiah did not show them.
³Then Isaiah the prophet came to King Hezekiah, and
said to him, "What did these men say? And whence did
they come to you?" Hezekiah said, "They have come to
me from a far country, from Babylon." ⁴He said, "What
have they seen in your house?" Hezekiah answered, "They
have seen all that is in my house; there is nothing in my
storehouses that I did not show them."

⁵Then Isaiah said to Hezekiah, "Hear the word of the
LORD of hosts: ⁶Behold, the days are coming, when all
that is in your house, and that which your fathers have
stored up till this day, shall be carried to Babylon;
nothing shall be left, says the LORD. ⁷And some of your
own sons, who are born to you, shall be taken away; and
they shall be eunuchs in the palace of the king of
Babylon." ⁸Then said Hezekiah to Isaiah, "The word of
the LORD which you have spoken is good." For he
thought, "There will be peace and security in my days."

This final chapter of Isaiah 1-39, in its present position,
helps form a bridge between Isaiah of Jerusalem of the
eighth century and Deutero-Isaiah, for, in its present form,
it foretells the Babylonian ascendancy which is the historical
background of the latter. Although this narrative follows
that of Sennacherib's advance on Jerusalem (chaps. 36-37),
chronologically the events of which it speaks were earlier.
The occasion most probably was the laying of plans for the
rebellion that led to the events of 701. No other biblical text
indicates that the Babylonians were involved in that revolt,
but Mesopotamian records do. Merodach-baladan
(Marduk-apal-iddina), a Chaldean (Neo-Babylonian)
prince, in concert with the Elamites, rebelled against Sargon
II at the very beginning of the latter's reign. He was driven
from his base in Babylon, but renewed the attempt to establish an independent Babylonia after the death of Sargon II
(705). His revolt in the east shortly after Sargon's death
coincided closely with that in the west in which Judah,
under Hezekiah, had a part. There is, therefore, no reason to

doubt that Babylon had a hand in fomenting the rebellion or this chapter (and in 2 Kgs 20:12-19). An occasion later than the events of 701 is certainly excluded because after that date there would have been no gold and silver in Hezekiah's treasury to show to the Babylonians; according to 2 Kgs 18:15-16 Hezekiah not only emptied the Temple and palace treasuries, but had also to strip gold from the Temple doors. Although the present narrative relates the Babylonian embassy to Hezekiah's recovery from illness (v 1), that is probably an editorial device to join the two stories; anti-Assyrian machinations would have provided sufficient explanation.

The Isaiah, the Hezekiah, and the relationship between them that we see in this narrative fit well into the atmosphere of chaps. 28-31 (those oracles of Isaiah which pertain to the time of Hezekiah's reign), something that could not be said of the other two narratives of this historical appendix. The Hezekiah who acts without consulting Isaiah (cf. 29:15; 30:1; 31:1), who is intent on rebelling against Assyria with the help of foreign powers, the Isaiah who condemns negotiations of this sort and the reliance on outside help that they imply, who sees such policies leading to disaster—these have a much more authentic ring. The more immediate question is whether we should credit Isaiah's prediction of the plunder of Jerusalem and the deportation of some of Hezekiah's descendants by Babylon. One reason for doubting could be that at this time Assyria loomed as so much more obvious a threat. Indeed, Assyria remained in control for more than another century and extended its power to even greater limits. Under Esarhaddon (680-669), Sennacherib's successor, Assyria conquered Egypt, in the process defeating Tirhakah (671), sacking Thebes (663), and establishing a new dynasty that ruled by Assyrian sufferance. It is true that Isaiah had on more than one occasion spoken of Assyria's limited role in Yahweh's plan and anticipated its end, so he could have seen the initiative eventually passing to the younger Mesopotamian power.

Yet there are difficulties involved. It is frequently said

that the reference to the carrying off of Judah's treasures and some of the royal line to Babylon (vv 6-7) reflects the events of 597 and therefore that it was composed *post eventum*. But this suggestion raises a number of problems. If the prophecy is *post eventum* it is remarkable that it refers to the deportation only of *some of your sons*, since that of 597 counted some thousands of persons (3,023 according to Jer 52:28). But it would be still more remarkable that an invented prophecy would place the responsibility on Hezekiah, whom the composers of the deuteronomic history judged very favorably (2 Kgs 18:1-5) and who has been idealized in the two previous stories we have dealt with (and whose fault in this matter is glossed over by the chronicler —2 Chr 32:25-31). It would also be difficult to explain how a fictitious prophecy, invented, on this view, more than a century after the events, provides the name of Merodach-baladan, a name which appears nowhere in the Old Testament other than in the two parallel versions of this story. There is also the fact that although the text speaks of all of Judah's treasures being taken off to Babylon (something which did happen a little over a century later), in Isaiah's own day, as a consequence of the transactions that lie behind this narrative, they were taken off to Assyria.

From the pooling of all these data another solution suggests itself. The embassy of Merodach-baladan did take place as reported (probably in 703) and it related to negotiations to coordinate the respective roles to be played by Judah and Babylon in the anti-Assyrian coalition. Judah's treasury is relevant in that it represents resources that could be called upon in the struggle. Isaiah learns of the negotiations and, true to the attitude manifested in the oracles preserved from this period (which relate mainly to Egypt), denounces the plan (trust in Babylon being no better than trust in Egypt), foretells its failure, and predicts that all these treasures would be taken off (not to Babylon but) to Assyria. As an oracle that was vindicated almost immediately, it was preserved by Isaiah's circle. Later, when Babylon became the threat, the oracle was recast to apply to the new situation.

Since Isaiah clearly saw Assyria as the real danger to Judah and would have considered pacts with Babylon likely to produce the same sort of fruit as pacts with Egypt, this reconstruction accords well with all we know. Thus the narrative does preserve an accurate historical remembrance of the Babylonian embassy and the sort of encounter that took place between Hezekiah and Isaiah.

Those who opt for a *vaticinium post eventum* and date it after 597 explain that the expression *some of your own sons, who are born to you* (v 9) can refer to grandsons or later generations; the Jehoiachin who was taken to Babylon was, in fact, the fifth generation after Hezekiah. This is indeed true, but the Hebrew expression (literally: "some of your sons who shall come forth from you, whom you shall beget") would more easily be understood of Hezekiah's immediate sons. If this were the case, it would simply represent Isaiah's expectation (probably to be seen also in 3:1-8) of deportation of members of the ruling class or the taking of them as hostages as part of the punishment for rebellion, and would not relate to Jehoiachin at all. On the other hand, the words of Hezekiah that interpret the prophet's words as implying *peace and security* in his days (v 8) would have to have been added at the time Isaiah's oracle was adapted to a later time, for by the adaptation the blow was, by a literary fiction, being transferred to a later century; in point of historical fact, the despoiling of Judah's treasures occurred both early and late. In spite of the apparent cynicism of Hezekiah's reply, expressing complacency with the ill fortune to come, since it will not occur in his time, the editor was probably intending to depict no more than the submission of a pious king to the word of the Lord.

Thus the collection of Isaiah 1-39 comes to an end with a prophecy of deportation to Babylon and so prepares for the collection that immediately follows, which opens with expressions of comfort for God's people. One reason that comfort can be offered is that "the word of our God will stand forever" (40:8). That "word" includes, in no small measure, Isaiah's promises of better times for God's people once sin had been punished (40:1).

SOME READING
SUGGESTIONS

Brevard S. Childs, *Isaiah and the Assyrian Crisis* (Studies in
Biblical Theology 2/3; London: SCM, 1967; Naperville,
IL; Allenson, 1970). A valuable investigation of the problems surrounding the Assyrian invasion of 701, with
special emphasis on form-critical study of the relevant
oracles of Isaiah.

Ronald E. Clements, *Isaiah 1-39* (New Century Bible Commentary; Grand Rapids, MI: Eerdmans; London: Marshall,
Morgan & Scott, 1980). A very compact and competently
done commentary, recommended but with reservations
on the author's hypothesis concerning a "Josianic redaction"
of Isaiah, a hypothesis which influences many of his judgments on dating, authenticity, etc.

Otto Kaiser, *Isaiah 1-12: A Commentary* and *Isaiah 13-39:
A Commentary* (The Old Testament Library; Philadelphia: Westminster, 1972, 1974). Translated from the
German of Vols. 17 and 18 of the series Das Alte Testament
Deutsch. A useful commentary, though the author is perhaps too quick to reject Isaiah's authorship and, especially
in the second volume, to see apocalyptic compositions.

William McKane, *Prophets and Wise Men* (Studies in Biblical
Theology 1/44; Naperville, IL: Allenson; London: SCM,
1970). Although, as the title indicates, the area covered is
broader than Isaiah, special attention is given to him.

Frederick Moriarity, "Isaiah 1-39," *The Jerome Biblical Commentary*, ed. R. E. Brown et al. (Englewood Cliffs, NJ: Prentice-Hall, 1968), I, 265-282.

Bruce Vawter, *The Conscience of Israel* (New York: Sheed & Ward, 1961). Pp. 162-207. Unsurpassed as a general discussion of Isaiah's teaching in general, with special emphasis on social justice.

J. William Whedbee, *Isaiah & Wisdom* (Nashville/New York: Abingdon, 1971). A helpful discussion of wisdom influence in Isaiah; for my reservations of various aspects of the book, see *Catholic Biblical Quarterly 34* (1972) 126-28.

Hans Wildberger, *Jesaja.* 3 vols. (Biblischer Kommentar Altes Testament 10; Neukirchen: Neukirchener Verlag, 1980-1982). These three volumes, containing over 1,700 pages, easily add up to the most scholarly and detailed commentary on Isaiah available. Careful and balanced judgment throughout.

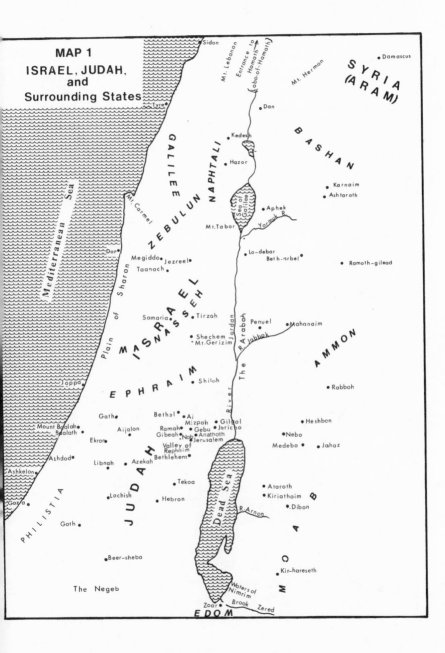

MAP 1
ISRAEL, JUDAH,
and
Surrounding States

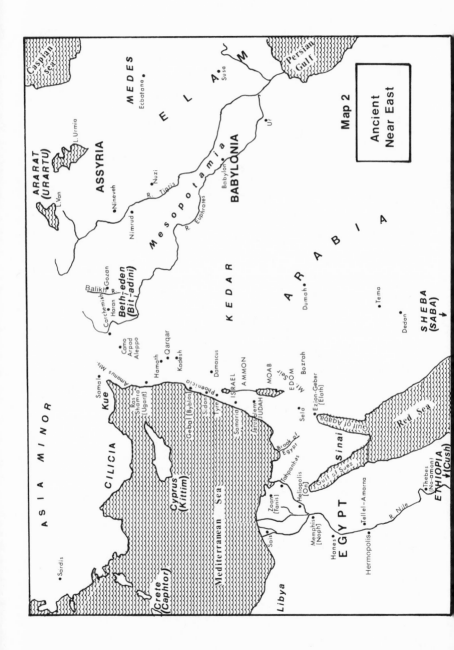

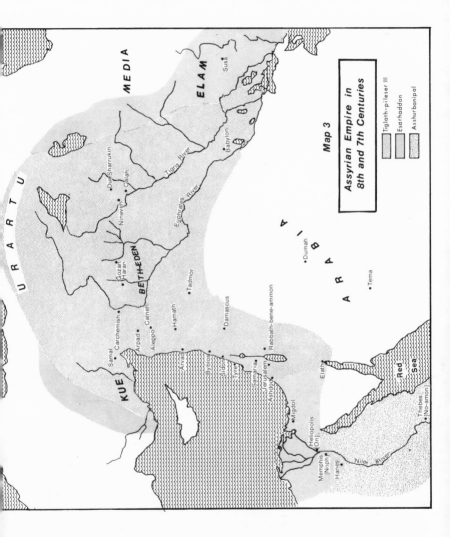

Map 3

Assyrian Empire in
8th and 7th Centuries

Tiglath-pileser III
Esarhaddon
Asshurbanipal